The Globalization of News

The Globalization of News

edited by
Oliver Boyd-Barrett and Terhi Rantanen

SAGE Publications
London · Thousand Oaks · New Delhi

First published 1998

SAGE Publications Ltd
6 Bonhill Street
London EC2A 4PU

SAGE Publications Inc
2455 Teller Road
Thousand Oaks, California 91320

SAGE Publications India Pvt Ltd
32, M-Block Market
Greater Kailash - I
New Delhi 110 048

British Library Cataloguing in Publication data

A catalogue record for this book is available from the British
Library

ISBN 0 7619 5386 8
ISBN 0 7619 5387 6 (pbk)

Library of Congress catalog card number 98–61246

Typeset by Type Study, Scarborough, North Yorkshire
Printed in Great Britain by The Cromwell Press Ltd,
Trowbridge, Wiltshire

Contents

Notes on Contributors

Oliver Boyd-Barrett, Ph.D. is Professor at California State Polytechnic University, Pomona. He has written and edited many books and articles on international communications and education. He pioneered international programmes in mass communications by distance learning at the Open University (UK) and at Leicester University (UK). His current research includes investigation into satellite broadcasting in the Middle East, the political economy of distance learning and the globalization of Hispanic media.

Derek Forbes is Head of the Department of Communication at the University of the North-West in South Africa. Former journalist and member of the South African National Editors' Forum (SANEF), he is working on the subject of news agencies for his doctorate. His previous theses dealt with foreign news reporting and the training of journalists for developing countries (City University, London). He teaches journalism and media criticism at the Department of Communication, University of North-West. His research – a survey of media training needs in South Africa – has contributed to Unesco's regional media training programme, the Independent Broadcasting Association's 1992 inquiry into regional broadcasting in South Africa, training at the South African Broadcasting Corporation, SABC, and the Truth Commission Inquiry into the role of the South African press (1997). His publication, *The End of the Mangope Regime*, records the 1994 Bophuthatswana Uprising in South Africa. He is engaged on committees looking at the training and research of journalists in South Africa.

C. Anthony Giffard is Professor and Director of the School of Communications at the University of Washington in Seattle, and founder and former Head of the Department of Journalism and Media Studies at Rhodes University, South Africa. He has been a visiting professor at the University of Wisconsin, Madison and Johannes Gutenberg University in Mainz, Germany. His books include: *UNESCO and the Media* and, with William A. Hachten, *The Press Under Apartheid: Censorship and Repression in South Africa*. His articles have appeared in *Journalism Quarterly*, the *Journal of Communication*, *Journalism History*, *Revue du Tiers Monde*, *The Journal of Development Communication*, *Newspaper Research Journal*, *Development Gazette*, *California Western Law Review*, and *Keio Communications Review*, among others.

Stig Hjarvard, Ph.D. is an Associate Professor and Head of the Department of Film and Media Studies at the University of Copenhagen. He has published books and articles about deregulation of broadcasting, the history of the Eurovision News Exchange, the development of local and commercial television in Denmark and audiovisual communication theory. Current research includes an investigation of historical changes in broadcast journalism.

Ullamaija Kivikuru is Professor of Journalism at the Swedish School of Social Science, the University of Helsinki, Finland. She has taught and done research in Eastern and Southern Africa since the late 1970s. Her fields of interest include journalism and development communication.

Michael Palmer is Professor and Director of the Centre for Research on Information and the Media in Europe at the University of Sorbonne Nouvelle, Paris. He has published extensively on news agencies and media policy. His books include *Le trafic des nouvelles* (1981) together with Oliver Boyd-Barrett, *Des petits journaux aux grandes agences* (1983) and *Media Moguls* (1991) together with Jeremy Tunstall.

Chris Paterson is a Lecturer at the Centre for Mass Communication Research at the University of Leicester. He has also taught at Georgia State University in Atlanta after receiving his doctorate from the University of Texas in 1996. His research concerns television news agencies and processes of news media globalization.

Terhi Rantanen, Ph.D. is Assistant Professor and Docent in the Department of Communication, Helsinki University, Finland. She has done research in several countries and published extensively on news agencies. Her books include *Foreign News in Imperial Russia: The Relationship between International and Russian News Agencies, 1856–1914* (1980). She is currently researching the globalization of media in eastern Europe.

Ingrid Schulze Schneider is Profesor Titular at the Departamento de Historia de la Comunicacion Social, of the Facultad de Ciencias de la Informacion, Universidad Complutense, Madrid. Her doctoral thesis was published in 1987: 'El Sistema Informativa de Bismarck: Su Proyeccion Sobre La Politica y Prensa Espanola' (Editorial de la Universidad Complutense de Madrid).

Jürgen Wilke is Professor at the Institut für Publizistik, Johannes Gutenberg Universität, Mainz, Germany. His research interests include the history and structure of mass communication, analysis of news production and international communication (especially Latin America). He has also edited and co-written books on news agencies.

List of Abbreviations

AAP	Australian Associated Press
ABU	Asian-Pacific Broadcasting Union
ADN	Allgemeiner Deutsche Nachrichtendienst
AFP	Agence France-Presse
AP	Associated Press
APS	Allied Press Service
APTV	Associated Press Television
ASBU	Arab States Broadcasting Union
CBU	Caribbean Broadcasting Union
ČSTK	Česka Slovenska Tiskova Agentùra
ČTA	Česka Tiskova Agentùra
ČTK	Česka Tiskova Kancelar
DANA	Deutscher Allgemeine Nachrichtenagentur
ddp	Deutscher Depeschen Dienst
DENA	Deutsche Nachrichtenagentur
DNA	Development News Agency
dpa	Deutsche Presse-Agentur
EBU	European Broadcasting Union
ECN	East Cape News
Ecna	East Cape News Agencies
FES	Friedrich-Ebert-Stiftung
GNS	German News Service
INS	International News Service
IPP	Independent Press Pool
IPS	Inter Press Service
ITAR-TASS	Informatsionnoe telegrafnoe agentstvo Rossii-Telegrafnoe agentstvo Sovetskogo Soiuza
MISA	Media Institute of Southern Africa
MTI	Magyar Tavirati Iroda

NANAP	Non-Aligned News Agencies Pool
NWICO	New World Information and Communication Order
NZPA	New Zealand Press Association
NZUPA	New Zealand United Press Association
PANA	Pan-African News Agency
PAP	Polska Agencja Prasowa
PST	Press Service Tanzania
RHEINA	Rheinische Nachrichtenagentur
SAPA	South Africa Press Association
SHIHATA	Shirika la Habari la Tanzania
SNB	Soviet News Bureau
SPTA	St Petersburg Telegraph Agency
SUDENA	Sudwestdeutsche Nachrichten-Agentur
TASR	Tlačová agentura Slovenskej republiky
TASS	Telegrafnoe agentstvo Sovetskogo Soiuza
UPI	United Press International
UPITN	United Press International Television News
URTNA	Union of National Radio and Television organizations of Africa
VWD	Vereinigte Wirtschaftsdienste
WTN	Worldwide Television News

1 The Globalization of News

Oliver Boyd-Barrett and Terhi Rantanen

It is commonplace to repeat that modernity is inherently globalizing, even if there is disagreement as to whether the process of globalization began before modernity or was solely its consequence, or whether modernity has merely transformed the nature of globalization. There is much discussion about the effects of globalization on consciousness and on the micro level of social behaviour (See Tomlinson, 1991, for one of the best of recent syntheses, and Giddens, 1990). Even though there is still a great deal of work to be done at this level (see Sreberny-Mohammadi, 1991 and Boyd-Barrett, 1997, for a discussion of the limitations of our existing knowledge, even in the realm of media) there is a danger that in the enthusiasm for charting the consequences of globalization, we marginalize or even forget about the role of the institutions, that is to say the question of the agents of globalization. When we focus on the institutions we often discover that there are diverse and competing interests at work, and that what may appear at one level to be 'globalization' in the sense of 'homogenization', may appear at another level as fragmentation and competition.

Our interest is as scholars (both as historians and as social scientists) of the role of news agencies. For some time the news agencies have been identified as agents of globalization, within UNESCO's (important, if unfashionable) discourse of the New World Information and Communication Order (NWICO). What we want to propose in this book is that the connections between news agencies, national formation and globalization are more profound and have a more substantial history than has been recognized up to this point in time. The news agencies are of considerable significance as the first international or, indeed, global media organizations and are among the first of the world's transnational or multinational corporations.

We regard the development of the concept 'news' as a process that lies at the heart of modern capitalism and which also illuminates processes of globalization which modern capitalism has helped to generate. 'News' represented the reformulation of 'information' as a commodity gathered and distributed for the three purposes of political communication, trade and pleasure, and directed in its generic form by technology (for example the telegraph), scientism (for example the belief in the value of 'facts'), and the development of mass media markets. News contributed to processes of the construction of national identity; to imperialism and the control of colonies; it was an essential lubricant in day-to-day financial affairs, both within and between domestic markets. The collection and dissemination of this commodity was organized and rationalized on behalf of media and non-media clients by a small group of powerful agencies, acting globally and as a cartel. Hence the links between modernity, capitalism, news, news agencies and globalization are an outstanding but neglected feature of the past 150 years.

In this volume we investigate the role of news agencies in the globalization and commodification of news. We also call attention not just to the tensions between the national and global levels of action to which these same organizations contribute simultaneously (both national formation *and* national deconstruction through the fomenting of transnational identities and activities), but also to the tension between commercialization (in response to freshly reinvigorated market forces on the global stage), public service regulation (representing the interests of the state, supposedly for the benefit of the community in democratic societies, and of the community itself, in resistance to the unfettered interests of international capital): indeed, in the news agencies we find pre-written much of the struggle between commercial and public service models and agendas which has also typified the history of broadcasting media throughout the 20th century. Thus even from their earliest days in the mid-19th century we find that the news agencies demonstrate models of business practice, professional ethics, and clientelism which are the heart of the study of all communications media.

One of the important themes of this book is the extent to which the news agencies represent models of multinational or transnational media enterprise (specifically) or even of such enterprise *in general*. It is easier to appreciate this in the light of the extraordinary mushrooming of the influence of Reuters which now ranks 48th of Europe's top 500 companies, is the 12th most valuable company quoted on London's stock exchange, is the linchpin of day-to-day financial market transactions worldwide, and operates as information provider or distributor in some 150 countries. In other words, we are proposing that the news agencies themselves have been major players in processes of globalization while they are also of increasing importance in underpinning the globalization activities of *other* players on world markets. What we want to argue in this book is not that globalization can be reduced simply to media or to capitalism or economics or to politics or to culture, but that globalization represents each and every one of these dimensions and that the news agencies can be seen to contribute to each dimension. But we shall also be arguing that what are sometimes called processes of globalization turn out on closer inspection to be less unidirectional, and that news agencies are also sometimes incorporated in trends that may have more to do with the consolidation of regional or institutional centres of power, where power is still fragmented and contested.

In the decade between the mid-1970s and mid-1980s there was a modest boom in the growth of news agency studies. Broadly speaking, these were of two kinds: one set of studies was largely descriptive, tended to be atheo-retical and unengaged with some of the major tendencies in social research of the period. But they did belong to a period in which there was growing interest in and sophistication of thought about journalism and news-production practices. In retrospect, much of that research could be located within a tradition of 'political economy of the media', that is to say, a tra-dition which concentrates on how media texts relate not solely to their con-ditions of production, but also to the broader political and economic structures of society. The news agencies fit particularly well into this approach because they so clearly mediate between other important social institutions, notably the retail media, state and capital. This political economy emphasis is easier to recognize in the 1990s because the develop-ment of 'cultural studies', especially that wing of it which focuses on audi-ences and reading practices, has tended to marginalize interest in media production. Before the Internet, 'retail' audiences did not exist for the agen-cies; their 'audiences' were institutions; in place of 'audience' studies there were 'gatekeeper' studies which looked at how client institutions selected the news they received, for further distribution. Another category of study, if 'study' is not too dignified a term, is represented by the rhetoric and con-troversy about news agencies which was stimulated within UNESCO by the NWICO debate and the McBride Commission (although significantly the role of news agencies was much less emphasized in the final McBride Report – see UNESCO, 1980) and which was often overtly partisan, and informed by rather simplistic dependency frameworks within a customary UNESCO discourse of nation states as independent operators.

In this book we argue that news agency studies are informed by and can contribute to both political economy and cultural studies approaches, in particular that they have much to say about the broad social, political and economic contexts of news agency operations, about their news-construc-tion practices, about their texts and how their texts may be said to function ideologically and, not least, about the social contexts and practices associ-ated with the reception and use of their services. But we are particularly concerned to foreground the significance of 'agency' (in the sense of being 'opposite to structure') in the theorization of processes of globalization because we believe that without a grounded understanding of agency, such theorizing tends to grow nebulous, even to be point of being classified as neo-liberal since it leaves under-theorized issues of dominance and inequal-ity (which was one of the strengths of older concepts such as media or cul-tural imperialism which globalization now seems to have replaced).

During the mid-1980s social scientists, having taken a brief look, rather lost their interest in news agencies. This perhaps underlines the extent to which the news agency topic was dependent on the NWICO debate for sus-tenance. The NWICO debate has largely collapsed, and so too, apparently, has social science interest. This is a pity because whatever its faults, and there were many, NWICO was at least a conscious, well-articulated and coordinated response to the reality of progressive globalization – even before the term itself was commonly used – at least as far as the media were concerned. However, building on the descriptive value of the 1970s and 1980s research, there has been a significant addition to the number of company histories available, most notably, that of Read's (1992) work on the history of Reuters. (Company histories have been the longest tradition in news agency research. The first company history was written by Eliassen in 1918, about the Danish news agency, Ritzau.)

In this time there have, in addition, been two important developments which we think would justify the renewal of social science interest in news agencies. The first concerns the ways in which the world itself has reconfig- ured with the collapse of communism and the cold war, the emergence of new political systems in central and eastern Europe, development of South Asia and China as major industrial forces in the world, and other develop- ments which challenge the validity or usefulness of the world maps as drawn by media news coverage. Second, there have been major changes in the world of news agency institutions themselves. It is no longer so clear, for example, that there are four or five major players as at least one, UPI, has changed ownership and its role appears in some respects to have greatly diminished on the world stage. Simultaneously, Reuters has become more and more powerful, being its own league compared to other major players.

There is also a theoretical and practical problem about how to con- ceptualize the other major players, given that the overall economic activity of Reuters far exceeds that of its nearest competitor, AP, that TASS is no longer a world agency, and that the operations of the French-based agency, AFP, are not so different in scale from those of the German news agency, DPA, or even the Spanish news agency, EFE. Additionally, there is a major new development with the emergence of a new breed of news-film or tele- vision news agencies. To the original news-film and video agencies, Visnews and UPITN (now transmuted into Reuters World Television and WTN respectively), which dominated the world market for some two or more decades, has been added APTV. But we have also to take into account the emergence of global television news, led by companies such CNN and BBC World Television, which, although they may subscribe to 'wholesale' ser- vices, have their own channels, distributed by satellite or by cable, or provide news to terrestrial broadcasters and through the Internet. These further undermine the validity of the distinction between wholesale and retail news suppliers, and they raise issues about the relative value of print as opposed to visual sources of world news supply. This latter development has stimulated a new wave of interest in global news in the late 1990s, mainly concentrating on video news sources. Placed alongside the mushrooming theorization of processes of modernity, post-modernity and globalization, these developments urgently require a revisit and reconceptualization and up-dating of our knowledge of the news agencies.

These processes of reconceptualization go to the very heart of our theme, and to the most fundamental of the concepts that have so far underpinned the study of agencies. For example, what do we mean by 'news'? What do we mean by 'news agency'? What do we mean by 'national', 'international', 'transnational' or 'global'; what do we mean by 'wholesale' and 'retail'? What are meant by key descriptive terms commonly paraded by the institutions themselves such as 'story', 'bureau', 'client', 'service'? So a part of our goal, both here and in the future, is to re-establish our terms.

But the more important part is to take a fresh look at how the news agencies have contributed to processes of what for the moment we will call 'globalization'. We want to argue that for this term to retain its force it must be concretized, related empirically to identifiable processes at work; the study of news agencies offers us a way of doing this. The news agencies were among the world's first organizations to operate, not only globally, but to operate globally in the production and distribution of 'consciousness', through the commodification of news, in ways which had very significant implications for our understanding or appreciation of time and of space (see, for example, Rantanen 1997). Part of this has to do with the territorial bonding of 'nation states' and the dialectic at the very heart of modernity between national formation and global formation. The agencies were vital components in the armoury of the nation state; then as now, agencies were among the range of institutions which new nation states came to feel they had to establish in order to be seen to be credible as nations and in order to project or to control the dissemination of their 'national image' on global markets. National agencies could also be regarded as the Trojan horses for globalization through the exclusive links which they were obliged to establish with the major 'global' news agencies of the 19th-century cartel, in particular Reuters, Havas and Wolff. This dialectic as it affects the news agencies is as much in evidence towards the end of the 20th century as it was in the second half of the 19th. Our volume explores this dialectic with reference to various instances of struggle over the past 150 years, between national governments, national agencies, global agencies and global regulatory bodies, with reference also to the political, economic and cultural interests which have helped to constitute the global agencies.

Through our focus on news agencies we want to problematize this concept of 'globalization': we certainly do not consider this can be legitimately used as a 'normative' concept (describing the world as many people would like it to be or as they think it already has become); nor do we think it refers to the homogenization of world culture; nor do we consider it is an inevitable 'one-way street'. Nor are we convinced as to its novelty: there are many instances of 'globalization' dating from long before modernity, including the influence of world religions, imperialistic conquests, and trade networks. Instead, we subscribe to the view that the forms of globalization change shape, direction and intensity from one epoch or phase of social development to another. Our focus is on the forms of globalization within 'modernity', that complex of cultural dynamics which embraces the formation of the nation state, industrialization, urbanization, techno-rationality and democratization (Giddens, 1990). This is both a physical and an ideological phenomenon; ideologically it has had the consequence of interpreting the world within the nation-state framework and, in the way of ideologies, of making seem 'natural' and 'inevitable' that which is constructed and fragile (Hall, 1982). It is not so much that globalization is a part of modernity that excites our interest, since globalization may be said to be part of other 'epochs', even if the introduction of the telegraph brought about an especially important intensification in the conquest of space and time constraints. We want to say that 'globalization' is in its very essence a process of dialectic, not least between the local, national, regional and global, a process of conflict and struggle both among the agencies of globalization and the alleged subjects of globalization. In addition to our focus on time, space, commodification, national and international formation (in particular the role both of the state and of major economic interests), ideology, interpretation and the social embedding of global texts, we also propose to look at the interrelationship between all these things and technology (telegraph, cable, telephone, radio, television, satellite, Internet, etc.).

Theorizing the News Agencies

Within the range of different media forms, news agencies are sometimes presented as among the least glamorous or interesting. They represent an extreme form of a 'journalism of information' in contrast to a more refined and creative 'journalism of opinion'. Although the Anglo-Saxon invention of 'journalism of information' has enjoyed increasing worldwide influence over the past century, in contrast to its more literary, discursive, and 'European' shadow, newspapers do still remain in many ways the media of overt partisanship, political commentary, invective, and analysis. The extent to which such characteristics invade 'news' as opposed to 'opinion' spaces within a newspaper varies, but the boundaries between these concepts are unclear even at the best of times – they have more to do with the construction of an appearance of credibility than with the actual and impossible expulsion of ideology from news texts. Specialist correspondents, including foreign correspondents, are credited with the creative task of making interpretive sense out of a range of diverse sources, which include, to varying degrees of visibility, news agencies.

News agency news is considered 'wholesale' resource material, something that has to be worked upon, smelted, reconfigured, for conversion into a news report that is suitable for consumption by ordinary readers. It has also suited the news agencies to be thus presented: they have needed to seem credible to extensive networks of 'retail' clients of many different political and cultural shades and hues. They have wanted to avoid controversy, to maintain an image of plain, almost dull, but completely dependable professionalism. This image has sat more successfully with major news agencies such as Associated Press or Reuters, than with government-owned or backed national news agencies where association with state-supported propaganda has compounded the sense of dullness, even while reducing perceptions of professionalism and dependability.

To some extent this image, nurtured by the agencies themselves over the past century and a half, has also asserted itself in the world of media history and media study, where agencies sometimes have been barely visible actors in analysis of print and broadcast news, and have often attracted the least theoretically inclined, though most historically inflected of academic analysis. Needless to say, the absence of overt theory does not signify the absence of *any* kind of theory, and in practice, we will argue, agencies have always been theorized, and the manner of their theorization corresponds to some degree, but not entirely, with more general movements in the history of communications research.

Some 19th-century references to news agencies, most famously that of the French novelist, Balzac in an 1840 article in *La Reveue Parisienne* (quoted in Levebre, 1992: 69–71), about Havas, indicate that they were viewed as both hidden but powerful. Balzac's observation indicated a concern that behind the apparent diversity of news channels in retail media, was a much more restricted range of sources.

Early, implicit theorization of news agencies sees them as powerful, but hidden, and, because hidden, perhaps even more powerful than commonly suspected. Added to the view of agencies as powerful, is the view of them as services of propaganda. This was manifest during the first world war when at least some of the resources and services of the agencies were placed at the disposal of government propaganda campaigns. The German Karl Bücher talked in 1915 of the dangers of monopoly holdings of services such as Reuters and Havas, which he considered official and thus biased sources of information, and which were partly responsible for war propaganda activities (quoted in Hardt, 1979: 21). This view was apparent throughout much of the politicking between state, national and international agencies in Europe during the second half of the 19th century, where agencies are seen as potential or actual sources of hostile propaganda, on account of the identity of their host countries, or as actual or potential channels for the transmission of such propaganda overseas. The Russian government's fear of the dominance of Wolff in the transmission of international news gathered by the cartel for distribution in Russia, is one such example (Rantanen, 1990). The propaganda value extended from the political to the economic: the mere presence or absence of the British news agency, Reuters, in certain territories during the 1930s was seen as relevant to British trade interests by both agency and state sources. Added to the view of agencies as vehicles of propaganda is the left-wing view, expressed powerfully by Villard (1930) in relation to Associated Press, that they were part of the apparatus of class oppression. His discussion directed attention away from the state itself, to a more general consideration of ideology through social class division.

Whether it is the state or social class, or both, that is identified as enemy, a polar opposition was proposed here between propaganda and truth. This did raise helpful questions and issues about the proper role of the state in news agency activities, and the advantages of alternative forms of ownership and control, including private or co-operative structures. But it was also somewhat simplistic in its model of social representation, insensitive to the subtleties of news construction and agenda-setting.

In summary, we would argue that up until the second world war the agencies belonged to any mixture of three prevailing discourses about media: media as powerful and influential; media as vehicles of nation-state or class propaganda; media as exemplars of a modern, technologically sophisticated professionalism.

The range of such discourses was amplified with the transition from British to American world hegemony. The American agencies had resisted and eventually defeated the cartel practices of the old ring combination, of which Reuters was the cynosure. The American agencies propagated effectively the models of both co-operative and private ownership which, they claimed, would guarantee unbiased news (see, for example, Cooper, 1942). They preached the advantages of an open market in news, a line supported by the US State Department, and which contributed to the formation of the 'free flow of information' doctrine later adopted by the UN, and which informed the UN's activity in the sphere of communications (Schiller, 1976). In practice, it has been argued, the doctrine supported the rights of western media, especially those of the US, UK and France, to continue distributing their media products throughout the world, while most countries of the world lacked the means to establish any kind of reciprocity of influence. Even national agencies in the communist block, set up for the purpose of preventing the intrusion of western ideas, still subscribed to the services of the major western agencies.

The UN, through UNESCO, consistently endeavoured to encourage the spread and development of national news agencies, and of news-exchange arrangements between them, especially during the great wave of independence in Africa during the 1960s. Setting up a national news agency became one of the essential things, part of the 'script', of what it meant to be a 'nation'. Through a national news agency, a state could lay down information links domestically and internationally which would facilitate the generation and exchange of news. National news agencies became the natural local business partners for the western-based international agencies: they provided a conduit, albeit government controlled, through which international news could be funnelled to local media, and domestic news released to the wider world. All this was assumed to contribute to national formation and national development, although these assumptions were rarely tested.

This then was a progressive, modernist discourse that treated news agencies as though they were public-service institutions, fulfilling positive functions for nation-building, including the local provision of international news and projection of national news on to a larger world stage through the international agencies. In this model, the news agencies forged closer links between communities within nations, and between nations, in a largely pluralistic world. It was a model which suited the literature of Schramm (1964), Pye (1963), Lerner (1958) and others, in which the media play a positive, even indispensable role in the process of modernization and the expansion of democracy. Little thought is given in detail to issues of media control, content or finance, or to the precise ways in which given kinds of content lead to the consequences attributed to them. It avoided some difficult questions: for example, do agencies really contribute to 'development', or might they be counter-productive to some definitions of 'development' (for example, where used to bolster the power of particular ethnic groups)? The tension between 'development' as positive news and traditional western news values was not addressed, and there was a confusion between 'western news criteria' on the one hand, and 'really useful information' on the other. This model still retained a view of media as powerful at a time when, in the western world, newer models prevailed, emphasizing the role of 'intervening variables' and the essentially limited character of media power (Klapper, 1960). The model stimulated interest in pluralism at global level, but casually tolerated monopolies at local level, offering little insight into the structural impediments to pluralism at either level.

The reality of news agency coverage, reflected in early content analysis of agency wires (IPI, 1953) did little to sustain the credibility of the 'free flow' model. National agencies were generated within a global news system largely controlled by the 'Big Four' western agencies (AFP, AP, Reuters, UPI), and by the two leading state agencies of the communist world, TASS (Soviet Union) and Xinhua (China) serving their allies in the eastern bloc and communist Asia. These provided international news which was dominated (at that time) by news of their own host countries and subscribed to specific sets of news values characteristic of western media and communist media. The national agencies often served as funnels for local distribution for the Big Four agencies (though AP more often contrived to remain independent). In this way the international agencies could reach a larger number of outlets, with less pressure on local foreign exchange, than probably would have been the case had they tried or been allowed to distribute directly to all local media. The national agencies, sometimes with editorial tutelage from the Big Four agencies whose services they received, provided a rudimentary service of local news dominated at least as much by urban and elite news as the services of the Big Four, because their resources for coverage of the rural majorities were slender or non-existent, and political controls too often reduced their coverage to sycophantic and superficial reports of the doings of heads of state and their ministers, and ministerial meetings with counterparts from other countries ('protocol news' – Harris et al., 1980). Together with the editorial staff of the national agency, acting as stringers for the international agencies, such a service could provide a source of cheap, local coverage, at least in non-crisis periods.

Post-independence disillusionment was best expressed in the 'dependency' theories from South America, which had experienced a comparatively longer period of constitutional independence, but extensive experience of US capitalist expansionism. The news agencies fitted dependency theory very well given the character of the world news system, and the way in which it could be seen to facilitate the integration of new states into the world capitalist economy and its values. They provided an example in the cultural arena of the tendency identified by Galbraith (1967/77) for industries to be dominated by a few big players, closely interlinked with a second tier of national or regional players, and with a much larger number of small local or niche-market players lagging well behind.

Dependency theory dominated the vision of countries of the second and third worlds in the NWICO movement as it spread its influence though the non-aligned movement and through UNESCO in the 1970s. For countries of the South, the role of the major news agencies was especially significant in provoking official anger at how the international news system favoured western definitions of the exceptional and significant, and seemed to obstruct the ability of new southern nation states to contribute to the representation of their national image and national interests in northern media markets, with potentially enormous implications, politically and economically. The McBride Report (UNESCO, 1980) placed all this in much broader context, focusing on the full range of media industries. But McBride came too soon to make sense of the extraordinary sensitivity of the western (political and media) world to southern criticism, which was soon to lead to the withdrawal of the US, UK and Singapore from UNESCO (the UK returned in 1997) and which, in retrospect, serves as a lesson – which cannot be emphasized enough – demonstrating the extent to which maintenance of world political hegemony is considered to depend upon a pliable global media system.

Dependency discourse had the merit that it focused attention on the global news system and on the political economy of news agencies. It explored the factors that have made it difficult for newcomers, especially newcomers with alternative ideas as to the functions and content of news agencies, to gain entry. It went some way towards exploring the dynamics between political economy and content, although this was achieved mainly through quantitative content analysis. Sophisticated qualitative analysis of day-to-day coverage was rare, although there were strong examples, among them Vietnam war coverage (see Boyd-Barrett, 1979: ch. 13; and Boyd-Barrett and Palmer, 1981: ch. 13), and agency coverage of the NWICO debate itself (Salinas, 1977). But it did not recognize the growing importance of the international video news agencies. Further on the debit side, the dependency framework as manifested in the NWICO debate still seemed to subscribe to the view that nation states were the most useful units of analysis, even though the integration of nation states into a global capitalist economy rendered it necessary to look at the relationship of national media to the local incorporation of elite social classes within the global economy.

At the level of concrete action within UNESCO, NWICO discourse about news agencies was undermined by an absence of empirical support for claims that agencies are indeed important contributors to national and economic development. The dynamics of this supposed relationship to development have never been clear. NWICO discourse could not shake itself free of the notion that the proper way to set up or to support a news agency was through governmental or intergovernmental action. Thus the Non-Aligned News Agencies Pool (NANAP) was supported by UNESCO, despite NANAP's heavy and unreasonably over-optimistic reliance on the participation of national news agencies that were themselves integral components of statist, authoritarian regimes. The pool was coordinated by a country (Yugoslavia) which was soon to collapse in on itself in an explosion of extreme bigotry. UNESCO assistance to the Pan-African News Agency supported an under-resourced creation of another intergovernmental body, the Organization for African Unity (OAU). PANA was committed to promotion of African unity, restricted in what it could say about member African regimes, and hopelessly dependent on inadequate, partial and impecunious government-backed national news agencies (Boyd-Barrett and Thussu, 1992).

Since dependency theory, in what further ways have news agencies been 'theorized'? The collapse of the communist east in the late 1980s coincided with a period in media research in which the influence of cultural studies predominated. This involved a welcome concentration on the semiotic construction of texts, and on processes by which actual readers make and take meaning from texts. This was a period which celebrated the notion of textual 'polysemy' and audience autonomy. Significant determiners of individual meaning were found in cultural contexts impinging on the use and consumption of texts. Cultural studies ignored news agencies, whose original texts could only be accessed with difficulty, and which lacked direct 'audiences'.

Temporarily, but remarkably, all this diverted mainstream attention from the fact that the global media industries were undergoing processes of concentration, deregulation, privatization and commercialization to a wholly unprecedented degree, and that for more than 99.999% of the world's population access to mass audiences was an extremely remote likelihood, the proclaimed universality of the Internet notwithstanding. In the same period, ownership of the former state-owned agencies in eastern and central Europe was transformed. New private agencies were founded, and major western agencies began to penetrate their markets. During this time, the modest level of interest in news agencies which had been sparked by the NWICO debates tailed off into insignificance, with the exception of a few new organizational histories. Interest was revived in the mid-1990s by the development of interest in global television and the role within it of the major video news agencies. Two of the three leading video news players had significant affiliation with existing global print agencies (Reuters Television, and AP Television) and the third (WTN, previously UPITN) had evolved from a partnership in which one of the previous Big Four had played a significant part (UPI). The speed of development of global television reinvigorated a political economy perspective, and the political economy approach has been influential in recent research by Boyd-Barrett, Palmer, Paterson and Rantanen, for example, whose work is also represented in this volume. This is a political economy moulded by a discourse of globalization – not the free-market globalization of neo-liberal apologists, but the oligopolistic hegemonic globalization of their critics. Like most political economy of media, its major weakness is in the analysis of content, although here too we have sought rectification.

Globalization theory, drawing alike on cultural studies and political economy, on processes of meaning as well as on economics of communication, posits a more complex world than political economy on its own, and may thus be able to build a bridge between the two approaches. There is a post-modern dimension here which distrusts systems and polarities. None the less, we want to argue in this book that globalization theory should not lose sight of agency, and that there is still considerable evidence of system: this is manifest in the patterns of dependent interaction among strong and weaker players, the advantages which favour western agencies, consistent inequalities in the distribution of resources, the application of a constant set of news values, and evidence of system capacity to adjust to a changing external environment.

Conclusion

This opening chapter has mapped the study of news agencies with respect to the development of the study of international communication and of globalization within media study. The introduction to each part will discuss particular contributions. Part I introduces the print-based, financial and television news agencies, with reference to developments and trends over the entire history of news agencies. It includes a chapter on the early development of business practices which forged relations between global and local agencies to consolidate the hold of both global and local players over their respective markets. The dynamics of struggle for control of domestic markets between local agencies, press groups, governments and international agencies is explored further in Part II, which traces the global–local dynamics of the evolution of national news agencies in periods of major political transition, represented here by studies of Spain, eastern and central Europe, east and southern Africa. The final part, Part III, looks at the role of the major global agencies in defining what is meant by 'news' in mainstream media around the world, and in imposing their definitions on other media, especially national news agencies. It is also about attempts to define news agencies that are 'alternative' to the western mainstream media: first, Inter Press Service, the radical third world news agency co-operative and, second, the practice of television news exchange between major public service broadcasters as an important alternative to the practices of commercial television news agencies.

Through this volume we wanted to achieve a number of goals. At the most basic level, we recognized that the field was in need of up-dating since the broad surveys of news agency activity by Boyd-Barrett (1980), Boyd-Barrett and Palmer (1981) and Fenby (1986). In addition, we wanted a volume that would demonstrate the continuing importance of news agencies, *theorizing* these institutions in relation to important theories and controversies of the late 1990s, embracing each major phase of news agency operation from production through text to distribution and consumption, integrating historical and contemporary research, and exploring the dynamics between local, national and international news agencies. We wanted to broaden a field that is no longer simply about general news agencies but about financial, video, photo, Internet, and other 'wholesale' operations that originate media product; we were also concerned to introduce some new considerations (such as that of quality control procedures) and to improve the ways in which some older questions (such as news agency content) are investigated and conceptualized. The current struggle for market share between the major agencies raises questions about the future scope for competition, and we wanted to throw some light on these issues, for example: Is the world market for video news big enough for three major players or can we expect it to reduce to two (which has indeed happened while this book was in press)? Is market deregulation good or bad for national news agencies? Last but by no means least, we have welcomed the opportunity to bring together in one volume a range of different voices, from different countries. News agency scholars have traditionally come from a variety of different fields, and have tended to work in isolation. Limitations of space are such that we have not been able to invite as wide a range of contributions as we would have wished. None the less, we believe this volume is recognition in itself that news agency study has reached a certain level of continuity, maturity and community, which it has not enjoyed hitherto. We would hope that a future contribution to this field could also bring about the integration of scholarly and practitioner perspectives.

References

Boyd-Barrett, O. (1979) 'Theory and practice: from Cuba to Vietnam', in O. Boyd-Barrett, *The World-Wide News Agencies: Development, Organization, Competition, Markets and Product*, PhD thesis, Milton Keynes: Open University Press, pp. 833–55.
Boyd-Barrett, O. (1980) *The International News Agencies*, London: Constable.
Boyd-Barrett, O. (1997) 'International communication and globalization: contradictions and directions', in Ali Mohammadi (ed.), *International Communication and Globalization*, London: Sage, pp. 11–26.
Boyd-Barrett, O. and Palmer, M. (1981) *Le trafic des nouvelles*, Paris: Alain Moreau.
Boyd-Barrett, O. and Thussu, K. (1992) *Contra-Flow in Global News*, London: John Libbey.
Cooper, K. (1942) *Barriers Down*, New York: Farrar & Rinehart.

Eliassen, P. (1918) 'Ritzaus Bureau 1866–1916. Et bidrag til det udenlandske og danske efterretningvaesens historie', Kobenhaun: Trykt hos Nielse & Lydiche.

Fenby, J. (1986) *The International News Services,* New York: Schocken Books.

Galbraith, J.K. (1967/77) 'The technostructure and the corporation in the new Industrial state', in M. Zeitlin (ed.), *American Society Inc.* (2nd edn), Chicago: Rand McNally College Publishers, pp. 202–13.

Giddens, A. (1990) *The Consequences of Modernity,* Stanford: Stanford University Press.

Hall, S. (1982) 'The rediscovery of ideology: return of the repressed in media studies', in M. Gurevitch, J. Curran and J. Woolacott (eds), *Culture, Society and the Media,* London: Methuen.

Hardt, H. (1979) *Social Theories of the Press: Early German and American Perspectives*, Beverly Hills, CA, and London: Sage.

Harris, P., Malczek, H. and Ozkol, E. (1980) *Flow of News in the Gulf,* New Communication Order Series no. 3, Paris: UNESCO, pp. 43–63.

IPI (International Press Institute) (1953) *The Flow of News,* Zurich: IPI.

Klapper, J. (1960) *The Effects of Television,* New York: Free Press.

Lerner, D. (1958) *The Passing of Traditional Society,* New York, Free Press.

Levebre, A. (1992) *Havas: Les arcanes du pouvoir,* Paris: Bernard Grassett.

Pye, L. (1963) *Communications and Political Development,* Princeton, NJ: Princeton University Press.

Rantanen, T. (1990) *Foreign News in Imperial Russia: The Relationship between International and Russian News Agencies 1856–1914,* Helsinki: Suomalainen Tiedeakatemia.

Rantanen, T. (1997) 'The globalization of electronic news in the 19th century', *Media, Culture and Society*, 19: 4.

Read, D. (1992) *The Power of News. The History of Reuters,* Oxford: Oxford University Press.

Salinas, R. (1977) 'News agencies and the new information order', in T. Varis et al. (eds), *International News and the New Information Order,* Institute of Journalism and Mass Communication: University of Tampere, Finland.

Schiller, H. (1976) *Communication and Cultural Domination*, New York: International Arts and Sciences Press.

Schramm, W. (1964) *Mass Media and National Development,* Stanford: Stanford University Press.

Sreberny-Mohammadi, A. (1991) 'The global and the local in international communications', in J. Curran and M. Gurevitch (eds), *Mass Media and Society,* London: Edward Arnold.

Tomlinson, J. (1991), *Cultural Imperialism,* London: Pinter.

UNESCO (1980) *Many Voices, One World: Towards a New, More Just and More Efficient World Information and Communication Order* (McBride Report), The International Commission for the Study of Communication Problems, Paris: UNESCO; London: Kogan Page.

Villard, O. (1930) 'The Associated Press', *The Nation*, 16 April/23 April.

Part I

NEWS AGENCIES AS AGENTS OF GLOBALIZATION

Introduction

Terhi Rantanen and Oliver Boyd-Barrett

Part I introduces the print-based, financial and television news agencies, and discusses their development and present status in relation to the questions which globalization theories have raised and thus introduces new approaches to analysis of the relationship between globalization and news agencies. In chapter 2 Oliver Boyd-Barrett traces the development of the major global agencies (Reuters, AP, AFP) from their origins until the present day by asking whether they and the global news system of which they are the centre are significantly different from their predecessors (the British Reuters, the French Havas and the German Wolff) that monopolized the world's news market, dividing it between themselves, some 100 to 150 years previously? If there are significant continuities, then here is a case not merely of a sustained manifestation of globalization of media industries but of a phenomenon which some globalization theorists prefer to think the concept of globalization displaced – that of media imperialism. Boyd-Barrett answers his question by showing that the global agencies' present hierarchy, smaller in number as far as the print agencies are concerned, is sustained by the accumulated benefits of market advantage rather than by formal agreements. Yet it is their continuing domination of these markets, not the subtle differences over time of explanations for that domination, that should hold our attention. Further, they each retain significant associations with particular nations: AFP with France, Reuters with the United Kingdom, and AP and WTN with the United States. If Reuters was one of the strongest agencies previously, it is now the strongest, mainly because of its financial news service.

While the major agencies are still concentrated in the world's prosperous nations, the Big Three enjoy a status which the rest of the world by and large now seems to tolerate: the 'dependency' NWICO discourses of the 1960s and 1970s have been conquered, temporarily at least, by a worldwide neo-liberal discourse that seems prepared to risk the dangers of monopoly where these are the outcome of 'free market' economics. The absence of strong, viable, alternative services reinforces the Big Three's status (AFP, AP, Reuters): instead of trying to resist them or to develop new concepts, most smaller agencies imitate the strategies of the majors. It remains to be seen whether this development actually leads to a decline in the overall number of news agencies, although as chapters in this book suggest, there are real dangers here for many of the older national news agencies.

The globalization of news was a reality for the 19th-century news agencies, and therefore long precedes globalization-by-television – the theme which has attracted most media scholars to date. As Terhi Rantanen shows in chapter 3, global and local were deeply interconnected in the globalization of news in the 19th century. The global agencies negotiated market entry through national agencies. Rantanen points out that although this relationship is often regarded as a one-sided affair in which the globals lorded over the local agencies, a better description would be 'bi-directional dependency' that involves exclusive use of news both in global and domestic markets. In order to secure compliant local partners it suited the globals to work through local monopoly structures. In the cases of the United States, Australia and New Zealand, local monopolies were achieved through strong local co-operatives which then charged high entry fees to outsiders. They secured the services of a global agency, in this case Reuters, through which they had access to news gathered by the members of the European cartel. The process of establishing local monopolies was not at all a smooth one, and there were sources of active competition and resistance. This is highly significant because it reinforces the argument which is advanced in the introduction to this book that the global system of news, which has been established through this critical nexus between global and national news agencies, has worked towards the simultaneous construction of discourses which we now take for granted as 'national' and 'international'.

The importance of the local is further emphasized by Jürgen Wilke in chapter 4. Here a local, media-owned co-operative agency – established, ironically, by the allies in the aftermath of the last world war – retains a strength on its own domestic market which can withstand full-blown competition from the global agencies and which has even had the curious effect of encouraging the globals to become more local. This is certainly an unusual case. There are not many markets where the competition for local media is quite so unrestrained. Were dpa stronger, it arguably could mount greater competition on international markets; the strength of the activity of global agencies in its domestic market is possibly one strategy to discourage such an outcome. This case demonstrates how the co-operative formula retains credibility and that in countries which have wealthy media systems it can withstand both private, non-co-operative competition from domestic sources as well as competition from the global agencies. Although this case is similar to Rantanen's study of Australia and New Zealand in revealing the importance of the local in global–local dynamics there are significant differences. In the case of Australia, the global agency (part of a global cartel) preferred to work with a local monopoly in a symbiotic partnership of mutual need (and even without the shadow of the cartel, this symbiosis is still a feature of global–local relations in some countries). The global agency still had the upper hand in so far as it could choose to opt for a different partner and such a choice would have consequences for the distribution of power on the domestic market. In the German example, however, the national agency is not so dependent on global suppliers – it maintains its own reporting networks – and can withstand the incursions of globals on its own market. The example demonstrates that it is possible for a domestic agency to struggle free of dependence on globals. dpa's co-operative structure lends it a credibility for domestic clients. Were it a government agency, the globals might have more success – in a deregulated market – in prising away clients. AFP of France, however, also manages to stave off the incursions of global and domestic competition, despite significant dependence on and links with the state. A wealthy media market and credibility are clearly important factors in supporting a strong national agency, but credibility need not require complete independence of the state. It can be still be achieved provided that the links with the state are sufficiently discreet and subtle – in the case of AFP, there is also a co-operative structure where government representatives sit with media owners and journalists. AFP's credibility, like dpa's, is also built on the strength of its independent reporting overseas.

Chapter 5 on financial news services by Michael Palmer, Oliver Boyd-Barrett and Terhi Rantanen fortifies the developments noted above. It is here that we see the agencies contributing directly to the construction and moment-to-moment facilitation, if not the very life-blood, of a system of global commerce which depends, first and foremost, on the collection and instantaneous dissemination of financial information that is believed to be absolutely secure and trustworthy. Financial news services have become more and more important in several respects. First, they help to support the general news services for media, including electronic news services. Second, they constitute an important source of economic support for the agencies themselves. Third, they have contributed to the shaping of western news ideology as 'impartial' and 'objective'. The agencies that control financial news markets are also Anglo-American. Among the major news agencies of what had once been a global cartel, only Reuters has dedicated the major part of its activity to reporting economics and financial news and data for the business community, while preserving its commitment to general news services. Reuters' present main rivals, such as the US Knight-Ridder, Dow Jones, Telerate and Bloomberg were set up solely to serve financial business markets. No single organization within the spectrum of Reuters' competition is thought to offer a range of services as broad as that of Reuters. It has penetrated the financial news markets in many countries – spectacularly, in recent years, in central and eastern Europe after the collapse of communism.

Boyd-Barrett also writes in chapter 2 about the growth of 'wholesale' television news services. Two of the traditional global agencies, AP and Reuters, are involved in services both of print news to newspapers and audiovisual news (APTV and Reuters Television) to broadcasters, thus increasing their overall influence. Boyd-Barrett adds World Television News (WTN) to the list of major agencies, although WTN is now exclusively a television news agency (in the process of being acquired by its rival APTV, in June 1998). International television news pictures are thus provided to broadcasters worldwide mainly by three commercial news agencies and a variety of co-operative news exchanges (about the latter Stig Hjarvard also writes in chapter 13).

In chapter 6, Chris Paterson focuses on the phenomenon of concentration in the supply of international television news, which he finds every bit as intense if not more intense than the concentration that has typified the print news agencies over the past 150 years, and with particularly worrying implications, among other things, for the quality of news from the developing world. Concentration in international television news reflects, first, the narrow bonds of professional consensus amongst influential first world journalists within the agencies and among their clients and, second, trends of corporate downsizing, media concentration and the opportunism of 'alliance capitalism'. Paterson concludes that electronic news is now determined and provided by a small number of culturally homogeneous news people in a very few similar, often collaborating Anglo-American organizations based in London.

2 'Global' News Agencies

Oliver Boyd-Barrett

In this chapter I shall review the prevailing features of the major 'global' news agencies, with a view to answering the following question: on the eve of the 21st century can we say that the major news agencies are significantly different than they (or their predecessors) were at the turn of the 20th century or before?

The global agencies are organizations whose main *raison d'être* is to gather and to sell news throughout the world for the benefit of 'retail' media (newspapers, broadcasters, on-line suppliers) and other outlets (business, finance institutions, governments, private individuals). The leading agencies of the 1990s are generally acknowledged to be Agence France-Presse, Associated Press, and Reuters. Two of these organizations, AP and Reuters, are involved in services both of print news to newspapers and audiovisual news (APTV and Reuters Television) to broadcasters. Because of the importance of television news, and of the agencies as suppliers of it, it is also necessary to add World Television News (WTN) to the list of major agencies, although WTN is now exclusively a television news agency (WTN is successor to UPITN, which had been jointly owned by the second major American agency, UPI, and the British television news station, ITN). Although these agencies are 'global' in the scope of their activities they each retain significant associations with particular nations, namely France (AFP), the United States (AP, WTN) and the United Kingdom (Reuters, WTN). WTN supplies still pictures to AFP, and the two organizations co-operate in the field, sharing a number of bureaux.

Continuities and Discontinuities

In a recent article (Boyd-Barrett, 1997) I have argued that the continuities in news agency history are at least as remarkable as the discontinuities. In that article I was looking mainly at the period 1980–1996. Here, I shall consider a somewhat longer time span, 1850–2000, although I am principally focusing on a comparison of the situation in the late 1990s with the state of affairs around 1900. The main criteria I use to establish a comparative framework for this exercise are as follows: diversity, location, autonomy, competition, clients, technology. I developed these categories in the introduction to my 1980 study, and I believe that these are still among the fundamental axes of concern in any analysis of these enterprises.

The issue of content *per se* I shall leave to later chapters. In general terms the agencies are still mainly providers of 'spot-news', following in the Anglo-Saxon tradition, developed in the 19th century and honed in the 20th, of a 'journalism of information', which privileges 'facts' together with the routines in which this style of journalism engages to convince readers of the authenticity of such 'facts'. The 'facts' thus privileged overwhelmingly favour certain categories of information and event over others, certain sources over others, and certain locations over others.

Diversity

In 1980, I argued that there were four principal global news agencies, active as general news gatherers and as news distributors through most of the world. These were primarily agencies for print news media. Two of the major agencies had associated television news services (Visnews and UPITN), and two supplied audio reports for broadcasters. By 1996, I argued that the number of major print news agencies had declined from four to three. Significantly, UPI was no longer considered equivalent competition by the largest agencies in the 1990s. Some other agencies, such as DPA (Germany) and EFE (Spain), which had been significant regional players, with particularly strong activity in certain markets, may have become stronger, but had not joined the league of the major players. Whereas in 1980 there were a number of developing 'alternative' regionally focused news agencies, the promise of these had largely evaporated by the late 1990s, due to their lack of credibility in the eyes of mainstream 'first world' newspapers, and financial insecurity (Boyd-Barrett and Thussu, 1992).

The agencies of the Soviet Union (TASS, now ITAR-TASS) and China (Xinhua) I had placed in a different category, on the basis, first, that there was no clear dividing line between their activities as news agencies and their functions as departments of government and, second, that they tended not to operate commercially, often providing news services free of charge. By 1996, the influence of ITAR-TASS (still a state agency) had diminished with the development of alternative Russian news sources, notably the privately owned Interfax and regional agencies of the Russian Federation; that of Xinhua continued much as before. These sources continued to be influential globally for information about Russia and China, but not as sources of news about other countries (other than to clients within Russia and China).

On the other hand there had been significant growth of 'wholesale' television news services. Visnews had been taken over completely by Reuters to form Reuters Television; UPITN had been through a succession of changes, leading to the formation of WTN, the second largest television news service and owned principally by Capital Cities Corporation, which in turn was taken over by Disney in 1996. (ITN has a minority stake in WTN, and Reuters has a minority stake in ITN; ITN subscribes to WTN and to Reuters TV.) Associated Press had added APTV to its services in 1994, putting downward pressure on prices and threatening the viability of the market for the three major players. (In May 1998, as this book was going to press, APTV announced its decision to buy WTN. The world market in television news will be controlled by two dominant players with the possibility that one of these may withdraw at some time in the future.) Eurovision and, to a lesser extent, Asiavision, the news exchanges organized by public service broadcasters in Europe and Asia, continued to be influential sources in 1996 as in 1980, feeding both 'wholesale' or commercial news agency footage to those agencies' subscribers, together with member footage to their respective networks. Some 'retail' global television news operations such as CNN, BBC World, and Sky news were also acting to some extent as 'wholesalers', by distributing channels to cable operators, providing footage to other broadcasters, and feeding 'print' news services via the Internet, while themselves continuing to be significant clients and users of conventional 'wholesale' agency television news.

In the case of financial news services, Reuters was one of the strongest global agencies throughout the entire 150-year period, and was certainly the strongest in the 1980s and 1990s. In 1980 the agency was clearly overtaking or had already significantly overtaken competitors such as Associated Press, Dow Jones, Telerate or Commodity News Service (CNS). By 1996 it was by far the strongest globally, but subject to both old (Dow Jones, Knight-Ridder) and new competition (Bloomberg, established in 1981). Bloomberg and WTN both have links with the French global agency, AFP, in provision of financial and television news. But against Reuters' 340,200 subscriber terminals in 1996, Dow Jones/Telerate boasted only 94,500 and Bloomberg 75,000 (Napoli, 1997).

Bloomberg's influence is greater than the number of its terminals may suggest, as it feeds financial data and economic news through the AP network to AP members and clients in the United States, and to many national markets through national news agencies. Indeed, it boasts having the second largest 'wholesale' news distribution in the United States, after AP. It has print, radio and television distribution in many countries: Bloomberg television is distributed via Astra satellite service in Europe. Media exposure increases the number of its clients for hard-core financial news services (for example bonds, equities). With 500 reporters in 70 countries by the mid-1990s, Bloomberg has extended beyond financial towards more general news (Bloomberg, 1997). Bloomberg exercised an influence beyond its actual size on account of the speed of its development, the main reason for which was its provision of sophisticated added-value data-graphics and manipulations to basic financial statistics which helped fund managers to take decisions. This kind of competition has stimulated greater attention by Reuters, for example, to the improvement of customer relations, and the sophistication of its services (for example Reuters 3000, a screen system that packages historical data and analysis with prices and news).

The most immediate characteristics of this apparently broader range of news sources are that the number of 'voices' which are represented among the providers is still small and that North American and western European interests dominate. West European voices amongst the global 'wholesale' giants are primarily represented by Reuters, Reuters Television and Agence France-Presse. Because London is the headquarters to both APTV and WTN, and is a significant hub bureau of CNN, there is an English inflection even to some of the US agency activities. The situation is not dramatically different from how it was in 1900 when the German agency, Wolff/Continental, probably played a more significant role internationally than DPA, its successor, does now, at least in first-world markets, on account of its membership of the global cartel. But Associated Press was only beginning to flex its global muscles, and was still a junior player in the world league.

Location

How far are the major news agencies still concentrated in the world's most prosperous nations? In 1900 and before, the location of major agencies represented the world's wealthiest nations: Britain, France and Germany, together with the United States (although at that time the US agency, Associated Press, was not as powerful as its European counterparts). By 1997 the American, English and French influence certainly contains news agency activity among the world's most advanced nations, but it is noticeable that nations even wealthier than England and France show little ambition (or capability, or both) to acquire first-rank position within the global agency business. This may be a realistic response to the advantages which established players enjoy from accumulated professional expertise, international credibility and worldwide networks. As Asia grows more powerful over the next 50 years we should expect certain challenges to this position: for example, Xinhua (China), which would have to operate commercially and without political fetters if it wished to join the inner club; or an Indian challenge, which in comparison with China would have the advantage of a tradition of greater media freedom and English-language usage. While Japan has been a leading economic power for many decades, its national news agencies, Kyodo (general news) and Jiji (economic news) have never become significant as global news providers. Key competitive factors at work that may help determine the success or otherwise of future challenges have to do with level of resource, actual and perceived independence from state and capital (that is, from political and business interest), an established culture of journalism, competence, and principal operational languages.

Autonomy

Autonomy is generally an important consideration for media scholars in assessing the interest, accuracy and credibility of information providers. It is often assumed that providers who are financially and politically independent have a stronger claim to credibility, impartiality and objectivity in their news reporting. According to western news values, news providers which are government or politically controlled are not trustworthy as impartial sources, and are incapacitated to act as effective sources of criticism or scrutiny of government actions. This view privileges concerns about formal political processes over concerns about economic and financial processes. The potential of the commercial media as guarantors of a 'public sphere' is challenged by those who argue that such media are compromised by their dependence on advertising and/or their need to maximize audiences in order to earn profit and to satisfy patrons, owners and shareholders. The limits to autonomy, therefore, are generally seen to relate variously to issues of ownership and sources of finance. Professional values are sometimes seen to act as buffers or mediators between the interests of owners, profit, audiences and the requirements of impartiality and objectivity, although at other times it is considered that professional values entail certain practices or routines which further compromise claims to impartiality (see Curran, 1991).

In terms of ownership, the leading agencies of the 19th century were Reuters, Havas and Wolff/Continental. These were independent companies; the strengths and personalities of their founders were significant influences in the early years. Earnings were generally derived from the sale of news services to media, financial or economic institutions, and governments. All were indirectly linked to their respective governments, which were important as sources of revenue and as sources of intelligence, and it is generally considered that their news services reflected their respective national interests. Read writes of Reuters, for example, that in the period 1860–1900 it functioned 'increasingly as an institution of the British Empire' (Read, 1992: ch. 3); Wolff was subsidized by the government of Bismarck who wanted to prevent Reuter from taking over the German agency. Havas also sold advertising space, acting as space-broker on behalf of client newspapers and advertisers or their agencies. A newer model of agency ownership and control was emerging in the United States, where Associated Press was a co-operative, formed by a significant number of US newspapers, and deriving all of its revenues from media sales. Later US agencies (INS to 1957, UP/UPI until the early 1990s, when it was acquired by Saudi-based Middle East Broadcasting Centre) were privately owned by newspaper chains owned by Scripps (in the case of UPI until the mid-1980s) and Hearst (in the case of INS).

I do not believe we know enough to be sure as to the balance of earnings between the different major sources of finance in this early period (that is, between media, financial and political sources) except to say that financial and political sources were considerable. (Political patronage was sometimes disguised in the form of 'excessive' payments for services rendered.) In 1919, Reuters earned a total of £63,000 (24% of its total earnings) from commercial and trade services, private-telegram and remittance traffic, and advertisements, as against £199,000 (76%) for news subscriptions at home and abroad. In 1924 these figures were £95,000 (28.5%) as against £208,000 (71.5%) (Read, 1992: 153). By 1933, commercial service subscriptions had overtaken UK newspaper subscriptions on the UK market; but income from economic services did not finally overtake news services, overall, until 1968.

This evidence suggests to me that, in the case of Reuters, the financial category was probably much more important overall than the political – despite significant instances of limited government subvention during the agency's history – and that news subscriptions were superior to both sources up to 1968, since when the relative importance of revenue from financial services has progressively increased. Political payments ceased in the mid-1980s: the last payment from BBC External Services ended in 1980 (the final payment was £250,000) and payments from the Foreign Office were drastically reduced in 1986 from £296,000 to their 'true' level of £20,000 (Read, 1992: 331). Financial service revenue was probably less important than political sources in the case of Havas and Wolff, and the political category possibly rivalled the media as a revenue source. The dominance of political sources of revenue has been sustained throughout the post-war history of Agence France-Presse, although there are no available figures which would allow an assessment of the proportion of state payments which could be regarded as 'subsidy'. Associated Press has been financed principally by subscriptions from its member newspapers and broadcasters, and from sales of services to overseas media and other clients.

During the first half of the 20th century this general pattern was sustained, except that the relative importance of the political probably increased: this was due to increased involvement of their respective states in the cases of Havas and Reuters. States had an interest in supporting the overseas reporting strength of these agencies in a variety of ways, especially in times of national crisis, as in the two world wars and during periods when the agencies would otherwise have been unable to sustain their reputations for worldwide coverage, or to sustain news coverage in those areas which were poor sources of revenue. The latter provided little news which was in media demand, but did supply news which was of interest to the agencies' home governments. A new source of state aid developed with the growth of broadcasting which, through much of the world, was state-owned – the state thus became an important purchaser of agency services both for state ministries and for state-owned broadcast institutions. State involvement in media was further intensified with the new wave of national news agencies which accompanied processes of decolonization in the 1950s and 1960s.

Today's agencies have more complex management structures. But none of them, with the exception of WTN, is part of a larger media or non-media empire, and news and information is still their principal activity. This particular continuity is very significant, given the trends in recent decades towards growing concentration and diversification of media empires, and the involvement of giant non-media corporations. In the case of Reuters, AFP and AP, their constitutions restrict the range of activities in which they can become engaged, and require impartiality and objectivity. AP is restrained from entering into activities which could compete against the interests of its members. Reuters has provisions to prevent the control of the agency by a single interest or group. Paterson argues in this volume that single, large clients such as Murdoch's media empire could exert leverage over an agency such as Reuters, although against this view it could be argued that because any interference in content could be construed as extremely damaging by the financial community, which accounts for over 94% of the agency's revenue, it probably would not be tolerated.

Havas has been succeeded by AFP. This agency has a co-operative ownership structure, representing newspapers, journalists and the state. The state accounts for over 40% of the subscription revenue, and this percentage has declined from over 60% since the late 1970s. Media clients are the next most important category. However, AFP is subject to government interference through state representatives on its governing council (for example influence which was exerted in 1975 to block the reappointment of Jean Marin as director-general, and again to prevent the re-election of Lionel Fleury as director in 1996, following the agency's 1995 coverage of a housing scandal which involved the Prime Minister) (Hoover's Company Profiles Online, 1996). Such intervention is sometimes a punishment for things which the agency has already done and which the government does not like, and can be interpreted as testimony to a spirit of independence within the agency. This spirit has the support of many media members of the governing council. French media have become more inclined to challenge the political establishment in the 1980s, with the adoption of more commercial and 'populist' practices, and media support for AFP independence may have strengthened.

The German agency does not rank among the world's 'global' agencies, although it is ranked as an important news source by many national news agencies. DPA is a co-operatively structured, media-owned agency which derives most of its revenue from media subscriptions and sales.

In general, it can be concluded that the categories of media and financial sources of revenue for the world's major agencies are now more important than the political in comparison with either 1900 or 1850. This is due to a variety of factors, principally (a) greater acceptance that political subvention of news agencies detracts from their credibility; (b) privatization and deregulation of broadcasting, together with the expansion of cable and satellite, has reduced the importance of state-owned broadcast institutions as clients; (c) the development of financial news markets has reduced the necessity for dependence on the state – completely in the case of Reuters, and partially in the case of AFP; (d) diminution of a tendency for Reuters and AFP to distribute exclusively through (usually state-controlled) national news agencies; (e) more generally, the expansion of new media and new media markets – including news-photos, radio, terrestrial television, cable, satellite, videotext, teletext and online services – has greatly diversified the range of media markets, which in turn, has reduced dependence on political sources.

Traditionally, dependence on political or state sources of revenue has been regarded as more problematic than dependence on corporate finance. The demand of the corporate sector for general financial and economic news and data, company information, stocks and commodity prices, has not been regarded as likely to lead to pressures in support of particular sectors or points of view. The corporate world has an insatiable appetite for timely and accurate information that is likely to affect in any way the prospects for profit and loss. This demand probably has positive benefits for the range of general news – profits from corporate clients help to finance stronger reporting networks. Any negative implications have yet to be proven. The most serious consequence, possibly, is that revenues from financial news services are increasing the ability of major agencies to compete with national and other smaller agencies on domestic markets, threatening a reduction in diversity of local news supply. The supply of financial information often has substantial and immediate implications for company earnings, and this sector of news agency work is extremely sensitive to speed, accuracy, and equivalence of treatment among clients. This does not overcome the problem of patterned inequalities of attention between different geopolitical regions or categories of news.

The continuing independence of the major agencies (none of them has been subsumed within larger companies with the exception of WTN, part of the Disney empire) can be regarded as a positive and reassuring feature, which probably supports the credibility and acceptability of these organizations throughout the world (although worries are sometimes expressed that the increasing importance of economic news, especially in the case of Reuters, may weaken the commitment to other categories of news). There is less likelihood that clients will feel that by subscribing to a particular agency service they may be subscribing to a competing or potentially competitive organization. The global agencies have tended not to enter into direct competition with their own clients. For example, Reuters withdrew from its involvement in the Spanish-language North American news channel Telenoticias, partly in order to avoid competing with its other broadcast clients in that market.

Competition

The principal feature of the world's news market in the second half of the 19th century and the first third of the 20th, was the cartel. This was an oligopolistic and hierarchical structure of the global news market controlled by Reuters, Havas and Wolff at the top tier, in partnership with an ever-increasing number of national news agencies. Each member of the triumvirate had the right to distribute its news service, incorporating news of the cartel, to its ascribed territories: these territories were determined by periodic, formal agreements. With some exceptions, the members of the triumvirate were prohibited from selling their news to clients in the others' territories, although they could gather news independently from those territories if they wished. The triumvirate of Reuters, Havas and Wolff supplied world news to national news agencies in return for a service of national news and payment of a subscription fee by the national agencies. In general (although the practice was rather more complicated) the national agencies had exclusive rights to the distribution of cartel news in their territories, and the cartel had exclusive rights to the national agency news services.

The global news system is still a hierarchical one, in which a small number of global agencies supply world news to clients throughout the world, including national news agencies, but this hierarchy is now kept in place by the accumulated benefits of market advantage rather than by formal agreements between the major players. These are, indeed, in intense competition with one another (there was also competition in the 19th century, despite the cartel), to the point of seeking to sell news in each other's domestic markets, even in the markets of client national news agencies, and they operate competitively in all markets. It is less common than it was for global agency services to be distributed exclusively through national news agencies, and in any case it is rare for all the major agencies to be distributed this way in any given territory. The collapse of communism in Russia and eastern Europe, together with other instances of dramatic political transition, have opened up those markets to competition from global agencies. But, equally, versions of news agency services are available through the Internet for individual as well as corporate clients, so potentially there is a loosening up of ties in both directions.

With the advent of television news services there is now a greater range of suppliers of 'wholesale' news. Reuters Television and Associated Press Television are in competition with WTN (which in a previous incarnation was jointly owned by the second major US agency, United Press International). Each agency has certain market strengths. AFP is particularly strong in France itself and in the ex-colonial territories of France. In recent years it has become much more aggressive in South-East Asia. Associated Press is particularly strong in the US, and in South America. Reuters is especially strong in the UK and in much of continental Europe. AP and AFP are still mainly general news providers, but also active in news photos, and provision of financial news (mainly for media clients, or of general news for financial news clients in association with financial news agencies such as Dow Jones or Bloomberg). Reuters is the world's leading provider of financial news and information and transaction services for financial news clients, where it faces a range of specialist competitors.

In 1964, AP revenues were £19 million as against those of Reuters' £4 million. AP in that year achieved revenue in excess of expenditure of £186,792 as against a loss for Reuters of £57,092. AP spent £2,678,571 on foreign news collection that year as against £1,256,000 in the case of Reuters (Read, 1992). In 1972 the situation was still very similar, with Reuters earning approximately half the revenue of Associated Press.

Yet by 1987 the two agencies were broadly equivalent in terms of revenue and expenditure (Boyd-Barrett, 1980: 38), and unlike AP, whose revenue was 80% from domestic services, most of Reuters' revenue (84%) was foreign. UPI in that year was third largest of the agencies (with revenues of $67 million) and AFP was fourth (with revenues of $43 million). Only 18% of AFP's revenues was earned outside of France, and 64% of the agency's revenues came from the French government (this had declined to 40% by 1996).

By 1980, Reuters' revenue had exceeded that of AP (Boyd-Barrett, 1980: 252), and in 1995 Reuters, with total revenues of £2,703 million (£2,914 million in 1996) had almost 12 times AP's £230 million turnover (£258 million in 1996); Reuters' media products' revenue of £153 million alone was worth more than half of the AP total, and probably worth more than AP non-US revenue. In 1996 Reuters was the 12th most valuable of all British companies quoted on the London Stock Exchange (Job, 1997), climbing to 11th place by 1997 (*Financial Times*, 10 April 1997). Reuters' pre-tax profit growth has risen from £94 million in 1985 to £701 million in 1996. The rate of increase in pre-tax profit from 1995 to 1996 was 17%. Annual profit increases of 20–30% have been common for much of the period 1985–1996 (Davidson, 1997).

The financial dominance of Reuters is accentuated upon looking at AP's operating revenue: this showed a loss of $25.8 million in 1995, reducing to a loss of $15.7 million in 1996. The company had total assets in 1996 of $229.4 million, and debt of $44 million. After-tax operating losses for APTV were $19.7 million in 1996, down from $24.6 million in 1995.

It should be taken into account that AP is a 'not-for-profit' co-operative, and that it presumably has some discretion as to how far a loss needs to be recovered from subscription fees to its members. It should also be noted that APTV revenue increased nearly five-fold in 1996 compared to 1995, and was projected to double in 1997; this rate of increase was considered in AP's 1996 annual report to have contributed to a reduction in the rate of loss. APTV clients include 100 international broadcasters. There is also a special services unit to provide technical and satellite support to APTV customers, and a Sports News Television service, in association with Trans World International. In 1996 it began to develop Electronic News Production System for the BBC, a newsroom management and research facility. In addition to APTV, AP has other non-traditional revenue streams, including AP AdSend, which distributes advertising digitally between advertisers, agencies and newspapers. This operation became profitable in the final quarter of 1996. The older AP–Dow Jones services of financial and business news outside the US is administered by AP. In 1996, amounts due to Dow Jones and Co. Inc., net of amounts due from customers, was $2.2 million.

AFP's total revenues in 1995 were equivalent to £147 million, suggesting that there has been a remarkable closing of the gap between the positions of AP and AFP in the last two decades as a result of more aggressive activity of the French agency overseas, especially in South-East Asia, and in economic and financial news. In 1977, AP revenue was approximately $100 million as against AFP's $43 million, a difference of 233% (Boyd-Barrett, 1980), whereas in 1995, AP revenue at £230 million as against AFP's £147 million was only 64% greater. In this respect, it can be said that in the last two decades, the major European (print) agencies have greatly increased their position with respect to the 'US' agencies, AP and UPI, of which the latter is now owned by a Saudi company.

Clients and Markets

Agency statistics must be treated warily as definitions of key terms such as 'bureau' or 'employee', for example, are not always provided or clear, and different agencies define and count things differently. None the less, statistics from the three major agencies provide some idea of the range of these services. These statistics are culled from a mixture of company reports and company publicity.

In 1995, Reuters claimed that its customers watched news and prices on more than 327,000 computer screens, in 42,000 locations, linked to a Reuters communication network spanning 154 countries, through 24 languages. It had 14,348 staff, gathering news from 197 offices in 207 cities in 90 countries. For Reuters media products the agency claims 1,200 journalists and photographers working in 120 bureaux in 74 countries. Reuters Television goes to 900 television broadcasters in 81 countries. The Reuters World Service news report sends a total of 150,000 words daily. One hundred news photos are distributed a day; there is also a graphics service.

In 1997, AP served 1,550 US newspaper members (plus 230 non-daily, non-English-language or college papers), as well as 6,000 US radio and television stations and networks, 750 subscribers to AP Network News (the largest single radio network in the USA) and 55 subscribers to All-News Radio. In addition it served 8,500 foreign subscribers, in 112 countries, through five languages translated by AP (with scores more translated by foreign subscribers). It had a total of 3,421 employees, of whom 536 were principally communications technology workers. Of the total staff, some 2,566 were based in the USA, and 855 were international. AP had a total of 237 news bureaux: 144 domestic and 93 international news bureaux across 71 countries. No figures have been provided for APTV.

Agence France-Presse had 12,500 clients, including 650 newspapers and magazines, 400 radio and television stations, 1,500 companies and public agencies and 100 national news agencies (which in turn served 7,600 other newspapers, 2,500 radio stations and 400 television stations) receiving AFP services in six principal languages, amounting to a total of 150,000 words, 250 photos and 20 graphics a day. The agency claimed 3,100 employees, including 150 photographers, 900 correspondents and 2,000 freelancers, located in 207 bureaux, reporting from 165 countries. This can be contrasted with the figures for a leading national agency which also has international distribution, the Spanish EFE, which covers news from 137 cities of 102 countries, with 23 bureaux in Spain and a total staff of 1,145.

I have noted that the main categories of client for news agency services are media, financial or corporate, and political. Media clients are newspapers, radio and television broadcasters (terrestrial, cable, satellite) and on-line service providers. Financial or corporate clients are distinguished by Reuters as clients for either information products or for transaction products. Information products deliver news and prices to customer screens, datafeeds to financial markets and the software tools to analyse data. Their clients are traders, brokers, dealers, analysts, investors, and corporate treasurers. Transaction products enable traders to deal from their keyboards. Political clients can be classified as government ministries or departments, and media and other industries which are primarily owned or supported by the state. Read (1992) quotes figures showing a decline in the relative importance of receipts from UK government sources to Reuters from 5% of total revenues in 1965 to 1.9% of total revenue in 1975, and this will have declined still further in subsequent years. In 1976 an internal Reuters inquiry estimated that AP and UPI derived respectively 2.2 and 1.6% of their income from the United States government. However, the category of 'state' client need not be restricted to the 'home' governments of the news agencies.

Earlier, I considered evidence with respect to the balance of the three main categories of client in terms of their importance as sources of revenues. Here, I will consider issues related to the relative importance of different client areas, expressed in terms of geopolitical boundaries, and issues related to the extent and manner of client participation in the areas covered by the agencies.

The most important markets for the news agencies tend to be their home or domestic markets, North America and western Europe. In this respect there has been no change for over a century. There have been substantial increases in overall revenue, and these increases have been most spectacular for Reuters in the past two decades: revenues multiplied some 40 times in the period 1977–1995, and revenues from media services grew approximately 16 times (Boyd-Barrett, 1997). The following discussion of the relative order of major geopolitical regions as sources of revenue has to be read in this context of very significant growth in overall income.

For Reuters, the UK is the single most important country, in terms of revenue (16% of the total in 1995). Altogether, the area of Europe, the Middle East and Africa accounted for over half (55% in 1995) of all revenues. The next most important markets are Asia/Pacific (18.1%), and the Americas (15.4%). Latin American revenue accounts for 10% of all American income (or 1.5% of total income). The figures for the Americas excluded income from Instinet (which provides agency brokerage services in global equities to securities industry professionals, and which accounts for 9% of total company revenue) and Teknekron (which provides trading-room software systems, and which accounts for 2.8% of total company revenue).

Media products in 1995 for newspapers, broadcasters and online services amounted to 5.7% of total revenue. Europe, the Middle East and Africa accounted for 58% of all media product revenue or 3.2% of total company revenue; the Americas accounted for 24% of all media product revenue or 1.4% of total company revenue; Asia/Pacific accounted for 17.6% of all media product revenue or 1% of total company revenue.

In 1918, from figures provided by Read (1992: 153) we can assess that the most important territories were then identified as the UK (18.6%), India (13.2%), Europe (11.9%), Far East (6.1%) and North America (0.3%). By 1938 the respective percentages, in order of size, were UK (28%), India (24.4%), Far East (14.1%), Europe (8.2%), and North America (0.3%). By 1979 Europe and the UK accounted for 59% of total revenue, followed by North America (17%), Asia (11%), Africa (7%), the Middle East (3%) and South America (3%).

From these figures we can deduce (a) that Europe today is far more important than it was before the second world war, as a market for Reuters; (b) that, however, the relative importance of Europe, the Middle East and Africa, if we treat this as a single region in the way that Reuters' company reports now do, has declined significantly in the period 1979–1995, from 69% to 55% of overall revenues, but may have declined somewhat less in the case of media product revenues, for which this region accounted for 58% (and the agency has exploited the opening up of markets in eastern Europe); (c) that Asia is relatively less important as a source of revenue today than it was in the pre-war years, but its importance has recovered substantially in the period 1979–1995, reflecting the booming economic growth of that region throughout the period; (d) and that in 1995, Reuters earned substantial revenues from North America in comparison with 1918–1938; the relative importance of North America, however, has actually declined, overall, in the period 1979–1995 – but only if profits from Instinet and Teknekron are excluded. North American media product revenues, on the other hand, are probably higher now than they were in 1979.

We do not have corresponding figures for AP and AFP. We can note that the domestic US and French markets are by far their most important; Europe and Asia are significant areas of activity. The importance of overseas revenue for Associated Press has generally increased in the post-war period. AFP's predecessor, Havas, was powerful in South America, because this continent was apportioned to Havas under the cartel agreements. On the demise of Havas as a news agency, under German occupation of France in the second world war, and with the temporary transfer of Havas markets to Reuters, the European presence in South America generally diminished, although post-war AFP may have had a stronger foothold than Reuters. The influence of the American agencies has been growing in South America since the 1920s and 1930s, and the American agencies, AP and UP(I) were generally acknowledged as the most important of news agencies serving South America for most of the succeeding post-war period, and may have achieved dominance as early as 1930 (Boyd-Barrett, 1980: 175). The post-war influence of both the major European agencies, AFP and Reuters, has been modest. On the other hand, that of the Spanish news agency, EFE, has been growing, and in the 1990s EFE was claiming to be the most used news agency in South America.

Ownership and management structure of both AP and AFP provide a privileged voice for their respective domestic members/clients. AP is a co-operative and has an elaborate structure for the participation and representation of members in decision-making. Full membership is limited to North America. Agence France-Presse has a communal governing council representing French media interests, the state, and journalist unions. Again, this structure ensures representation only for its domestic client base. Reuters has a board of directors. The chair in 1995 had links with a variety of (non-media) industrial interests. Of five non-executive directors, three had media connections, among others. The five executive directors were all full-time employees of the company. At one time, following a restructuring of the agency in 1944, Reuters was partly owned by the news agencies of India, Australia and New Zealand (the connection with PTI of India ended in 1949, and the status of AAP and NZPA was transformed when Reuters was floated on the stock exchange and restructured in 1983). There is now no structure for client participation; but considerable attention is afforded to client needs and demand, in a context where market dominance in itself can be a source of client grievance.

Technology

All major agencies have been at the forefront, sometimes the pioneers, of new communications technologies. This was true of the early days of cable, when Reuters, among others, was active in the laying of cable. Then came radio, later largely displaced by telephonic cable, itself largely displaced by satellite communications and computer. Photo services developed in the 1920s, and are now common to each of the main agencies; television began in the 1950s. Today the agencies are complex multi-media organizations principally using satellite for delivery of print, audio and television news and online news services. With respect to technology, then, it can be said that (a) the agencies have been major users of communications facilities, and major clients of state and private telecommunications networks, making their voices heard in international user and regulatory forums; (b) they themselves have been active in the customization of telecommunications networks, in research and development of communications technologies, and sometimes in the sub-leasing of such facilities for other users; (c) through technologies they have developed new forms of communications, as for instance in the development of Reuters' monitor services in the 1980s which for the first time provided a transactional facility between money market providers, in essence providing an electronic 'dealing floor'; (d) through technologies they have streamlined ways in which news could be fed through to retail media unedited, as for instance in the services of AP to client media in the United States where for decades it has been possible for client newspapers to feed AP news into news pages without editorial intervention; in more recent years, computerization has facilitated greater specialization of news services, news markets and client choice; (e) the agencies' motives for investment in communications technologies have consistently related to intensifying speed of news processing and delivery, competitiveness, serving new markets, and cost efficiency; (f) particularly in the case of Reuters, investment and application in technology for the delivery of information services and software, and facilitation of trading transactions, has played a significant role as lubricant to the maintenance and growth of international financial markets and activity.

Conclusion

In this chapter I have reviewed some of the major continuities and discontinuities that emerge upon examination of the history of global news agencies over the past 150 years in terms of diversity, location, autonomy, competition, clients and technology. In very general terms I have concluded that we have seen greater diversity in terms of numbers of players, but not necessarily in terms of location or of interests represented; the major players are probably more autonomous than they were, and competition between them is more intense; they have a much larger and broader range of clients whom they serve with increasingly sophisticated technology. While it would be quite wrong to ignore many significant developments and transformations in this long period of time, it is also apparent that this is an arena of continuous dominance by North America and western Europe, and that the influence of the UK and France, in particular, is now out of proportion to the economic significance of these powers. This may signify that through a process of accumulated advantage, these European enterprises now enjoy a status which much of the rest of the world, the 1970s era of NWICO protest notwithstanding, is inclined to accept. This rests in part on the increasing spread – as part of the process of globalization, and intensified by processes of democratization in South America, Africa, Russian and eastern Europe – of a western ideology of news and news-making. The new technologies of the emerging 'superhighways', which also constitute part of the globalization process, may indicate a less certain future, although early evidence does not suggest any immediate threat to the established balance of news power.

References

Bloomberg, M. (1997) *Bloomberg on Bloomberg*, New York: John Wiley.
Boyd-Barrett, O. (1980) *The International News Agencies*, London: Constable.
Boyd-Barrett, O. (1997) 'Global news agencies as agents of globalization', in A. Sreberny-Mohammadi, D. Winseck, J. McKenna and O. Boyd-Barrett (eds), *Media in Global Context,* London: Edward Arnold.

Boyd-Barrett, O. and Thussu, K. (1992), *Contra-Flow in Global News*, London: John Libbey.

Curran, J. (1991) 'Mass media and democracy: a reappraisal', in J. Curran and M. Gurevitch (eds), *Mass Media and Society*, London: Edward Arnold.

Davidson, A. (1997) 'The Davidson interview – Peter Job', *Reuters Business Briefing,* 22 July.

Giddens, A. (1990) *The Consequences of Modernity*, Stanford: Stanford University Press.

Hoover's Company Profiles Online (1996) 'France: Agence France-Presse', *Business Briefing*, 21 December.

Job, P. (1997) 'Reuters talks, the market listens', in *Blue Wings, Finnair Inflight Magazine*, February-March.

Napoli, L. (1997) 'Profile: Bloomberg, a man and his information machine', in *The New York Times, CyberTimes*, 29 April.

Read, D. (1992) *The Power of News. The History of Reuters*, Oxford: Oxford University Press.

3   The Struggle for Control of Domestic News Markets (1)

Terhi Rantanen

> It is probable that before many months are over, telegraphic communi-
> cation will be established with Great Britain in a form so perfect that what
> happens in the metropolis of the Empire will be known in its extremities
> in one or two days or in fact in a few hours, according to the arrangement
> rather than distance. (*Sydney Morning Herald*, 26 May 1871)

The relationship between global and local is becoming an essential focus in
study of the globalization of news. Most articles in this volume concentrate
on very recent developments, but the process of news globalization had
begun already in the 19th century when electronic news was commodified
(Rantanen, 1997) for the purpose of selling news to newspapers and other
clients, among whom national news agencies were particularly important –
because they also represented a cheap supply of national news which could
be traded as part payment towards their subscription for the services of the
global agencies.

Traditionally, when studying the relationships between national and
global agencies in their historical context the main emphasis has been on
showing how the former were dependent on the latter (see, for example,
Ingmar, 1973; Rantanen, 1990, 1997). This is understandable since the
precise details of the global news cartel formed by Reuters (British), Havas
(French) and Wolff (German) in 1859 had been relatively unknown even
for scholars. So the first scholarly task was to reveal the detail of the agreements that were formerly held secret by these global agencies. Such studies
showed how the major agencies divided up the world's news market
between themselves (and after 1927 with the US Associated Press) and
made national agencies contractually dependent on them. The global agencies restricted other agencies from operating in their exclusive territories,
until 1934 when the cartel was breaking down. Meanwhile, a national
agency in its home territory achieved an exclusive right to the cartel's news,
but lost the right to send its news to any other news agency except to the
global agency with which it had signed the agreement.

But why did the national agencies approve this policy? To answer this
question it is important to study the domestic markets of different national
agencies. In my earlier work on the historical development of the US news

agencies I wrote that the segregation of news agency studies into two dis-crete fields – international communication and the history of journalism – has led to a basic misunderstanding of news agency operations. So, researchers in international communication have tended to emphasize the subordination of national to global news agencies – as if competition in the internal, domestic market was not an important factor. Historians of jour-nalism, on the other hand, have committed the opposite sin – they have focused exclusively on the relationships between domestic agencies while ignoring their foreign connections. Hence the national and global markets have been treated as independent variables. I concluded that the starting point for a new line of research must be a strong, bi-directional dependency between the national and global markets (Rantanen, 1992: 4).

We cannot completely understand the globalization of news if we sepa-rate foreign and domestic markets from each other. When electronic news became commodified and monopolized in the global market, the same hap-pened in the domestic market. The crucial link here is the transformation of news from a public to an exclusive good. As Shmanske (1986: 55–80) has shown, the success of the US co-operative news agency, Associated Press, can be understood by analysing the economic and marketing problems associated with private-sector production of common goods. According to Shmanske, in news provision the news quickly becomes common property, so in order to survive economically the news agency must be able to exclude from using the news those newspapers which do not pay for it. His contri-bution has been to show how this happened in the domestic market and how the co-operative ownership supported that development. Shmanske pays due attention to the fact that co-operative ownership has a strong advan-tage over other ownership forms (private, state) in marketing and protect-ing collective goods. He asserts that there is nothing *morally* superior in the co-operative ownership form; it was superior only in the way that the US Associated Press(es) practised price discrimination and restricted their membership.

Earlier research has neglected to note that this process occurs simul-taneously in global and domestic markets. Both global and national agen-cies adopted the principle of exclusivity. Although national agencies could not operate in the global market, they exercised the policy of exclusivity in their home market. This explains why national agencies were willing to accept the global agencies' policy and why the cartel system survived for over 60 years.

Hence, it is not only a question of combining two different approaches, but of understanding that the concept of bi-directional dependency consists of two elements, namely two different kinds of exclusivity. First, global agencies had exclusive access to national agencies' news. Second, and this is often forgotten, national agencies had access to global agencies' news in their home territory. While the global agencies were able to monopolize the world's news market, one national agency in each country could monopo-lize the delivery of foreign news in its own country. The exclusive contract a national agency had with the global news cartel effectively denied its domestic competitors access to the cartel's foreign news. Hence, a monopoly was created both in the global and national markets. To make the distinction between the two types of exclusivity that have so far been neglected I shall call them global and domestic exclusivity. As I hope to demonstrate here, it is the inseparable relation pertaining to these two spheres of activity that is most noteworthy.

This chapter illustrates these points by using as an example the early development of Australian and New Zealand press associations. It offers an interesting case in studying the concept of bi-directional dependency between the global and domestic markets. There are certain similarities here with the US Associated Press and the case sheds light on the role of co-operative agencies in protecting the exclusivity of telegraph news. In these countries there was a need for foreign news, but their geographical location burdened the media with expensive transmission costs. As a result, newspapers decided to share these costs by forming co-operative ventures. As a matter of fact, the Australian and New Zealand news agencies adopted the structure of a co-operative news press association from the US Associated Press.

The chapter has three aims. First, it illuminates the historical development of the Australian and New Zealand press associations' relationship to Reuters, a topic that has hardly been broached by scholars. Second, it shows how the question of exclusivity was embedded both in the agreements with the global agencies and in the articles of the co-operative agencies. And third, it provides material to develop further the concept of bi-directional dependency and to understand the role of exclusivity in the global and domestic news markets. Since the Australian Associated Press destroyed its archival files (except the minutes of the meetings of the Board) in the 1960s, I have relied heavily on the materials from Reuters' archive in London and the Alexander Turnbull Library in Wellington.

Global and Domestic Exclusivity Created

> It will been seen by reference to our Telegrams that the cable has been repaired between Port Darwin and Java, and that direct telegraphic communication between Australia and Great Britain has been restored. . . . As soon as the necessary repairs were completed, a telegram was sent to Mr. Reuter, and a congratulation message was dispatched from Adelaide to England. The line is now open for the dispatch of public business. (*Sydney Morning Herald*, 22 October 1872)

When the global agencies Havas, Reuters and Wolff divided up the world's news market, Australia became Reuters' territory as a part of the British Empire. These agreements gave Reuters the exclusive right in relation to other global agencies to operate in Australia and New Zealand. The relationship between Australia and Reuters had got under way in 1859 when

Reuters provided the first telegram detailing sailings of the *Columbine* into Sydney. The transmission of the telegram took more than six weeks, because the telegrams were sent from London by steamer. The *Sydney Morning Herald*, Australia's first daily (established in 1831) and the *Melbourne Argus* (established in 1834) were sufficiently prosperous to appoint a representative to serve them both in London. This arrangement set a precedent for Australian newspapers having their own regular staff members in London (Desmond, 1978: 288). By 1861, Reuters already had an agent in Australia, although news from there was very rare (Storey, 1951: 35). This agent was probably Mr Greville, who later opened his own telegraph agency in Australia.

In 1871 Reuters informed the Australian newspaper proprietors that after the submarine cable was opened the company would establish a branch office in Melbourne to offer a news service to the colonial press. Immediately the *Sydney Morning Herald* announced that it had formed, together with the *Melbourne Argus*, the Australian Associated Press (the Argus–Herald Association) which would sell the Reuters' news to other newspapers (Walker, 1976: 205). It was the first press association, and there were many more to come as competing newspapers founded one association after another.

The agreement was signed between the proprietors of the *Argus* and *Herald* newspapers and Reuters in June 1871. Reuters agreed to 'despatch daily by telegraph by retransmission from India, Jawa or Singapore . . . the same telegraphic intelligence as shall be dispatched by the Company to the Indian Press . . .'. The average daily number of words was to be 50. The association got exclusive rights to Reuters' news in Australia and New Zealand. Hence, the association's domestic exclusivity was created. In the second chapter of the agreement Reuters undertook 'not to despatch any intelligence whether general or special directly or indirectly to any other person or Newspaper in the said Colonies'.

As a result of the opening of the Eastern Cable and the Overland Telegraph from Darwin, the first submarine cable message from London reached Sydney in October 1872 (Barty-King, 1979: 39). The *Sydney Morning Herald* published its first foreign telegrams under the headline 'Latest Intelligence. Reuter's Telegrams to Australian Associated Press' in October 1872. The papers that took the initiative in organizing the cable service protected their investments with domestic exclusivity, and outsiders complained from the outset about the monopoly. Entry to it was then offered to the *Evening News* on condition that it did not print cables before the *Sydney Morning Herald* had used them (Mayer, 1964: 27).

Global and Domestic Exclusivity Extended

In New Zealand in May 1865 the completion of the telegraphic line from Bluff to Christchurch also saw the start of the General Telegraphic Agency.

In the following year it was followed by The *Otago Daily Times* agency. Some New Zealand papers started to use Greville's Telegram Company which operated as Reuters' agent in Australia. Greville was an Australian journalist who obtained the agency for Reuters and also received his international news from it. Both services continued to the second half of 1872 when the first non-competitive agency, the Holt and McCarthy Agency, was founded (Day, 1990: 189–210; Sanders, 1979: 3).

Julius Vogel, Colonial Treasurer and newspaper proprietor in New Zealand, concluded an agreement with Hugh George, manager of the *Melbourne Argus* and the Australian Associated Press, for reception of the Reuters agency in New Zealand in 1872 (Day, 1990: 212). With this agreement the Holt and McCarthy Agency was able to achieve a monopoly in New Zealand until 1878 when a new agency, the New Zealand Press Association, was founded. After a short but intensive period of competition the two agencies were amalgamated. A new co-operative agency, the New Zealand United Press Association (NZUPA) started its operations in January 1880 (Day, 1990: 216–29; Sanders, 1979: 8). It immediately made an agreement with Reuters for the delivery of foreign news. Hence, by 1880, Reuters had established direct contacts with both Australian and New Zealand press associations.

Reuters' exclusive right to New Zealand had already been confirmed in its agreements with the Australian press associations which included New Zealand as one of the colonies. Meanwhile, a similar relationship was created between the Australian newspapers and the NZUPA. It was the Australian press associations that transmitted Reuters' and Australian news to New Zealand. This relationship was strengthened in 1887 when the NZUPA decided to make an agreement with a new press association, the Australian *Argus–Age* Association (Fenwick, 1929: 14), instead of with Reuters. This decision did not change the fact that Reuters provided foreign news to both associations, but made the Australian press association Reuters' representative through which the New Zealand papers received their foreign news. Instead of signing agreements with Reuters or paying commissions, NZUPA simply paid the Australian press associations for the delivery of Reuters' news to it.

The NZUPA was not allowed to use any other sources except the one provided by the Australian press associations. Up to 1913 all the agreements signed with them had included an article that said the NZUPA was not, during the currency of the agreement, to publish or cause to be published in any of the newspapers subscribing to its association any European or foreign cable messages other than those supplied by the Australian newspaper association. After 1913 the NZUPA was granted the right to use supplementary services provided by other Australian newspapers.

The articles of the NZUPA did not specifically mention that its members were not permitted to receive news from other sources. However, the association made individual contracts with its members and subscribers. The fourth article of the 'cable' agreements declared that the proprietor of the paper would not directly or indirectly, during the currency of the agreement, enter into any arrangement, with any other company, organization, association or person for the supply of cable news to the proprietor or to any other person on his behalf.

In this way, the NZUPA could make sure that no other foreign sources were used except that of the Australian press associations (including Reuters' service). It could also control the admission of new members to the association by setting them higher entrance fees. This led to the establishment of a parliamentary committee in 1896 to investigate the situation in which the whole cable service of the colony had fallen into the hands of the NZUPA. The committee ascertained that

> a combination of the leading papers exists in Australia to supply the associated journals with the Australian combination, receiving news from them, and thus a monopoly exists between New Zealand and Australian colonies, the information being received by the Combination in Australia, and then passed on to the Press Association in New Zealand.

Seeing that the newspapers could not obtain a cable service from any other source than the Press Association, the committee regarded the heavy entrance fees as inimical to the interests of the colony (Reports of Select Committees 1896: i).

Domestic Exclusivity Divided

Compared to many other countries the Australian newspaper market was not only especially wealthy, but also extremely competitive. Because of the high transmission costs incurred in sending foreign telegrams, there was a need for joint operations to cut the costs. Australia has a long tradition of co-operative efforts – press associations – although they were often controlled by only two or three metropolitan newspapers. It was also typical for Australian news agencies that there were periods when there were several competing press associations, often consisting only of a couple of papers. The biggest metropolitan newspapers also played a major role in these organizations. They could afford to have their own offices in London and agreements with foreign newspapers. Sometimes, the agreement with Reuters was concluded between these major newspapers instead of with an association. In addition, national agencies usually received their news directly into their home countries. The Australian news agencies considered it important that from the outset the selection of news (from Reuters) was made in London by Australian journalists.

Storey (1951: 119), Reuters' company historian, mentions that Australia failed to develop a domestic news agency that would have served both capital and provincial newspapers. Instead, the newpapers allied themselves in groups and established the principle of buying the Reuters service in

London at the discretion of their London representatives. Storey complains that the arrangement deprived Reuters of the advantage of a news-distributing organization in Australia and prevented the agency from having a close and intimate relationship with its newspaper customers.

What this meant in practice was that the Australian market was divided on the one hand between the members of the different press associations, and, on the other, between them and Reuters. This is quite exceptional compared to Reuters' agreement with other Dominion agencies. In India and South Africa, for example, the inland service was entirely in its hands – Reuters had the rights solely in relation to the country or provincial papers (Read, forthcoming). The first agreement with Reuters to reserve the country press for Reuters was concluded by the *Argus–Age* Association in 1891 (Report of Select Committee on Press Cable Services, 1909, appendix).

The Australian Press Association (also called The United Cable Association) that was formed in 1895 by merging two rival press associations, the *Argus–Herald* Association and the *Age* Association, partly changed this situation (*A Century of Journalism*, 1931: 280). Previously, each of the associations had received its own independent service of news from London. It was found that the competing associations expended considerable sums of money and wasted much energy in obtaining what practically amounted to the same news (Report of Select Committee on Press Cable Services, 1909: appendix). The new association consisted of seven newspapers but the management of the association was in the hands of the *Melbourne Argus* and the *Sydney Morning Herald*. It had a news-collecting agent in London that obtained news from the leading newspapers and Reuters (*A Century of Journalism*, 1931: 752).

According to the agreement made by the two associations between themselves when they founded the association, its main purpose was to share the costs and expenses of organizing the reception of cable messages from Europe. Their delivery was exclusive and restricted in two ways. First, its members agreed not to use any European cable services other than Reuters. Hence, the association protected Reuters' global exclusivity by prohibiting the use of other foreign news agencies by its members. Second, no messages were to be supplied to any other newspapers in Sydney, Melbourne, Adelaide or Brisbane without the unanimous consent of the members of the association. The members protected their own exclusive territories and maintained their domestic exclusivity to Reuters' news. There was only one exception to the rule: the messages could be sold to provincial newspapers within the scope of the agreement with Reuters (Report of Select Committee on Press Cable Services, 1909, appendix). The association did not, in effect, have exclusive rights to its domestic market; rather, its exclusivity was limited to the big cities and it shared its provincial market with Reuters.

The association protected its own exclusive rights effectively by prohibiting the participation of other metropolitan newspapers in the organization without the unanimous consent of all the members. Many newspapers, especially pro-Labour papers were denied supply by the association, and the setting of an alternative agency was simply too expensive (Walker, 1976: 206–7). As a result, there was practically no other source to supply news for Australia and New Zealand. The situation led to the establishment of a special committee in 1909 to investigate the accusations over the monopoly (Report of Select Committee on Press Cable Services, 1909). Unlike the corresponding committee in New Zealand, it was unable to reach an unanimous decision, but the Government did act on its recommendations (Putnis, 1998).

Global Exclusivity Shaken

> Mr. Murdoch attacked Reuters, and our service. He described your Editors in London as a 'lot of broken down University men and snobs, arrogant and British, with no conception of Australian requirements'. He said we were a Foreign (i.e. non-Australian) Agency, that our news was influenced by foreign governments, and that what Reuters needed was an Australian staff in London. (Reuters' General Manager in Australia to the Company's General Manager in London in 1924)

In 1911 Keith Murdoch's (the father of Rupert Murdoch) *Melbourne Morning Herald* seceded from the Australian Press Association and joined forces with the *Sydney Sun*. The two formed the United Service (*Sun–Herald* Cable Service, United Cable Service). The new association obtained Australian rights to the *Times* and *Sun* materials in London and opened its own office there. Hence, it entered into competition with the Australian Press Association and also indirectly with Reuters.

The mutual competitiveness of Australian newspapers opened up a situation in which Reuters could choose its Australian counterpart. The Australian papers were now competing over the agreement with Reuters – to its advantage; Reuters could simply accept the best offer. In 1916 Reuters decided to sign an agreement with the United Service instead of the Australian Press Association. Accordingly, Reuters' service was telegraphed to the *Sydney Sun* which delivered the messages to other papers of the United Service Association. The Australian Press Association was forced to receive its news from the minor agencies that operated outside the cartel such as the British United Press, Central News, Exchange Telegraph and a number of London and New York dailies. The majority of the provincial papers in Victoria and New South Wales switched to the United Service following the rift between the Australian Press Association and Reuters.

Reuters switched again seven years later. With the contract between Reuters and the United Service due to expire in 1926, Reuters made an agreement with the Australian Press Association instead of the United Service, because the latter was reluctant to accept the conditions offered by Reuters. The agreement was non-exclusive for the Australian Press Association, because it gave Reuters the right to sell its own and the Australian

Press Association service to newspapers outside the association and to retain 25% of the subscriptions, the rest going to the association. However, it was exclusive in the sense that Reuters agreed not to sign an agreement with any other Australian press associations. At that time Reuters had 60 subscribers in Australia, among them the *Melbourne Herald* which had by that time broken away from the *Sydney Sun*. The latter was invited to join the service but refused the terms offered. The contract between the Australian Press Association and Reuters was made for three years.

At that time there were three different groups in the Australian newspaper market. The *Melbourne Herald* and the *Sun* group (United Service) operated outside the Australian Press Association. However, in 1924 the Australian Press Association, the *Sun* group and the *Melbourne Herald* group decided to join forces. The main reason was to pool the cable costs. They had gathered that the two foreign news services to Australia cost about £70,000 each year (*The Imperial Press Conference in Australia*, 1925: 61). The 'Combine' also decided to organize an Interstate News Bureau to serve provincial papers that had previously been served by Reuters. Some papers, afraid of Melbourne and Sydney domination, remained outside the Combine.

There was a growing sense of dissatisfaction among Australian newspapers with Reuters. A meeting was arranged in Melbourne where Reuters' service was criticized as being 'largely propaganda' and there were objections to Australian papers being plastered over with acknowledgement to Reuters. The speakers expressed doubts as to Reuters' independence. Since the United Cable Service–Reuters contract was due to expire, the Reuters' general manager in Australia warned his headquarters in London that there was an effort to drive Reuters out of Australia, if the rival associations managed to join their interests and turn joint forces against Reuters.

The Combine was also interested in establishing its own independent foreign news coverage and even had plans to form a British Dominions Combine. This was expressed at the Empire Press Union Conference in Australia in 1925 in which the Australian participants criticized the paucity of news items on Australia and other Dominions published in British newspapers. Sir Hugh Denison of the *Sun* said:

Those of us who have been in recent years in the Old country have felt almost humiliated, if I may use the term, when we took up those splendid morning and evening papers day after day and looked for some news of the Dominions, the places we came from, and in very few instances could we get any information at all. I made up my mind that on my return to Australia I would have a talk to other friends of ours who constitute these news services, and see when the opportunity arose whether we could not create a return service from Australia to England upon the same lines which we have from Great Britain to this country. . . . by the creation of a news service from Australia to Great Britain we may be able to give all those other Dominions the same class of news so that in those Dominions they will have the same knowledge of Australia Great Britain gets. I see no reason why South Africa should not know more of Australia than it does, nor why Canada,

India, and the Strait Settlements should not know also. (*The Imperial Press Conference in Australia*, 1925: 63)

Although the plan was never realized, it expressed an articulate criticism against Reuters' position in controlling news to and from Australia. This criticism was not passed without Reuters' notice and the headquarters warned its representatives in the Dominions about Australians' efforts.

Earlier, Reuters had been able to use the clashing interests of the rival Australian newspapers in its negotiations. In the new situation in which the newspapers had been able to overcome their differences, Reuters felt that it had to accept any offer from the Combine or otherwise be driven out of the country. As the general manager of Reuters in Australia wrote to Sir Roderick Jones, Reuters' general manager: 'The situation is most difficult, delicate and dangerous, and I am most strongly of opinion that you should deal with it in person'. As a result, Sir Roderick Jones came to Australia in 1926 to negotiate a new agreement.

Domestic and Global Exclusivity Strengthened

For forty years Australia has been one of the weak spots in our world arrangements, and a frequent source of worry and trouble. By reason of this fifteen years' Agreement, binding up practically the whole press of Australia and New Zealand to us, it now should become one of the cornerstones of our overseas edifices. Strengthened and fortified as we now are in Australia, and relieved of all the friction and rivalry which in the last few years especially have consumed so much of our time and energy, we should be able to adopt a more confident and a more resolute policy, if and when necessary, in Canada, South Africa, and elsewhere, including not least of all the Far East. (Jones: 1926)

The two years that preceded the 1926 agreement between Reuters and the Australian press associations was a critical period in their relations, because it was the first time Australians had articulated any joint need to change the prevailing conditions. Given Reuters' exclusive access to Australian news, Reuters could decide what Australian news was to be transmitted abroad and that the Australian agencies were not permitted to use sources other than Reuters. This was now questioned and, to a certain extent, resented. However, the two associations decided to sign a joint agreement with Reuters in 1926. By that time there were only a couple of newspapers that stood outside the Combine. The agreement was to have a long-lasting influence on the future relations between Australian newpapers and Reuters, because when the two Australian press associations merged into one in 1935, the agreement was simply transferred to the new organization, the Australian Associated Press, AAP.

The question of domestic exclusivity (that also involved New Zealand) was still central in defining the relationship between Reuters and the associations. The agreement was framed as follows:

1. The ASSOCIATIONS shall have placed at their disposal for exclusive use in Australia and New Zealand the sole rights to REUTERS' NEWS SERVICES existing or to be established from all parts of the world and the use and sale of the said NEWS SERVICES in Australia and New Zealand shall be reserved exclusively and absolutely to and for the financial advantage of the ASSOCIATIONS: REUTERS engaging not to supply any news services to or for publication in any newspaper in the said country.

2. REUTERS shall ensure that any agency in Europe, America or elsewhere allied to REUTERS does not assist with news or otherwise either directly or indirectly any organization or newspapers in Australia and New Zealand which competes with the ASSOCIATIONS or any of their Members or NEWSPAPER SUBSCRIBERS. (Memorandum and Articles of Association of AAP 1935: 14)

In other words, Reuters' news was only exclusive to the members of the association because Reuters agreed not to transmit its messages to any other newspapers outside the associations. Furthermore, Reuters agreed to ensure that no other member of the cartel would supply its news to Australia. However, in contrast to agreements with other national agencies, there was no article that explicitly defined the associations' service to Reuters as exclusive. The agreement only stated:

12. To place at the disposal of REUTERS' correspondents at the earliest possible moment for transmission from Australia the Australian and New Zealand news available before publication in the Offices of the Newspapers published by members of the ASSOCIATIONS. . . . (Memorandum and Articles of Association of AAP, 1935: 21)

Although Reuters later insisted that it had exclusive rights to the AAP's news, the AAP maintained Reuters' right as non-exclusive. This became a matter of dispute over the interpretation of the 1926 contract in the coming years. It is important to note that Reuters delivered the copies of its messages to the London office of the Australian Press Association and United Service. Again it was Australian agencies who decided which Reuters' news was to be sent to Australia. While the associations paid Reuters £11,000 per annum for its service (£12,000 from 1931), Reuters paid the associations £4,000. The agreement was to continue until 1941 and thereafter until the expiry of a year's notice given by either party.

The agreement with Reuters cannot, as such, help us to understand the concept of exclusivity. Since the co-operative ownership form has been the most common in the history of Australian news agencies, the AAP's company act (Memorandum and Articles of Association of AAP, 1935) reveals how exclusivity was embedded in the articles of co-operative news associations. First, access to the association was strictly controlled. While any applicant interested in the objects of the Association could become a member, a voting majority consisting of not less than three-quarters of the total votes of all the members was required for admission. Second, the members were not allowed to give the news they obtained from the association to non-members. And lastly, the members were not allowed access to any other services except those provided by the association. This is how Reuters' global exclusivity in Australia was protected. As the article phrased it:

> 104. No Member or Subscriber shall alone or in connection with other Members or Subscribers or other persons establish or obtain a Supplementary Service, and no Member or Subscriber shall permit a company controlled by him or by him in conjunction with other Members or Subscribers or other persons to establish or obtain a Supplementary Service. . . . (Memorandum and Articles of Association of AAP, 1935: 65)

In other words, the AAP had the Australian newspapers thoroughly tied up. No AAP member newspaper was able to take other agency services as a supplementary service without sharing it with other members and still remain a member of the AAP. Together with the agreement with Reuters these articles formed an iron-clad protection of the home market. The domestic news was now entirely in the hands of Australian Associated Press who no longer shared it with Reuters. Still more important, the agreement with Reuters was not explicit in defining Reuters' exclusive rights to the AAP's news.

Conclusion

News agencies in the 19th century and the beginning of this century can be divided into three different categories: (a) the global agencies; (b) the middle-sized agencies; and (c) small national agencies. While the global agencies operated outside their national borders, the small national agencies could only operate in their own home country. The middle-sized agencies, such as the US Associated Press and the Austro-Hungarian Korrespondenz-Bureau, operated primarily but not exclusively within their home countries (Rantanen, 1990: 50). Although the Australian press associations did not achieve the status that the AP and Korrespondenz-Bureau enjoyed in the agreements with the global agencies, their status was different from that of small national agencies. While the Australian news agencies were contractually dependent on Reuters, they themselves made the New Zealand agencies contractually dependent on them. The latter were not only dependent on Reuters but on the Australian agencies as well. In this way, the Australian agencies were allowed to operate outside their own home territory in a way similar to that in which the Korrespondenz-Bureau operated in eastern Europe or the US Associated Press operated in North and South America. The Australian agencies could secure for themselves a second 'home market' and thus a second source of income.

As Oliver Boyd-Barrett (forthcoming) writes, a prosperous, media-wealthy domestic market appears to be a necessary if not sufficient condition for a global agency. His argument could even be applied to those national agencies that extended their markets beyond their national territories such as the Austro-Hungarian Korrespondenz-Bureau, or the Australian press associations. The US AP that began as a national agency, was only finally able to become a global agency because of its wealthy home market and its expansion from North to South America.

It was the national co-operative press association that included almost every Australian paper that finally was able to protect the entire home market of the Australian newspapers. Before the Australian newspapers could join their efforts they had to share their home market with Reuters. The New Zealand Press Association bound its members from the beginning to its rules, thus preventing new domestic competitors from operating. At the same time, it became dependent on Reuters and the different Australian press associations. It did not matter which one it chose, because all Australian press associations were also dependent on Reuters.

The major change took place in the global news system when the news cartel was abolished in 1934. The US United Press Association had resented the concept of exclusivity from its early days, refused to join the cartel and started its worldwide expansion. The US Associated Press then adopted the policy of its domestic competitor and objected to the concept of exclusivity in its agreement with Reuters. The AP and UP signed an agreement in which they undertook not to compete against each other by refraining from signing exclusive agreements (Rantanen, 1994: 28). After exclusive territories were excluded in the agreement between the AP and Reuters, many national agreements followed their example. However, because of the longevity of agreements, the question of abolishing exclusivity became a reality in the relationship between Australian Associated Press, New Zealand United Press Association and Reuters only in the 1940s. Exclusivity was eventually abolished, when the AAP and NZPA (in 1942 the NZUPA was renamed the New Zealand Press Association) became Reuters' shareholders in 1947, but this is already beyond the scope of this article.

The Australian and New Zealand cases show that the co-operative ownership form was advantageous for national agencies in the protection of the exclusivity of news in their domestic market. Global and domestic exclusivity were protected both in the agreements between the global agencies and the national press associations and between the latter and their members. This partly explains why the cartel lasted so long and why co-operative ownership gradually gained worldwide acceptance.

Acknowledgement

The author wishes to thank the University of Western Sydney for the scholarship that made this research possible. She would also like to thank Frank Garfield for his invaluable help.

References

Archival sources: Reuters' Archive, London. Alexander Turnbull Library, Wellington.

Barty-King, H. (1979) *Girdle Around the Earth*, London: Heinemann.

Boyd-Barrett, O. (forthcoming) 'Constructing the global, constructing the local', in A. Kavoori (ed.) *The Global Dynamics of News*, Ablex.

A Century of Journalism. The Sydney Morning Herald and its Record of Australian Life, 1831–1931 (1931) Sydney: John Fairfax & Sons.

Day, P. (1990) *The Making of the New Zealand Press. A Study of the Organizational and Political Concerns of New Zealand Newspaper Controllers 1840–1880*, Wellington: Victoria University Press.

Desmond, R. (1978) *The Information Process. The World News Reporting to the 20th Century*, Iowa City: University of Iowa Press.

Fenwick, G. (1929) *The UPA. Formation and Early History*, Dunedin: *Otago Daily Times and Witness*.

The Imperial Press Conference in Australia (1925) London: Hodder & Stoughton.

Ingmar, G. (1973) *Monopol på nyheter. Ekonomiska och politiska aspekter på svenska och internationella nyhetsbyråers verksamhet 1870–1919*, Uppsala: Esselte Studium.

Mayer, H. (1964) *The Press in Australia*, Melbourne: Lansdowne Press.

Memorandum and Articles of Association of Australian Associated Press Proprietary Limited (1935) Melbourne: Harston, Partridge & Co.

Memorandum of Association and Articles of Association of the United Press Association Limited (1939) Wellington: Blundell Bros.

Putnis, P. (1998) *The Integration of Reuters into the Australian Media System in the Late Nineteenth and Early Twentieth Centuries*. Paper presented to the IAMCR General Assembly and Conference, Glasgow.

Rantanen, T. (1990) *Foreign News in Imperial Russia: The Relationship between International and Russian News Agencies, 1856–1914*, Helsinki: Federation of Finnish Scientific Societies.

Rantanen, T. (1992) 'Mr Howard goes to South America. The United Press Associations and foreign expansion', *Roy W. Howard Monographs in Journalism and Mass Communication Research*, No. 2.

Rantanen, T. (1994) 'Howard interviews Stalin. How the AP, UP and TASS smashed the international news cartel', *Roy W. Howard Monographs in Journalism and Mass Communication Research*, No. 3.

Rantanen, T. (1997) 'The globalization of electronic news in the 19th century', *Media Culture & Society*, 19 (4): 605–20.

Read, D. (forthcoming) Reuters in India, manuscript.

Report of Select Committee on Press Cable Services in Commonwealth Parliamentary Papers (1909). Parliament of the Commonwealth of Australia, *Journal of the Senate*, 1: 287–401.

Sanders, J. (1979) *Dateline – The New Zealand Press Association, 1880–1980*, Auckland: Wilson & Horton.

Senate Journals and Sessional Papers, vol. 1, Victoria: J. Kemp. Reports of Select Committees. Copyright Telegrams Committee (1896). New Zealand Appendix to the House of Representatives of New Zealand, vol. IV, Wellington: John Mackay.

Shmanske, S. (1986) 'News as a public good: cooperative ownership, price commitments, and the success of the Associated Press', *Business History Review* 60 (1): 64–9.

Storey, G. (1951) *Reuters' Century 1851–1951*, London: Max Parrish & Co.

Walker, R.B. (1976) *Yesterday's News. A History of the Newspaper in New South Wales from 1920 to 1945*, Sydney: Sydney University Press.

4   The Struggle for Control of Domestic News Markets (2)

Jürgen Wilke

In present-day Germany there is strong competition among the news agencies providing the mass media with both domestic and foreign information. This situation is almost unique in the world. The Deutsche Presse-Agentur (German Press Agency/dpa) is of prime importance, however, and it is the continuing strength of a national, co-operative news agency in the face of global competition that is the principal feature of this study. The three world agencies Associated Press (AP), Reuters and Agence France-Presse (AFP) each operate a German-language service. In addition, there are other agencies, especially those offering specialized services, for example economic news (Vereinigte Wirtschaftsdienste or United Economic Services/VWD) or sports news (Sportinformationsdienst or Sport Information Services/sid). Further, there are the agencies run by the large Christian churches: the Katholischer Nachrichtendienst (Catholic News Service/KNA) and the Evangelischer Pressedienst (Evangelical Press Service/epd). The Allgemeiner Deutscher Nachrichtendienst (General German News Service/ADN), which held a monopoly in the former GDR, merged with the Deutscher Depeschen Dienst (German Dispatch Service/ddp/ADN) after German unification.

The keen competitiveness between the news agencies in Germany today has, on the one hand, historical roots and, on the other, is a result of the ever-increasing number of players in the German media market. In order to remain competitive, the agencies are forced to diversify their services in a very distinct manner. In the following, the reasons for this and the development of competition among the news agencies in Germany today will be examined.

Reconstruction of News Agencies after the Second World War

The news agency business, as it currently exists in Germany, is a consequence of the second world war, even though the Telegraphisches Bureau (WTB) founded by Bernhard Wolff in Berlin in 1848 was one the first news agencies established in Europe (Basse, 1991). However, this agency soon became dependent on the state, and after the National Socialists seized power it was merged with a second agency, the Telegraphen Union (Telegraphic Union/TU) in 1933, and then nationalized. The latter was founded around the first world war, mainly by industrial corporations. In the Third Reich, the Deutsches Nachrichtenbüro (German News Office/DNB), which was the result of this merger, was an important instrument in the National Socialist propaganda apparatus (Reitz, 1991; Uzulis, 1995).

The reconstruction of Germany after the second world war was carried out in order to prevent the re-emergence of the circumstances prevalent during the National Socialist dictatorship. Broadcasting media, radio, the press, as well as the news communications industry, were key targets of this operation, which was initiated by the occupying allied forces. In each occupied zone, a news agency was established under military control to supply newspapers and broadcasting stations in those areas with news (Kristionat, 1991). In the American zone, the German News Service (GNS) was created. This agency was renamed DANA (Deutsche Allgemeine Nachrichtenagentur or General German News Agency) shortly thereafter and was later given the name DENA (Deutsche Nachrichtenagentur). In the British zone, there was the German News Service – British Zone (GNS–BZ), which soon received the name dpd (Deutscher Presse-Dienst or German Press Service). In the French zone, the Rheinische Nachrichtenagentur, RHEINA, later to be known as the Sudwestdeutsche Nachrichten-Agentur (South Western German News Agency/SUDENA), was established. In the Soviet zone, the Sowjetisches Nachrichtenbüro (Soviet News Bureau/SNB) became active. These four agencies began distributing their news between the end of June and the end of August 1945.

As of 1947 the news agencies in the three western zones were handed over, in a gradual process, to the newspaper publishers there. Thus, the responsibility for supplying news was slowly handed over to the Germans themselves. After lengthy negotiations, the agencies active in the west of Germany were unified to form the Deutsche Presse-Agentur (dpa), which distributed its first bulletin on 1 September 1949 – just a few weeks before allied control of the press in Germany finally ended. Another path was taken in the Soviet-occupied zone. On 5 October 1946, the Soviet News Bureau became the Allgemeiner Deutscher Nachrichtendienst (ADN), which was soon to be granted a monopoly, thus becoming an instrument of the state-guided media in the Soviet zone (Minholz and Stirnberg, 1995).

The fact that the dpa assumed a leading position in West Germany was due to its organizational structure: for the first time in Germany, a news agency founded on a co-operative basis and owned by the mass media themselves was established. The size of the member publishing houses or the broadcasting companies did not play a role in the distribution of the shares. Nearly all German newspapers, several journals, and the broadcasting companies were co-operative members of dpa throughout and became its clients.

Foreign News Agencies Returning to Germany

However, dpa's dominance in the Federal Republic of Germany did not mean that it had a real monopoly. Such a situation would no longer be tolerated by the newly established political system based on liberal-democratic principles. Foreign news agencies therefore re-entered the newsmarket in which they had been present earlier.

Paul Julius Reuter, the German founder of the British news agency, had tried as early as the 1850s, even after having settled in London, to gain a foothold in his country of birth. This opportunity, however, was denied him by the authorities (Wunderlich, 1991). Under the agreements of the cartel, which was established by the founding agencies in the 1870s, competitors were kept away from other countries' home markets. None the less, before the cartel collapsed in 1933 after being extended several times, the agencies had begun employing their own correspondents in the countries of the cartel members. Associated Press sent its first correspondent to Berlin as early as 1898 (Höhne, 1977). On 2 June 1931, AP was entered in the trade register as a limited company (GmbH) under German law. However, plans for establishing a German-language news service were abandoned when Hitler seized power. Nevertheless, German newspapers were still able to receive AP bulletins, although AP's focus in Germany was on collecting German news for its services in the United States and other parts of the world.

The situation was better for United Press (UP). As this agency had not been a member of the cartel agreement, it was in a position to offer its world service (even before 1933) in direct competition with the domestic agencies in Germany (Höhne, 1977). The British agency, Reuters, is supposed to have supplied to even more German newspapers than the American agencies AP and UP put together (Koszyk, 1986: 213). When the National Socialists took power in Germany, the situation became difficult for foreign news services. With the outbreak of the second world war, the situation was made worse. Fearing that their own correspondents would be interned, Reuters, for example, removed all except one of its people from Germany and resettled them at first in Amsterdam and Budapest, and then in other places. Whenever necessary, such as during the Munich Agreement negotiations, they preferred to fly in their own group of correspondents. When the United States entered the war in 1941, AP had to close down its operations in Germany and its staff were forced to leave the country.

The occupation of Germany by the allied forces after the capitulation on 8 May 1945 not only led to the founding of the news services by the occupying powers, but also opened the gate for the return of American, British and French (as well as Soviet) news agencies. However, this return was mixed. In the American zone, the GNS and later DANA acquired their foreign bulletins from the Allied Press Service (APS), which was established in 1944 in London as an Anglo-American enterprise. APS was supplied by AP, UP, Reuters and AFP. After APS closed down, DANA acquired its foreign news from AP, UP and International News Service (INS) directly. According to the agreements signed, those news agencies made their world news available to DANA. In exchange, they had access to DANA's German news. While INS and Reuters decided to sign such exchange contracts with DANA, AP rejected this idea; it wished to maintain business relations with newspapers on an individual basis only. UP was not keen on supplying a competing news agency with UP news either. They had no interest in becoming part of a news monopoly for reasons both of professional ethics and economic profit. In September 1945, INS concluded a contract with DENA also.

In late 1945, AP began courting the German newspapers licensed by the occupying authorities. It even signed anticipatory contracts which were to come into force once the papers' obligations to DANA expired. In this way, the agency prepared the ground for supplying news direct to its German clients, the first of whom was the *Wiesbadener Kurier* on 9 January 1946. In June 1946, AP began publishing its German-language service in Berlin. At first, this could only be sold to newspapers in the American zone and in the American sector of Berlin. AP did not receive permission to offer its services in the British zone until July 1947 or in the French zone until spring 1948. In the late summer of 1946, contracts were even signed with newspapers in the Soviet zone. These came to nothing with the introduction of the German mark in the western zones on 20 June 1948 (Höhne, 1977: 159f.). The American occupying powers denied the British and French agencies access to their area until they issued permits to the American agencies for their zones. In February 1946, UP started its service in Frankfurt as an independent subsidiary of the American agency. Thus, AP and UP became serious competitors in those zones in which they were based. After DENA was discontinued and dpa was founded, AP settled its German subsidiary in Frankfurt. From then on, the agency produced its German service there. While the foreign news was transmitted from New York or borrowed from the English-language European service of AP's central editing office, AP had its own German correspondents who were responsible for domestic services (Wilke and Rosenberger, 1991, 1994).

The Reuters agency, which served the British zone, first went a different way after 1949. It signed an exchange contract with dpa whom it thus supplied with foreign news, and even received German news from (Read, 1992; Bauer and Wilke, 1993). This excluded direct competition. However, Reuters also tried to gather and distribute economic news in Germany, traditionally a focal point of its activities. Through its subsidiary, Comtel Bureau Ltd, Reuters actually did participate in the Vereinigte Wirtschaftsdienste (VWD), founded in 1949/50 by a number of important economic organizations interested in this type of news (Merkl and Wilke, 1993). One of the partners in this venture was once again dpa.

However, in the course of the years, Reuters found these forms of activity on the German news market to be confining. The obligations under the exchange agreements prevented the corporation from creating its own dynamics. When the American news agency UPI (which emerged from the joining of UP and INS in 1956) gave up its re-established presence on the German market owing to its growing financial troubles, Reuters disengaged itself from its ties to dpa in order to provide a German-language service of its own. This service has now existed since 1 December 1971. In addition, another consequence of the closing of UPI's German service was the establishment of yet another news service. The German employees of the American firm wanted to continue their work and, hence, established a new agency, the Deutscher Depeschen Dienst (ddp). Upon expiry of the existing contracts in 1978, Reuters withdrew from the economic agency VWD too. It was no longer a shareholder as of 1980. This provided the British agency with even more scope for activity in Germany.

The development of Agence France-Presse (AFP), established in 1944 in newly liberated France (as the successor to Agence Havas), was different again. Naturally, the RHEINA (later SUDENA) in the French occupied zone, received news from AFP until merging with the other zone agencies in 1949. Afterwards, AFP distributed news bulletins in Germany only indirectly. Although a German-language service was established in Paris in 1948, it was only for Alsace, in the vicinity of the German border. None the less, news from Paris was later offered to the German media as well. Under these circumstances, however, the service had only limited success. In 1986 AFP was decentralized and the decision was made to relocate the German-language service to the German capital of Bonn. A subsidiary company was founded in order to facilitate this. The AFP wire has been sending out its German-language news from there since 25 April 1987 (Huteau and Ullmann, 1992; Schmid, 1993).

Growing Media Demand

A prerequisite for the presence of three world agencies offering German-language news in Germany today, in addition to the Deutsche Presse-Agentur (and other, more or less specialized agencies), is the existence of a sufficient demand for this product. This demand is created by a very dense media system. After 1945, the German media sector was initially built up under the control of the occupying allied forces. Some older German traditions were nevertheless respected in this process.

In Germany, the demand for the supply of news from news agencies results primarily from a multi-faceted, locally and regionally diversified newspaper system with a relatively high total circulation. Although press concentration has taken place since the 1960s, this has not had negative effects for the news agencies. The victims of this process, who suffered as a result, were mainly low-circulation newspapers. The remainder consisted of stronger newspapers who were more likely to have the financial means to subscribe to more than one news agency.

After the second world war, the allies introduced public stations, modelled on the BBC, to the broadcasting sector in Germany. In this case as well the regional spheres of responsibility of the occupying forces influenced the older German tradition of regional broadcasting corporations, which had been replaced by a centralist system under the National Socialist dictatorship. Hence, several broadcasting companies emerged in 1945, each broadcasting to a particular region of the country and each obtaining a monopoly within its respective region. Moreover, the financial situation of the public broadcasting companies, which were financed primarily from fees and later from additional advertising, was good. Thus, they could easily afford to use all the major news agencies in Germany.

Since the mid-1980s, private, commercial radio and television stations have come into being in Germany. This is partly because the technology – in the form of a cable system and satellites – was then available, but was mainly due to the deregulation of the media industry, a process which also occurred in other countries. This has led to an expansion of the radio and audiovisual sectors in the media system. The news agencies were able to profit from this expanded market. At the same time, though, the demands on their services grew.

If this expansion was due to the evolution of the media system, then an impetus of a different type was given with German unification, after the fall of the Berlin Wall in 1989. For political reasons, and because of the socialist economy, the number of newspapers and magazines had remained limited in the German Democratic Republic (GDR). As there was no private property, state or party newspapers dominated, in particular, those of the ruling SED (Sozialistische Einheitspartei Deutschlands or the Socialist Unity Party of Germany). In the course of unification of the GDR with the Federal Republic of Germany on 3 October 1990, newspapers in former East Germany were taken over by West German firms. However, this new news market remained strongly concentrated. Newly created enterprises soon failed. The existing West German news agencies, though, found a new market in East Germany. ADN, the former GDR agency, quickly lost its previous standing and was only able to survive by merging with ddp, a smaller West German agency. Nevertheless, it is still of particular importance in the new federal 'Lander' because of its old ties and its local knowledge. After 1990, the radio and television landscape in East Germany soon became very similar to that in West Germany, with the coexistence of public and private stations.

The increased demand for news from news agencies in Germany can be shown quantitatively. Table 4.1 shows how the number of subscriptions to dpa, AP, Reuters and AFP developed over time.

Subscriptions to news agencies by the daily press increased by 40% from 189 (1975) to 317 (1994). While nearly all West German newspapers (except one) already received dpa, the agency was not able to win more than 16 additional subscriptions following German unification, whereas the other three services fared much better. AP moved up to 39, Reuters 33 and AFP 21 newspapers. In particular, the German-language services of the world

TABLE 4.1 *Subscriptions to news agencies by German newspapers*

Year	dpa		AP		Reuters		AFP		Total sub-scription	Total daily newspaper
	n	%	n	%	n	%	n	%		
1975	120	99	54	45	12	10	3	3	189	121
1983	124	98	73	58	28	22	8	6	233	126
1988	121	99	81	66	33	27	9	7	244	122
1991	148	99	92	61	57	39	32	21	329	150
1993	139	99	93	66	53	38	27	19	312	140
1994	136	99	93	68	61	45	27	20	317	137

Source: Resing and Höhne, 1993; Höhne, 1995

agencies profited from the fact that more newspapers in Germany started using more agencies. In 1983, 28% of newspapers subscribed to only one news agency. Ten years later, only 18% still did so. Above all, the share of newspapers subscribing to four and more agencies has increased markedly over the same time – from 6% to 18% (Höhne, 1995). Meanwhile, it would seem (data are still lacking) that several publishers, under the pretence of economy, have begun to drop subscriptions to news agencies, indicating that there might be a reverse.

If one adds the Sunday newspapers and the TV and radio stations in public and private hands to the daily newspapers, then the four news agencies had over 530 clients in 1994 (these data are partially estimates). Among these, one can count more than 100 clients from the private broadcasting and television sector alone who did not exist 10 years earlier and whose demand has been added to the market in the meanwhile. However, these stations draw their news mainly from dpa. dpa received approximately half of these new subscriptions (54). The shares of the other three agencies in 1994 were all about the same (AP: 20; Reuters: 17; AFP: 17).

Comparing the Profile of the News Services

There are journalistic and economic aspects to competition in the German news market. In order to survive in this market, the news agencies have to give their services a certain profile, which must be attractive enough for their clients to want to pay for it. By what means do the four agencies in Germany try to achieve this?

In order to answer this question, a content analysis of all four news agencies was carried out. Some data are available from earlier studies (Wilke and Rosenberger, 1991; Bauer and Wilke, 1993; Schmid, 1993). The results presented in Table 4.2 are from a content analysis organized in the context of the current international News Flow Study in which more than 40 countries are involved. Ours was based on the basic services of dpa, AP, Reuters and AFP in the week of 3–9 September 1995.

TABLE 4.2   *Amount of news*

	dpa	AP	Reuters	AFP
News bulletins weekly	3,472	1,276	1,679	1,863
Daily average	496	182	283	266
Words per week	592,437	283,771	217,914	282,525
Daily average	84,634	40,539	31,131	40,361
Words per news bulletin on average	171	187	130	152

As expected, dpa offers the most extensive news material in Germany. On average, dpa submits nearly 85,000 words per day, more than twice that of its three competitors. Whereas AP and AFP vary only slightly from each other in terms of number of words daily (Reuters has more), there are differences in the length of bulletins. The dpa bulletins were on average 171 words long. The length of the bulletins of other three agencies varies considerably: AP supplies more extensive bulletins with an average of 187 words; Reuters has much shorter bulletins with an average of 130 words; and AFP is in between with 152. Each of the four agencies tends to submit reports which are shorter than in earlier years. But on the other hand there are changes in the amount of German-language services compared with some years before. dpa has increased its output of news bulletins by 14%, AP by 25% and AFP by all of 43%. Reuters has remained relatively stable here. On the other hand, the amount of words increased only in the services of dpa (7%) and AFP (21%). AP and Reuters seem, on the contrary, to be stagnant or even slightly reducing the number of words in their German services.

The topic areas of the bulletins are coded according to specifications which the news agencies themselves make. Obviously there are differences according to the topic areas. dpa offers not only the largest, but also the most diversified service. In addition to political news, which makes up one half of its reporting, there is also soft news, economic, sports and cultural news. In contrast, the foreign news agencies do not offer sports news and,

TABLE 4.3   *Topic areas in the German services of dpa, AP, Reuters and AFP*

Topic area	dpa (n = 3,472) %	AP (n = 1,276) %	Reuters (n = 1,679) %	AFP (n = 1,863) %
Politics	51	58	48	51
Soft news	16	25	10	11
Economics	12	8	27	4
Culture	6	2	—	—
Sports	15	—	—	—
Others	—	8	15	34
Total	100	101	100	100

apart from AP, have no cultural bulletins. Their German services have certain focal points though. Relatively speaking, AP has the most soft news; every fourth report falls into this category (in 1989, it was every fifth). Reuters has the highest share of economic news. In contrast, it provides little soft news. AFP stands out for its share of other topic areas (but Reuters does too). They include material which does not belong to 'classical' news agency offerings. For example, AFP supplied its German clients with a 'historical calendar' containing short references to events which took place on the same day 50, 20 or 10 years ago.

News by Region

How does the reporting of the agencies differ with regard to news origin and regions covered?

Every second news bulletin from the Deutsche Presse-Agentur is German news. Their preference for their home country is obviously very strong. AP and Reuters report somewhat less about Germany, but still devote nearly half of the news bulletins to Germany. Only a quarter of AFP's news bulletins refer to Germany. That means that AFP offers the most information from outside Germany. In the week examined, AFP had more news from EU countries, but even more from some other countries

TABLE 4.4   *Regions covered in the German services of dpa, AP, Reuters and AFP*

Regions covered	dpa (n = 3,472) %	AP (n = 1,276) %	Reuters (n = 1,679) %	AFP (n = 1,863) %
Germany	57	46	45	27
EU countries	13	12	11	22
Other European countries	8	9	9	10
USA	6	5	8	8
Asia	4	7	6	6
Russia	3	2	3	4
Australia/Oceania	2	4	3	4
Middle East/North Africa	2	5	5	6
Latin America	2	2	2	3
Africa (other countries)	1	—	1	2
Other CIC countries	—	—	—	—
North America (without USA)	—	—	—	—
Others (international organizations)	3	5	7	8
Not recognizable	—	—	1	—
Total	100	100	100	100

(USA included). Next to Germany, other European countries are reported in proportion to their regional importance. There is very little reporting about Africa and Latin America. The fact that more news originated from Asia may be a result of the Women's Conference which took place in Beijing in the week examined. The higher Australia/Oceania reporting coincided with the French underwater testing of atomic bombs.

Comparison of this pattern with data from earlier studies (Wilke and Rosenberger, 1991; Bauer and Wilke, 1993; Schmid, 1993), affords little evidence that the German services of the four news agencies have become more globalized. On the contrary, the amount of non-German news has declined in recent years – 6% in dpa, 3% in AP, 13% in Reuters and 4% in AFP. Nevertheless, dpa reported from 106 different countries in the world at least once in the week examined, AP from 94, Reuters from 86 and AFP from 112. Hence, the German services of dpa and AFP are the most globalized, perhaps even more than comparable ones in other parts of the world. (It should not be forgotten that AFP offers in total only about half as much news as dpa.)

Concluding Remarks

Only basic findings of the content analysis can be presented here. Conclusions are still possible about the competitive strategies used by news agencies in Germany. As we have seen, dpa is the main agency for the German news media. It offers the largest and most diversified service. Its co-operative structure gives the agency such a strong position that there is no obvious viable alternative. It can thus be said that dpa currently outstrips its rivals in the news market. This does not mean, however, that it is safe from competition. Indeed, journalists clearly are able to gauge the dpa's service by comparing it to that of the other agencies.

The news agencies' strategies are based on two factors: on the one hand, dpa's competitors do, of course, offer bulletins about the same important domestic and foreign events. This makes sense for the journalists in the newsrooms as the reporting of the same event by different agencies indicates its news value and, perhaps, has an influence on selection. At the same time, different versions make it possible to compare reports, evaluating them against each other, maybe even using several of them when writing the story. Therefore, in principle, drawing upon several agencies helps the journalist to fulfil his or her obligation to be accurate and to offer variety of content. On the other hand, more work is required of the journalist when different agency bulletins have to be pieced together. That is certainly not economical but, none the less, can improve the journalistic product.

A decisive factor for competition may be that the competing agencies have different focal points. For instance, AP offers more soft news, Reuters concentrates on economic reports, and AFP on foreign bulletins. In these areas, the agencies are obviously trying to offer something complementary to dpa's reporting. AP's motives in this respect probably have to do with the emergence of private radio and television stations in Germany, which are particularly fond of soft news. The media can subscribe to agencies other than dpa if they feel an additional news requirement exists in other areas. According to the distribution found, the most frequent combination of two agencies is dpa/AP, and of three, dpa/AP/Reuters.

The strong competition between news agencies in present-day Germany is definitely not confined to the strategy identified here. The news bulletins offered vary in other respects as well. Other characteristics also constitute important competitive factors: how fast the agencies can provide reports; their reliability; the fees; the 'quality' of information (Hagen, 1995); the style of the news; and the language – indeed, the whole 'service' supplied by the agencies to the editors of press, radio and television. 'Previews' of events and news expected on a particular day can be included in the reporting as well as summaries or features and spot news (especially for broadcasting stations). All four of the agencies supply news pictures. Reuters Television (and more recently AP) supplies newsfilm. dpa supplies private radio stations with an audio service. AFP was the first to include information graphics, and others followed. Thus, the news agencies have been forced to extend the range of their services to suit the German media market (Rosenberger and Schmid, 1996, 1997). Only by doing this will they be able to survive. In particular, the dynamics of technological change require the development of innovative products in the future.

References

Basse, Dieter (1991) 'Wolff's Telegraphisches Bureau 1849 bis 1933', Agenturpublizistik zwischen Politik und Wirtschaft, München, New York, London, Paris: K.G. Saur.

Bauer, Felix and Wilke, Jürgen (1993) 'Weltagentur auf dem deutschen Nachrichtenmarkt: Reuters', in Jürgen Wilke (ed.), *Agenturen im Nachrichtenmarkt*, Köln, Weimar, Wien: Böhlau, pp. 13–56.

Hagen, Lutz M. (1995) *Informationsqualität von Nachrichten. Messmethoden und ihre Anwendung auf die Dienste von Nachrichtenagenturen*, Opladen: Westdeutscher Verlag.

Höhne, Hansjoachim (1977) *Report über Nachrichtenagenturen. Vol. 2: Die Geschichte der Nachricht und ihrer Verbreiter*, Baden-Baden: Nomos.

Höhne, Hansjoachim (1995) 'Wenig Spielraum', *Journalist*. 45 (4): 19–23.

Huteau, Jean and Ullmann, Bernard (1992) *AFP. Une histoire de l'Agence France-Presse 1944–1990*. Paris: Robert Laffont.

Koszyk, Kurt (1986) *Pressepolitik für Deutsche 1949–1949*. Berlin: Colloquium.

Kristionat, Andreas (1991) 'Von German News Service (GNS) zur Deutschen Presse-Agentur (dpa)', in Jürgen Wilke (ed.), *Telegraphenbüros und Nachrichtenagenturen in Deutschland. Untersuchungen zu ihrer Geschichte bis 1949*, Munchen, New York, London, Paris: K.G. Saur, pp. 267–331.

Lefebure, Antoine (1992) *Havas. Les arcanes du pouvoir*. Paris: Grasset.

Merkl, Martina and Wilke, Jürgen (1993) 'Produktion und Verarbeitung von

Wirtschaftsinformation: VWD und dpa', in Jürgen Wilke (ed.), *Agenturen im Nachrichtenmarkt*, Köln, Weimar, Wien: Böhlau. pp. 107–60.

Minholz, Michael and Stirnberg, Uwe (1995) *Der Allgemeine Deutsche Nachrichtendienst (ADN). Gute Nachrichten für die SED*, München, New Providence, London, Paris: K.G. Saur.

Read, Donald (1992) *The Power of News. The History of Reuters*, Oxford: Oxford University Press.

Reitz, Jürgen (1991) 'Das Deutsche Nachrichtenbüro', in Jürgen Wilke (ed.), *Telegraphenbüros und Nachrichtenagenturen in Deutschland. Untersuchungen zu ihrer Geschichte bis 1949*, München, New York, London, Paris: K.G. Saur. pp. 213–66.

Resing, Christian and Höhne, Hansjoachim (1993) 'Die Nutzung von Nachrichtenagenturen durch Tageszeitungen', in *Bundesverband Deutscher Zeitungsverleger (BDZV)*: Zeitungen '93, Bonn: BdZV, pp. 276–302.

Rosenberger, Bernhard and Schmid, Sigrund (1996) 'Agenturen unter Druck', *Sage & Schreibe* 4, pp. 48–9.

Rosenberger, Bernhard and Schmid, Sigrun (1997) 'Die Konkurrenz fest im Visier. Wettbewerbsstrategien von Nachrichtenagenturen im gewandelten Medienmarkt – ein systematischer Problemaufriss', in Günter Bentele (Hrsg.): *Die aktuelle Entstehung von Öffentlichkeit*, Konstaz: UVK Medien.

Schmid, Sigrun (1993) 'Weltagentur auf dem deutschen Nachrichtenmarkt: Agence France-Presse (AFP)', in Jürgen Wilke (ed.), *Agenturen im Nachrichtenmarkt*, Köln, Weimar, Wien: Böhlau, pp. 57–105.

Uzulis, André (1995) *Nachrichtenagenturen im Nationalsozialismus. Propagandainstrumente und Mittel der Presselenkung*, Frankfurt am Main: Peter Lang.

Wilke, Jürgen (ed.) (1991) *Telegraphenbüros und Nachrichtenagenturen in Deutschland. Untersuchungen zu ihrer Geschichte bis 1949*. München, New York, London, Paris: K.G. Saur.

Wilke, Jürgen (ed.) (1993) *Agenturen im Nachrichtenmarkt*, Köln, Weimar, Wien: Böhlau.

Wilke, Jürgen and Rosenberger, Bernhard (1991) *Die Nachrichten-Macher. Zu Strukturen und Arbeitsweisen von Nachrichtenagenturen am Beispiel von AP und dpa*. Köln, Weimar, Wien: Böhlau.

Wilke, Jürgen and Rosenberger, Bernhard (1994) 'Importing foreign news: a case study of the German service of the Associated Press', *Journalism Quarterly* 71: 421–32.

Wunderlich, Christine (1991) 'Telegraphische Nachrichtenbüros in Deutschland bis zum Ersten Weltkrieg', in Jürgen Wilke (ed.), *Telegraphenbüros und Nachrichtenagenturen in Deutschland. Untersuchungen zu ihrer Geschichte bis 1949*, München, New York, London, Paris: K.G. Saur. pp. 23–85.

5 Global Financial News

Michael Palmer, Oliver Boyd-Barrett and Terhi Rantanen

Information Vendors, Financial News/Data Services

The Reuters' company historian, Donald Read, has pointed out that Paul Julius Reuter, the founder of Reuters news agency,

> was never primarily himself a reporter. He was a great news entrepreneur. During the second and third quarters of the nineteenth century news was becoming an opportunity commodity of the industrial revolution. If he had been in business in the early twentieth century, he might well have become an oil-man. (Read, 1992: 5)

Reuter provided brokers and merchants in London and Paris with twice-daily reports of the opening and closing prices of the stock exchanges of both capitals. Likewise, Reuter's first agreement of 1856 with the French and German agencies, Havas and Wolff, concerned the exchange of stock market prices (Boyd-Barrett, 1980: 221; Tunstall and Palmer, 1991: 52). Hence, Paul Julius Reuter identified a market that numerous agencies continued to target more than 130 years later.

'News moves markets . . . news is a market.' The interconnection between these two aphorisms of the news business is nowhere more apparent than in economic and financial news services. In 1997 Reuters was the market leader in this regard, and it is on Reuters that we shall concentrate. Competition is fierce: the opportunities for revenue are considerable, but so too are expenditures: research, development and related investment costs concern systems and networks as much as services. The application of state-of-the-art-technologies, in the 1990s (as indeed in the 1830s and 1840s) aims at providing reliable and relevant datafeeds fast so that end-users may make decisions – whether or not to conclude a 'trade', to make a transaction – on the basis of the most accurate and recent information available. It is not just the information that counts. News and data vendors promote themselves as providing 'added value' to information: they provide 'analysis' – the 'analytics' – as well as the data, the price signals, etc. For example, in 1995, Reuters, citing its '143-year tradition of accuracy', described itself thus: 'Reuters informs the world instantly by the latest electronic means. We help our customers to analyse the facts and trade on them'.

The Study of Financial News Services

What justifies the inclusion of financial news services within a volume on the news agencies? Arguably, the two concepts of 'general' and 'political' news are inseparable. Carey (1987) argues that the establishment of the popular daily press in the United States followed the logic of the market: news has to be up-dated daily because the opening of stock markets each day presages a new round of decisions to be made. Decisions about money are not taken simply in relation to strictly financial factors. Outbreak of war between two countries, for example, inevitably threatens some investments (for example key manufacturing installations in the war zone), while signalling an up-lift in demand for certain products (oil, armaments) with consequent implications for prices. Changes of government will be scrutinized by financial analysts for their market implications. Is the new government committed to higher spending on social services? If so, then this may indicate a possible increase in national debt, which in turn may have implications for prices of government bonds and interest rates, which in turn will affect sales of a wide array of retail goods. Market movements are typically anticipatory. Investors may not wait for the election results before deciding to sell stocks in bonds or commodities for which demand is likely to fall. Instead, they look for advance evidence of the most likely outcome of the election before it actually happens. If they believe they can anticipate the outcome, and can do so before most other people, then they can sell stock when demand for it is still relatively buoyant and they can get a good price for something whose value, they believe, will soon fall. Almost anything that passes as news in print, broadcast and electronic media is likely to have some financial implication for somebody, somewhere.

The very invention of news represents a coming together during 19th-century Europe and North America of at least four (overlapping) kinds of demand: for information which has political significance to those who consider themselves as belonging in some sense or another to 'civic society' or the 'public sphere'; for sports results (for sports fans and those who bet on sport); for information which both titillates and satisfies curiosity ('human interest' news; news of crime); and for financial news. News agencies have been intimately involved in developing provision of each of these major different categories of news. In particular, the provision of financial markets with financial news was a significant aspect of their activities from the earliest days:

> Reuters and Havas were conceived as business operations, and the origins of both lie in the demand for financial intelligence from an increasingly international European business community. Charles Havas had a background in contracting and banking before he started his agency, and business clients were among his most important in the first eight years of the agency's life. First location for L'Agence Havas was close to the Bourse de Commerce in Paris. Julius Reuter worked in banking before establishing his first service of commercial news in Paris

and his first London office was established in the Royal Exchange Building (Stock Exchange) where he installed one of his first correspondents. For the first seven years of the agency's history the most important clients were financiers and merchants, who took a service that was primarily economic. Dr. Bernhard Wolff (in Germany) first specialized in commercial news to brokers and businessmen, and later added general and political news; Wolff's agency (CONTINENTAL) was supported by both the Prussian government and banking houses. The first exchange agreement in the history of the three major European agencies was for an exchange of news of Bourse and trading activities.

. . . Competition in the sale of economic news was intense: it was the reason why Reuter left the continent of Europe and came to London. . . . Economic intelligence was also one of the agency's major attractions to the English press. One reason why *The Times* was last of all Fleet Street papers to subscribe to Reuters was because it had its own service of market prices; one of the first advantages of a subscription to Reuters that attracted *The Times* was the possibility of an American money service. Reuters' most important and earliest groups of clients in eastern Europe, India and South America were generally merchants. Before South America was signed over to Havas, Reuters ran a commercial service between Rio de Janeiro and the main continental markets. In Australia the market for economic news and the private telegram service was more profitable than newspapers. Much later, when Reuters switched to radio from cable, the first wireless services dealt in commercial news, followed by general news services some eight or nine years afterwards. (Boyd-Barrett, 1980: 220–1)

The demand for financial news from financiers, banks and brokers, was such that it spawned many smaller specialist services, both then and now, many of whose histories have been neglected. Bloomberg news service, which in the 1990s has constituted a threat to the much larger Dow Jones and Reuters wire services, started in much the same way as Reuters, largely on the back of securing a deal with the *Wall Street Journal* and Associated Press to furnish them with bond prices, electronically, in place of manual delivery from the Federal Bank of New York. Like Reuters, Bloomberg moved from financial to general news.

The data-like quality of the more quantitative forms of financial news had little appeal to the 19th-century journalistic community, which was still in the process of weaning itself away (in the USA and UK) from a 'journalism of opinion' to a 'journalism of information', and did not enjoy the status of political and general news reporting. Until recently, financial and economic news has generally had low status among journalists. Not until it became big business for Reuters in the 1970s, boosted by digitization and flexible exchange rates, did financial and trade information for non-media markets become fashionable even within Reuters itself. Previously unremarked, it had generally made a significant contribution to the organization's finances (around 30% in the mid-1960s – rising to 95% by 1997). Simultaneously many newspapers began to capitalize on the potential of advertising revenue from more extensive economic news and established financial news sections.

Among the major news agencies of what had once been a global cartel, only Reuters has dedicated the major part of its activity to reporting economics and financial news and data for the business community. Reuters' main rivals, such as Knight-Ridder, Dow Jones, Telerate, and Bloomberg, were set up mainly to serve financial and business markets. AP and AFP provided economic news for news media but also branched out to provision for non-media clients. AP is allied with Dow Jones through AP–DJ economic news service outside the USA. During the 1980s, AP was also allied with Telerate, which is now owned wholly by Dow Jones. A senior AP executive told Oliver Boyd-Barrett in 1996 that the contribution of such ventures has never accounted for more than 25% of AP revenues. No single organization within the spectrum of Reuters' competition is thought to offer a range of services as broad as those of Reuters.

Financial news services are important in several respects. In the first place, this activity accounts for most of what Reuters does, but at the same time it helps to support the general media services of Reuters, now one of only three major global print agencies, and one of only three (now two, 1998) major wholesaler providers of video news for television. The provision of financial and economic news, secondly, constitutes an important part of the agencies' services for their media clients, contributing to the growing recognition of such news as central to mainstream news coverage and understanding of global affairs. The demand for such news from both media and non-media clients has probably been the single most important stimulus to competition in speed of delivery, and has contributed to the shaping of western news ideology as 'impartial' and 'objective' – that is to say, news-as-information, with commodity value, for dissemination impartially and on equal terms to a wide array of different clients of various beliefs and interests.

The growth of financial news markets, and the consequent mushrooming of revenue, lay behind decisions that led to the change in the company's status and debut on the London Stock Exchange in 1984. One may argue that commercial profit is a more acceptable and invigorating alternative to hidden state subsidies of the kind that have marked various periods of Reuters' earlier history (Boyd-Barrett, 1980; Read, 1992). Financial news revenue has ensured a strong presence of a British-based agency in the world market for international news, helping to off-set what might otherwise seem to be American dominance, while public quotation has led to a broader ownership. (Headquartered in the city of London, Reuters presents itself as a 'news vendor' and 'news organization', as a transnational company that finds it convenient to be located in the British capital but does not identity itself as 'British'.) Profits have funded a considerable expansion in technical and personnel resources for all categories of news reporting, including radio, television, graphics, photography and historical data.

Financial news has become an important activity for many smaller agencies, sometimes operating at national or local levels, especially in the wake of deregulation of state agencies, and subsequent pressures on such media to be more self-sufficient financially. The combination of traditional news agency work with modern electronic networks has helped to reformulate the character of international trade and finance, and places the agencies so involved at the very heart of modern international capitalism and globalization.

The evident importance of news agencies in the supply of financial and economic information and transaction services raises significant issues about the adequacy of structures and operational controls that the agencies put in place to help ensure that the information which they supply is free of vested interest, whether exerted by internal or external sources. There are critics who worry that news agendas in general are being driven by economic and financial angles, which the agencies are increasingly skilled in providing. Such critics agree that such news is important, but they fear that the agencies and sections of the media find themselves increasingly allied to particular ideological positions related to finance, including issues to do with the merits or otherwise of free markets, currency stability, industrial concentration, and globalization of finance and trade.

Transaction Products and Information Products

The rhetoric of actors involved in the 'universe' in which information vendors operate is suggested by the following extract from a (three-page) advertisement placed by Nippon Telegraph and Telephone (NTT) in the *Financial Times:* 'In the nano-second nineties . . . the currency of the future is not the pound, the deutschmark, the franc, the dollar or the yen. IT'S INFORMATION'.[1] Reuters, in the mid-19th century as in the late 20th century, secured a competitive edge over its rivals by garnering substantial revenue from non-media clients; it did so by providing accurate reports fast from stock exchanges and other market venues that reflected movements in capital flows, commodities and related price signals. In 1851, Paul Julius Reuter – after failures in 'continental Europe' – opened a telegraphic institute in London the very year that the City was linked by telegraph with Paris. Thenceforth, it was possible for London and continental stock exchanges to receive news or price signals about 'stocks and shares' at the 'opening' of a given day's trading before the 'closure' of the same day's session in Bourses elsewhere in Europe: the 'quantum leap' towards what the late 20th century would call 'real time' trading had begun.

In the late 1960s and early 1970s, a combination of factors made Reuters well-placed to profit from the advent of real-time trading by operators interconnected with Bourses and financial centres around the clock and around the world – across the world's time zones. The much-vaunted 'technological convergence' did indeed mean that via computers and telecoms networks, 'electronic conversations' between traders serviced by Reuters and other information vendors led to the conclusion of transactions within seconds on the basis of information appearing on Reuters screens, and at a time when the introduction of flexible exchange rates and a boom in the level of activity in international trade created a growing market for such services.

The Stockmaster, developed by Reuters in the early 1960s, represented a major advance towards computerized stock-market information: 'for the first time, businessmen over a wide area could receive news simultaneously' (quoted in Read, 1992: 296). There followed Videomaster (1968) providing datafeeds accessible via screen-display; Money Monitor in 1973 – the first of a series of Monitor products, providing datafeeds of 'real-time current information' for, about and from foreign exchange and money markets; and an interactive Dealing Service in 1981, enabling dealers to exchange information and conclude transactions in under five seconds.

These interrelated developments in technology, financial and economic data flows, and market conditions underpinned Reuters' success from the 1970s to the early 1990s; it was generally a move ahead of potential competitors – either established media-oriented news agencies or specialist vendors of financial and economic data and newsfeeds. Its relationship with banks and brokers, and with treasurers of international businesses, was sometimes strained: brokers, especially, feared that Reuters' systems, products and facilities might undermine their traditional role; occasionally, banks promoted other networks (developed by competing news vendors or by the banks themselves), partly so as to reduce their 'dependence' on Reuters terminals.

Initially, from the 1960s, Reuters developed its own proprietary systems (hardware and software), or bought up companies (generally US-based) whose systems dovetailed with its needs. By 1994, Reuters accepted that 'the way of the world is open. Software and hardware are becoming so inflexible and interchangeable that no one wants data vendors to dictate their choice'.

Reuters helped create 'the world electronic marketplace', and profited from its development; Michael Nelson, one of the first within Reuters to identify and champion the agency's potential role, noted for example in 1975 how 'a dealing system is different from Reuters present business. It is information handling, but makes Reuters an instrument in the execution of a transaction which we have never seen before' (quoted in Read, 1992: 308).

Reuters – and competitors subsequently – provided both the data and the analytics that inform the data (thereby providing added value) and indeed the systems that enable electronic conversations between buyers and sellers and other market actors that lead to the conclusion of transactions or 'trades'. Dealing 'by dialogue' ultimately led to 'matching', the automatic conclusion of deals based on instructions from clients. (Subsequent competition, as in the case of Bloomberg, has focused on the added-value component to information, much of which is already available in the public domain, by increasingly sophisticated provision of historical data and software for manipulating data calculations and presentations.)

From the 1960s, Reuters computer services included market quotation systems serving clients in the UK and Europe, traditionally Reuters' most important markets. No less important were geopolitical and geofinancial factors: in the course of the 1970s, the volatility of currency movements intensified as the system of fixed currency rates, linked to the Bretton Woods arrangements concluded at the end of the second world war, collapsed; in 1971, trading in currencies soared when the United States president, Richard Nixon, floated the dollar off the fixed exchange rate; the oil embargo, decreed by the Organization of Petroleum Exporting Countries (OPEC), made currencies even more volatile. 'Forex' – foreign exchange transactions – became a worldwide electronic marketplace, served first and foremost by systems developed by Reuters – the Money Monitor, launched in 1973.

Banks, multinational companies, 'electronic brokerages' of all kinds – traders, speculators, governments and central banks – monitor price movements via Reuters terminals, served by Reuters systems; these include trading-room facilities and related transactions products. Transactions products became a major revenue earner for Reuters Holdings plc, the company floated on the Stock Exchange in 1984. Reuters serves multinational media and non-media clients worldwide by offering real-time multi-media and on-line systems and services, and is itself midway between Mammon and Mercury: the latter, the winged messenger of antiquity, is patron saint of journalists and of commerce.

In 1996, Reuters Holdings plc ranked 138 in the *Financial Times* list of the world's top 500 companies by market capitalization, and 35th on the *FT* list of Europe's top 500.[2] The Money Monitor, and related systems and services developed by Reuters during the 1970s and the 1980s, to serve non-media clients in the developed world (and, later, in the emerging market economies of the developing world), underpin much of the company's prosperity of the past 20 years. The 'globalization' of the economy, with the attendant increase in volume and pace of capital flows – and, in particular, of currency transactions – stimulates this trend. Thus, currency volatility in Europe in the early 1990s led to a host of 'electronic conversations', and the conclusion of transactions, via Reuters systems and services: during the debate and referenda held within the European Community and Union over the Maastricht Agreement, currency volatility was intense – notably in September 1992, when the British pound sterling and the Italian lira ultimately left the European Monetary System.

By 1996–1997, the position was somewhat different: the advent of the adoption of the 'Euro' currency, scheduled for 1999, led to consolidation by banks and an anticipated reduction in the volume of trading in European Union national currencies; this was perceived as affecting the number of trades likely to be conducted via Reuters and other electronic 'forex' systems. Another difficulty lay in the sometimes fraught relationship between stock exchanges, electronic brokers and information vendors. Stock exchanges compete with each other, as venues for transactions in a wide range of commodities, stocks and shares, and financial instruments.

Sometimes they co-operate, and indeed form joint ventures with third parties; sometimes they fall out.

These, therefore, are some of the issues we shall address in discussing the development of Reuters' financial services and support systems over the past quarter-century. Reuters is the market leader: it has competitors on various fronts, but no one competitor can match it on all the fronts where it does battle. None the less, we shall first mention what was at best a 'half-success' – Globex, an automated matching system for futures contracts, intended initially to facilitate automatic trading around the clock, around the world, that is, after the hours of open outcry trading, or regular trading hours.

Globex

In the late 1980s, two traditional rival exchanges in Chicago – the Board of Trade (CBOT), a major commodity futures exchange, also trading in financial futures, and the Mercantile Exchange (CME), which calls itself 'the world's largest marketplace', asked Reuters to develop 'an international electronic system for futures and options': CME, it seems, was the prime mover. Called Globex, the system began trading in CBOT and CME products in June 1992: one novel feature was that it allowed for electronic trading of futures and options after the close of the exchanges' open outcry trading hours. Thus participating exchanges listed their products for trading outside 'regular opening hours', and – given the various time zones across the world – made it possible for 24-hour, round-the-clock, round-the-world trading. A 20-year agreement between Reuters and the CME/CBOT joint venture gave the Chicago exchanges control over what contracts could be traded and who could participate. In 1993, the French exchange MATIF (Marché à terme international de France) joined the two Chicago exchanges trading via Globex. By mid-1994, total Globex volume had grown – 3 million deals were done via the systems in the first 14 weeks of 1994 compared with 4.3 million in the whole of 1993; however, an average 85% was generated not by the Chicago partners but by MATIF. For various reasons – including intra-exchange politics, and questions of the compatibility of systems – that which was possible technically encountered resistance from stock exchanges: the volume of trades never reached the target figures initially envisaged. In 1997, it was announced that the CBOT and CME were withdrawing from Globex: the preliminary statement of Reuters Holdings plc for 1996 expressed matters thus:

> Globex, the automated matching system for futures contracts built with the Chicago Mercantile Exchange and the MATIF futures exchange in France, is not likely to continue beyond 1998 as the original partners develop their own systems. The product has never been particularly successful and its closure will not produce any material impact on the company's results.[3]

Thus, it does not appear that Globex may be included among the host of successful Reuters electronic transaction products of the 1990s.

Instinet

Pride of place, in this regard, fell to Instinet: according to the Reuters Holdings plc 1995 annual report, this provided agency brokerage services in global equities to securities industry professionals in more than 30 countries. Instinet was a US corporation (founded in 1979), which became a Reuters subsidiary in 1987. In the mid-1990s, Instinet was the company's fastest-growing product line.

Thus, since the flotation of Reuters in 1984, the major growth in the company's fortunes has continued to lie in what it calls 'information' products and 'transaction' products, as opposed to 'media' products. Revenue from media products grows, but proportionately less so than that of the first two categories. Some people describing the position of media products within Reuters refer to Lewis Carroll's *Alice in Wonderland*: although tall, when she took a draught of a magic potion Alice found herself much reduced in size compared to other people. In Reuters, media products account for some 6% of company annual revenue. Comparisons of figures can be invidious: the company continually stresses its commitment to increasing the size and quality of its news-media resources. For instance, Reuters' editor-in-chief, Mark Wood, remarked in 1996 that the number of journalists had increased by 600 during the previous six years.

This said, company data for revenue by product category in 1995 show the importance of information and transaction products:

'information products' – £1,879 million (69 per cent of total)
(Information products deliver news and prices to customer screens. They provide datafeeds to financial markets, and the software tools to analyse data. They cover currencies, bonds, futures, options and other instruments. Triarch and Teknekron (subsequently renamed TIBCO) systems offer customers the means to manage their own information flows.)

'transaction products' – £671 million (25 per cent of total)
(Transaction products enable traders to deal from their keyboards in such markets as foreign exchange, futures and options, and securities. Foreign exchange dealers can either converse with chosen trading partners, or use an automated matching system.)
(*Customers*: many users of information products use transaction products too.)

'media products' – £153 million (around 6 per cent of total)
(Media products deliver news in all the dimensions of the multimedia: text, television images, still pictures, sound and graphics.)

(Reuters Holdings plc, annual report 1995)

For screen-based non-media clients, reliability and speed (as close to 'real-time' as possible (logistically and technically) is of the essence, even more so than for media clients. In the 'nano-second nineties', Reuters' quality controllers of services for non-media and media clients regularly remind Reuters' journalists in-putting material for both client categories that the 'econ' version of a breaking news story should come first, but of course a version for media clients should follow within a matter of a few minutes. However hackneyed the phrase, time really *is* money.

Transaction products epitomize this – even more than information products. In 1996, they included Instinet ('US' and 'International' – the former being the most developed), Dealing 2000-1, Reuters conversational dealing product, and Dealing 2000-2, Reuters automated matching product. In 1994, Peter Job, Reuters' chief executive, observed: 'since electronic brokerage is in its infancy outside the US, the world is Instinet's oyster, but cracking it open to find the pearl will take a while'. The company's international news release of 11 February 1997 stressed that the equities trading subsidiary was indeed propelling the growth of the company's transaction products. This news was all the more welcome in that the growth of the company's foreign exchange dealing products, the propellor of previous years, was slowing down, as the forex market began to flatten out.

Reuters' prosperity over the past quarter-century has come from its leading position as a supplier and vendor of systems and products feeding and fuelling the 'electronic conversations' and 'trades' in forex. Forex has accounted for much of its growth – in 1996 forex revenue share was about 33% of total company revenue. In 1990, when global forex turnover was reckoned to be $640 billion a day, it was estimated that about a third of the trades were conducted on 11,000 Reuters monitors, with the company earning revenue in more than 50 currencies. An article in the August 1991 edition of *Reuters World*, celebrating 10 years of the Monitor Dealing Service, noted that the service regularly carried over 1 million dealer 'conversations' each week: 'its primary benefits are an international dealer-to-dealer contact speed of between two and four seconds, service reliability and cost-effective communications'. This requires some comment. In September 1995, central banks reported that global forex turnover topped a trillion dollars *a day* – according to the tri-yearly survey of forex activity carried out by the Bank for International Settlements; in March 1996, *The Economist* put the figure at over $1.2 trillion.[4] As for trades, in June 1995, Dealing 2000–2, the automated trading system for foreign exchange, reached its 20,000 target for the number of trades concluded daily across the system; Reuters' chief executive referred to an ultimate target of 40,000 trades per day.

Periods of volatility, of sharp fluctuations in currency exchange rates, accelerate the pace and volume of conversations and trades. Events in western Europe in the summer and early autumn of 1992 were a case in point: markets were sensitive to the contradictory signals emerging from referendums (June – Denmark; September – France) and parliamentary votes on European integration; in September, the British and Italian governments withdrew the sterling and the lira from the exchange rate

mechanism of the European monetary system partly as a result of speculative movements against currencies that were seen to be 'over-valued'. The
Reuters 1992 company report noted both that exchange rate fluctuations
accounted for around one-third of total revenue growth and that

> in the financial arena, the EMS crisis, which we were the first to report, signalled
> the decline, at least for the time being, of rigid notions of value and the unques-
> tioned ability of EC central banks to stand behind them. Reuters products flour-
> ish in a world of free news flow and freely fluctuating values. (Reuters Holdings
> plc, annual report, 1992)

Writing from a different perspective, a financial journalist of the French
daily *Le Monde*, subsequently observed:

> The free circulation of capital and the development of sophisticated financial
> instruments make it possible to anticipate changes in parity rates, thereby
> unleashing tornadoes on the financial markets. One cause of the fragility of the
> EMS lies in its transparency. As the exchange-rate of each currency has to remain
> within the tightly controlled narrow band . . . market movers and financial oper-
> ators can monitor the exchange rates in order to see whether a crisis is imminent.
> (Lazare, 1993)

Reuters, like other news vendors, is organized to report breaking news
and market-moving news. It organizes the logistics of coverage so as to
anticipate likely developments (though not, of course, to report them before
they occur). Provided that they are certain of the safeguards necessary to
ensure accuracy and reliability, journalists and news vendors seek to report
less *when* things happen than *as* they happen; economic and financial journalists are particularly attentive to 'market impact'. Serving traders for
whom time is money, they appreciate market actors who deliver their
message in a user-friendly manner, showing an understanding of the
mechanics of news processing and an awareness of the possible impact of
the message – the pithy news-nugget or sound-bite, for example. Evaluating the performance of various central bankers in this regard, some tend to
prefer Alan Greenspan of the US federal reserve, to Hans Tietmayer of the
German Bundesbank. There are many set pieces in the events which economic news reporters cover – Group 7 meetings, World Bank meetings, and
the like: while some actors wish journalists to be consigned to the role of
scribes, the latter seek to identify what is newsworthy, so as to beat the competition with a story that moves the markets. There is of course a fine line
between accurate reporting of what is said and done, and piecing the story
together (often from a host of venues across the world) with a sense of its
possible implications.

All manner of fail-safe mechanisms are observed by reputable news agencies and financial news vendors: their commercial reputation depends on
their journalistic professionalism. As journalists they thrill to the impact of
their story. Three examples from mid-1995 highlight this; in relating them,
we shall respect the anonymity of our sources.

Market-moving News: Mid-1995

In mid-June 1995, the Organization of Petroleum Exporting Countries (OPEC) met in Vienna. Assessing agency coverage of the meeting, a quality controller observed on June 20:

> We set the tone, providing the agenda that others had to follow – journalists and ministers alike. On Sunday, we beat the competition with a story from 'M' based on a Gulf source stating that OPEC did not rule out raising the level of authorised production in 1996, and that it wanted to prevent non-OPEC producers from threatening its market share. On Sunday, our text – a 'snap, dateline O8 46' – stating 'Venezuela (an OPEC member) does not rule out the possibility that quotas may be suspended next year' led to a sharp fall in oil-prices. The markets feared that OPEC was using its muscle against non-OPEC countries that it considered were undercutting the market-price.
>
> We alone had the scoop. Competing agencies, and the next day's newspapers, had to react to our story. OPEC ministers stated that the Venezuelan minister had been misunderstood/misquoted. In fact, they succeeded, via us, in sending an involuntary shot across the bows against non-OPEC producing countries, even if they were not yet ready to take action against them. They used us to make their point.

A month later, a quality controller celebrated an agency scoop in the coverage of a meeting of the International Monetary Fund:

> In a time of ever more sophisticated economic reporting, requiring mastery of market techniques and jargon, nothing can beat a good old-fashioned scoop, which moves the markets and leaves our competitors breathless, desperately trying to catch us up.
>
> I refer here to the story we put out today, from 'X', dateline Washington, 25 July 04H 25 GMT: 'US hits out at Japan at secret IMF meeting'. The story tells how the US sharply criticised Japan during a secret meeting of the IMF board last Friday: the US claimed that Japan was responsible for the strong Yen which was hurting the American economy, and urged Japan to do more to stimulate growth by cutting interest rates and by increasing the budget deficit. Our story weakened the dollar, and the Bank of Japan intervened in its support. Some traders read our story as evidence that the US was not really committed to defending its currency and that it relied on Japan to do so.

The same quality controller was no less pleased to note that the competition, reporting on the story from Frankfurt, Sydney and Asian stock exchanges, was left chasing after traders' reactions to his agency's story: this was read to mean that the 'Fed' – the US central bank – was not going to support the existing dollar/yen rate; traders on the intraday market sold dollars for marks. The controller added: 'we beat the competition hands down. Great stuff!'[5]

The third example dates from 21 September 1995. A quality controller noted appreciatively how co-operation between a news reporting bureau and central editorial desks tightened up a story, improved its presentation and thus had market impact – 'can move markets':

> The Bonn bureau did well in unearthing an official summary of the proceedings of a select committee of the German Parliament. It contained sensitive remarks in undiplomatic language on the improbability of Italy meeting the criteria necessary to qualify for the first stage towards European Economic and Monetary Union (the so-called 'Maastricht criteria').
>
> These remarks did not figure in the 'lead'. In London, 'S.N.' of the money desk did well in picking them up in the fourth paragraph of the Bonn piece. The desk checked it out with Bonn, got some direct quotes, and issued a 'snap' or alert at 14 39 GMT. The lira fell, other agencies ran hard to catch us up, and we had a good market-moving scoop.
>
> Official reaction today showed the value of our story. At 10 20 GMT we put out a snap: 'Theo Waigel, the German finance minister, states that the Parliamentary report containing his remarks about Italy was unauthorised'. This reads as an embarrassed confirmation of the accuracy of what we said. Better still, the Italian budget minister stated today that these remarks were 'unwise and unacceptable'.
>
> Looking beyond these political considerations, it looks likely that this subject may well dominate the European monetary agenda this autumn, while the Bundesbank battles during the coming weeks to enforce strict adherence to the Maastricht criteria that set the preconditions for the first stage of EMU.
>
> Better still, our screen competitors were left standing.

These examples of 'market-moving stories' suggest, among other things, that vendors of financial and economic news and data are motivated, like journalists generally, by the hunt for a story; they strive to discover an angle or 'news-nugget' in an arena in which photo opportunities and press conferences notwithstanding, so often they consider the news offered and packaged by officials to be dull or contrived. However specialist their understanding and knowledge of financial markets, they remain journalists grounded in a culture where they have to be both 'economic roundheads' and 'general news cavaliers': this metaphor, dating from the English civil war, was used by Reuters journalists writing of the need for 'econ' and 'generalist' journalists to be *au fait* with each other's requirements, skills and publics.[6]

This view of economics and financial reporting as a proper sphere for the traditional 'nose for news' is at the heart of a long-standing tension which has persisted within Reuters since the reformulation of economics news reporting by Gerald Long in the 1970s; he created a temporary division of 'general news' and 'economic news' journalists, a division which has long since been abandoned as a formal feature of the company's structure. The 'general news' lobby is mostly made up of those who entered Reuters as journalists, usually with some previous experience of journalism, rather than as economic or financial experts or technicians. The current success of Reuters is sometimes attributed mainly to the combination of strong financial markets and state-of-the-art technical economic wizardry, with the company's original and traditional activity, general news reporting, coming up as a very poor third. Yet as the above examples demonstrate, journalistic skills are extremely important contributors to the success and credibility of financial and economic news to Reuters' information and media services. None the less, the 'general news' journalists worry that it is those whose origins lie mainly in finance or technology who rise to the top of the company and exert most influence, and that the values and skills of traditional journalism will be neglected, to the ultimate detriment of the company's success.

Similarly, the importance of traditional journalistic skills can be seen in the context of a different agency, AFP. The head of AFP's economic news desk in Paris in 1997 was previously based in Bonn; his predecessor had moved on to a posting in Asia; similarly, the journalist who headed the development of the AFP financial news service, AFX (developed first with Extel, then with the Pearson group that took over the Extel news agency), moved on to Hong Kong in 1994, as AFP Asia Editor and to oversee AFX expansion in Asia as well.

Agency journalists continually walk the tightrope of marshalling specialist knowledge – sports and science, just like economics and finance – and writing for a wide range of publics or markets. Some agencies, indeed, build on a reputation for specialist expertise in reporting economics and finance to expand into the provision of more general services. Bloomberg, the agency set up in 1981 by a former employee of the New York bank Salomon, Michael Bloomberg, and which is seen by many as the coming force in economic and financial news, was initially valued in the bond and corporate markets for its technical analysis, graphs, background and historical information; in 1989 he launched Bloomberg Business News, which by 1994 had over 300 journalists. Bloomberg expanded into television in the early 1990s, offering general news as well as business news services. Bloomberg, like Reuters, presents itself as offering business and general news for professionals – many of whom watch up-market and specialized television channels. 'Products for the media and financial community share a common base', observed Reuters' Peter Job (Reuters Holdings plc, annual report, 1994).

Market sensitivity to economics and financial news reporting clearly predisposes agencies to reflect free-market thinking, however scrupulous their attachment to factual reporting. Deregulation of financial markets, globalization, and other trends that became buzz-words of the late 1980s and the 1990s, hastened the flows of capital and of related data – as the success of Reuters Monitor (services and systems) and the growth of the forex market testified. In 1996, forex dealers were concerned at 'the slump in volatility', and that 'liquidity was drying up in the currency markets'.[7] Peter Job himself referred to the 'dull state of the foreign exchange market, an important segment of the company's business' (Reuters Holdings plc, preliminary statement for the year ended 31 December 1996). Some dealers put part of the blame on the growth of electronic brokerage systems, including Reuters Dealing 2000–2, and EBS, funded by a consortium of money-centre banks, including Citibank, JP Morgan, and Swiss Bank Corporation: voice brokers resented the loss (some 40%) of spot forex business to electronic broker-ages.[8] Reviewing the factors influencing the forex market, Peter Job listed positive and negative trends:

+ electronic systems increasing share and transparency
+ more electronic transaction opportunities
+ trading in new currencies
+ consolidation already well advanced
+ short-term volatility around EMU
+ EMU stimulates European money market development
+ world trade investment flows up[9]

– market transparency reduces market profits
– market concentration among big players

– more consolidation expected

– EMU eliminates currencies

EMU was a particularly contentious point. Across Europe, futures exchanges were perturbed that 'the rationale for many of Europe's exchange-traded currency and interest-rate products will disappear as local currencies give way to the Euro, and the interest-rate curves of participants' bond markets mesh more closely'.[10]

For Reuters, an electronic broker, volatility represented trades on its systems and, as the examples above suggested, market-moving stories. The possible reduction in the number of currencies was addressed by Peter Job in an interview with investors included in Reuters 1994 annual report:

> The market cannot be forced against its better judgment to accept a single value for currencies in Europe. There is no real sign that this is happening. In the immediate future, any attempt to introduce a single currency against market consensus will merely create volatility in European instruments.

Reuters' New Market: Eastern Europe

The collapse of communism in eastern and central Europe is a good example of Reuters' ability to operate as a global company. When central planning collapsed in these countries, and capitalism was introduced, newly established private enterprises needed information on currencies and prices. There was an instant demand to create electronic domestic money markets and to participate in the international money market. The difficulty was, of course, that this took place in the countries where no money markets had previously existed. Simultanously, national news agencies in eastern Europe through which and through whose communication networks western news agencies had delivered their news, lost their monopoly, thus making it possible for the latter to enter the markets. Two things were needed, and neither of them was available: reliable information and advanced communication technology. Reuters could combine its news and information service with its well-developed networking skills. It set up its own communication networks, for example satellite dishes, to distribute its services. Reuters acted instantly and was the first to enter the new markets. As a result, it was able to provide its services practically at the same level of speed, capacity and reliability as elsewhere in western Europe.[11] As one of its clients put it: 'It has become the fashion to have the Reuters Domestic Dealing service. Every bank wants it'.[12] Hence, Reuters' financial news service became a symbol of modernization among the new financial elites in the countries which had just entered the era of capitalism.

For Reuters the territories of the former Soviet Union soon became attractive, and it rapidly achieved a strong foothold there. Reuters' manager in central and eastern Europe commented, saying, 'In the biggest country, Russia, our business has not grown, it has exploded'.[13] By 1994, Russia had become Reuters' sixth most important market for Dealing 2000. There were more Dealing 2000 customers in Russia than in centres such as Frankfurt, Milan or Luxembourg. Reuters had clients in 25 different cities and also in most of the rest of the old Soviet Union. In Moscow alone Reuters has more than 110 staff members. In 1995 it launched a Russian-language economic news service using Cyrillic characters, thus extending into domestic markets.[14]

Reuters has more non-media than media clients in eastern and central Europe. For example, it had 100 non-media clients in Poland compared to 29 media clients in 1994, in Bulgaria 40 banking customers and 17 media clients in 1993.[15] Reuters has provided an ever-increasing number of services in about 20 national languages. It relies heavily on local staffs hiring the best qualified journalists and other specialists by providing salaries that are often better than domestic media can provide. As Rantanen points out in chapter 8, in eastern Europe Reuters does not compete with national agencies in the general news service, but it does do so in financial news services. The newly reformed national agencies which have lost their state subsidies and are trying to become independent, are desperately seeking new sources of revenue. Reuters' presence in eastern and central Europe indirectly prevents national agencies from expanding their activities into financial news services. Some of them still try to compete with Reuters while others have established joint enterprises with Reuters. It is highly unlikely that they can compete successfully against Reuters. Since other global news agencies have not been as active as Reuters in central and eastern Europe, it has for the time being become Reuters' territory. In countries such as Russia, a 'nationalist' press sometimes protests at this dependence on a western news and data provider.

Conclusion

Knight Ridder, AP-Dow Jones, Bloomberg, AFX and Telerate are among the companies that have competed in recent years with Reuters as vendors of financial and economic data, news and analysis, and in the provision of platforms and programmes, software and hardware. In the mid-1990s several of these companies jostled for position, as internet and intranet information flows promised to modify patterns of 'electronic conversations' and the market position of established actors. Some observers wrote of 'the death of money', 'the twilight of sovereignty', 'technopoly', and 'the real-time electronic marketplace'. Some agency executives employed such rhetoric; others were more reticent. Some agency journalists worried about *'la financièrisation du monde'*, and the gap between 'the real economy', and the value-added information-transaction economy of market-players and market-moving news. Mercury is the god of all types of exchange.

Towards the close of the 1990s, the position of the biggest player, Reuters, seemed a little less overwhelming than it had at the start of the decade. The rate of growth was showing signs of decline by 1997. This was partly sterling-related; sterling entered a period of considerable strength in 1996–1997, while Reuters continued to earn about 80% of its revenue from overseas. Price (1997) considered that the growing complexity of the company's end-user software slowed down installations to existing customers upgrading to the new 3000 series. Stiff competition restrained increases in price. The advent of the single European currency in 1999 indicated a possibly less volatile market in currency transactions, the forex market, which in some years had accounted for 30% of overall revenue. There were also concerns about the cost of adjusting systems for the so-called 'millenium timebomb'. Other factors of concern (Davidson, 1997) included the pace of banking consolidation, and the continuing difficulties the company faces in making further headway in the US market.

Such developments are a reminder that the company's own financial fortunes are much influenced by the very trends on which it reports. The company's in-built protections (for example the 'golden share' controlled by trustees of the Reuters Trust to ensure the company's independence and integrity, and to protect it from takeover) look reassuringly strong to most of those who have commented on them. Within the global compass of its activities, as we have seen, there are concerns about its market strength, its expansionism, and the consequences of this for the market opportunities of smaller companies within national markets. These concerns echo similar worries in other media markets, where the activities of multinationals undermine the possibilities of survival and growth of local and locally responsive companies. They confirm that Reuters is at once a business and a cultural force, with a particularly significant role within global capitalism.

Notes

1. *Financial Times*, 25 March 1997.
2. *Financial Times*, 24 January 1997.
3. Reuters Holdings plc, preliminary statement for the year ended 31 December 1996.
4. 'Illiquid lunch', *The Economist*, 30 March 1996.
5. Intraday refers to within the day and is thus any point at which a price or rate is noted in market trading between the opening and the close with particular reference to a high or a low during trading. Common intraday intervals include tick, five-minute, half-hourly and hourly (see Reuters, 1994).
6. ' "Gen news" man gets immersion course in "econ" ', *Highlights* (Reuters in-house journal), April 1992, quoted in Palmer (1996).
7. See for example, 'Forex dealers hit by stability', *London Financial News*, 8 April 1996.
8. According to an estimate based on returns compiled by regulators in Tokyo, Singapore and London (March 1996), around 40% of all dollar/yen business and 70% of all dollar/Deutschmark business trading through the broker market in Tokyo went through either Reuters or EBS, as did around 52% of all spot forex business trading through the broker network in Singapore and around 40% of all business brokered in London. See *Risk*, 9(4) April 1996.
9. P. Job, chief executive, Reuters Holdings plc, presentation to analysts, London, 11 February 1997.
10. Gerard Pfauwadel, chairman of France's Matif SA, France's futures exchange, quoted in 'Europe's futures markets scramble to cash in on the single currency', *Wall Street Journal/Europe*, 3 March 1996.
11. 'Reuters changing face in CIS and eastern Europe', *Reuters World*, Issue 86, May 1992.
12. 'Building the free market economy in Poland', *Teamtalk*, Issue 6, June 1994.
13. 'Glancarlo Orlando. Manager, Central and Eastern Europe. Executive Interview', *Reuters World*, Issue 106, December 1995.
14. 'Russia. Multimedia superpower', *Teamtalk*, Issue 9, December 1994.
15. 'Boom in Bulgaria', *Teamtalk*, Issue 3, September 1993.

References

Boyd-Barrett, O. (1980) *The International News Agencies*, London: Constable.

Carey, J. (1987) 'Why and how? The dark continent of American journalism', in R.K. Manoff and M. Schudson (eds) *Reading the News,* New York: Pantheon.

Davidson, A. (1997) 'The Davidson Interview – Peter Job', *Reuters Business Briefing,* 22 July.

Lazare, F. (1993) 'Les Douze cherchent à dédramatiser les dévaluations', *Le Monde*, 25 May.

Palmer, M. (1996) 'L'information agencée, fin de siècle', *Réseaux* 75 (Paris, CNET), Jan. – Feb.

Price, C. (1997) 'Go-go Reuters turns go-slow', *Financial Times*, 26–27 July.

Read, D. (1992) *The Power of News. The History of Reuters*, Oxford: Oxford University Press.

Reuters (1994) *The Reuters Glossary of International Financial and Economic Terms*, London: Longman.

Tunstall, J. and Palmer, M. (1991) *Media Moguls*, London: Routledge.

6   Global Battlefields

Chris Paterson

Television news pictures are provided to broadcasters worldwide by three commercial news agencies and a variety of co-operative news exchanges (the largest being Eurovision, based in Geneva). The television news agencies are the audiovisual counterparts to the wire services, and in two of the three cases (Reuters and Associated Press) are one and the same. These three companies exercise considerable control over the world's television news agenda, for most broadcasters have no other non-local sources for these influential and ideological products – the visual component of TV news. There has been little study of these companies, their processes of news selection and production, or the effect of this concentration of sources.

The three television news agencies which originate much of the international television news used by most of the world's broadcasters are Reuters Television, formerly Visnews, Worldwide Television News (WTN), formerly UPITN, and the relatively new Associated Press Television (APTV). The television agencies, all based in London, gather videotaped pictures and sound and story information continuously from a dozen or more bureaux, a far larger number of stringers, and from client television stations worldwide. The largest, Reuters Television, claims 70 worldwide bureaux and over 260 client broadcasters in 85 countries.[1] They also pull stories from the European Broadcasting Union's (EBU) news exchange mechanism and other exchanges.

They then edit together their own story 'packages' consisting of video and 'natural' sound (that is, no added narration), and transmit them via satellite to clients in any of several daily 'feeds', and via the EBU. Some audio commentary and electronic text (or 'scripts') are also provided to clients, providing information to accompany the visuals, and occasionally finished stories that a broadcaster can put right on the air are offered (for the broadcaster unwilling to invest in actual journalism). Many new commercial stations around the world have been designed from the outset to rely heavily on the agencies in this way (see, for example, Helland, 1995).

Clients pay the agencies from tens of thousands to several million dollars yearly, depending upon a variety of factors including the size of the station's audience, the number and type of newsfeeds received, and the amount of stories the station contributes to the agency (Waite, 1992). Currently, among the British and US networks (the most wealthy and influential of news agency clients) the affiliations are as follows: the most popular US newscast (for most of the last decade), that of Disney's American Broadcasting Company (ABC), receives WTN footage as majority owner of WTN.[2] NBC subscribes to Reuters. CBS has switched from WTN to Reuters and back to WTN (and has for some time syndicated a small amount of their video internationally as CBS International). CBS and NBC also subscribe to APTV.[3]

Time-Warner's CNN produces much of its own international material, but also subscribes to all three agencies. In the UK, the BBC's long-standing alliance with Reuters has metamorphosed to dependence on WTN and APTV. ITN has shifted from long-time supplier WTN (of which ITN owns a piece) to Reuters (which owns a piece of ITN), and may now shift back. News Corporation's Sky and Fox news networks depend entirely on Reuters for international coverage. Strict copyright rules are observed to ensure that no station broadcasts and no agency distributes news video which they have not either paid for or produced themselves. As Waite (1992) observes, at the heart of the international television news business is the goal of gaining the greatest possible exclusivity of news images for the lowest possible cost.

Barring major shifts in ownership or corporate policy, these agencies are likely to remain the dominant providers of international television news, especially from the developing world (where broadcasters rarely go; see, for example, Gonzenbach et al., 1991; Wallis and Baran, 1990), for at least the next several years.[4] Tunstall (1992) observed that Visnews (the predecessor of Reuters Television) claimed over 1.5 billion people saw its pictures around the world every day, a figure presumably based on the approximate audience of each of its subscribers.[5] He argued (1992: 89), 'TV foreign news professionals would probably agree that Visnews has some claim to being the most widely consumed, if least recognized, world brand'. That claim might now rightfully belong to WTN, since Reuters was a recognized name even before it took over Visnews, and it now aggressively markets its name to television audiences wherever possible.

Concentration of television news provision is the result of two significant trends in global electronic media. The first is the concentration of power over news selection at the individual and organizational level. The second is the industrial level trends of corporate downsizing (Auletta, 1993; Dominick, 1988) and media concentration (Bagdikian, 1992; Schiller, 1991; Smith, 1990; Vanden Heuvel, 1993; Waite, 1992), mixed with new forms of competition and alliance. The first trend may be termed 'gatekeeping concentration', to mix theoretical metaphors. As put by veteran British television anchorman Jonathan Dimbleby (in Harrison and Palmer, 1986: 76), 'as we're technically capable of becoming more and more informed and better and better informed, we're at risk of becoming less and less informed by fewer and fewer people'.

Organizations at the first tier of the television news sector are essentially 'wholesalers' of TV news visuals, sounds and textual information. With the commercial television news agencies are also several regional co-operative news exchanges and, in the US, commercial news exchanges.[6] Organizations at the second tier are 'packagers' and distributors of news constructed from the raw material of the first tier. The 'retailers' are primarily the television networks and their surrogate newsfeed operations providing news to affiliates. As in other information industries, they can be seen as simply adding value to existing information, and reselling it. CNN effectively overlaps both tiers, and other major players such as Reuters are attempting to do so as well. The literature has neglected this crucial internal structure, although its key elements are revealed in the more substantial recent analyses (Cohen et al., 1996; Hjarvard, 1995a, 1995b; Johnston, 1995). Boyd-Barrett (1980; Boyd-Barrett and Thussu, 1992) has described a wholesale/retail model in the context of print news agencies.

Figure 6.1 presents a model of international television news flow based upon this conception of a two-tier television news distribution structure. It shows the major providers and broadcasters of television news, and indicates the flow of television news pictures (and related sound and data) among them.

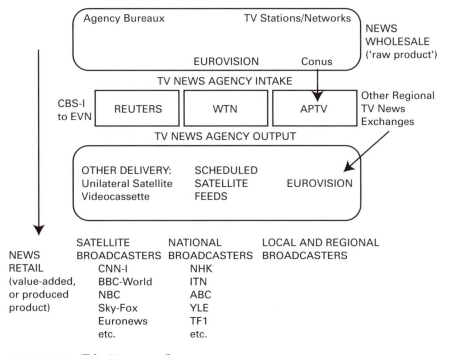

FIGURE 6.1   *Television news flow*

Manufacturing a Global Reality

Many studies of television news are based upon the concept of a shared reality manufactured by the social practices of journalists, and this is the perspective I have taken to examine how the global TV image of the world is created. People who do not live in or routinely travel to other countries generally have little or no opportunity to test or challenge their conception of the (mass media-provided) 'reality' of those countries. Mass media are almost wholly responsible for shaping that reality, and among mass media, international television news agencies are especially influential (for they alone provide contemporary visual representations of most of the world to the entire world) (see, for example, Behr and Iyengar, 1985; Larson, 1984; Ogundimu, 1992).

Research into the production of television news has demonstrated that there is an ideological component – a way of seeing the world – built into the very work routines used to produce television news stories. Altheide (1976: 24) contended that, 'The organizational, practical, and other mundane features of newswork promote a way of looking at events which fundamentally distorts them'. Golding and Elliott (1979: 210), argue that through its invariable neglect of the power relationships between people, nations and cultures, television news does provide a distinctive kind of world view. In so doing, television news will 'reinforce skepticism about . . . divergent, dissident or deviant beliefs' (Golding and Elliott, 1979: 211). Similar arguments have been advanced in regard to American media by Tuchman (1978), Gans (1980), Altschull and Herbert (1984), and Schudson (1992). Television news agencies, in their desire to please all of their clients, all of the time, must work even harder than their broadcast station clients to create the appearance of objectivity and neutrality. In so doing, they manufacture an ideologically distinctive and homogeneous view of the world.

The agencies are agenda-setters and more, for they make the first decisions on how and if international stories – particularly those from the news flow fringes of the non-industrialized world – will be covered for tele-vision. This is done through the choice of where to allocate their resources, the selection of stories they distribute to clients, the amount of visuals provided, and the nature and amount of accompanying audio and textual information. Broadcasters write their stories around the video these organizations offer, and if they are not offered video images, they generally do not report, or at least will minimize, an international story. Many studies of television newsrooms have reported that the availability of visual images is an important factor in determining whether a foreign news story is included in a newscast (Cohen et al., 1996; Golding and Elliott, 1979; Helland, 1995; Molina, 1990; Rodriguez, 1996; Schlesinger, 1987). Molina notes that at Mexico's Televisa, 'Television stories whose visual element is available through any of the news exchanges stand a better chance of being included in the programme agendas than those where only text is available'.

As put by Cohen et al. (1996: footnote 12, p. 82), 'in many instances a [European broadcast] service decides to present a story only because it has footage available'.

My research demonstrates a bi-directional agenda-setting effect (McCombs and Shaw, 1972; McCombs, 1981, 1988) between television news agencies and other mass media. Other media set the agency agenda by what they report and by what coverage they request from the agencies. The agencies set the agenda for other media through their choice of topics to cover heavily and first-time coverage of new topics.

An agency's decision to cover a story in the developing world may be influenced by the general interest of international media, but the choice of what to photograph (or even who to choose to shoot the video) is an ideological one, as is the choice of who to interview, of how many seconds to give each aspect of the story, and who to send the story to. The ubiquitous argument that any broadcaster can put their own spin on an agency story is specious, for broadcasters are constrained by the choices which the agency has already made – the choice of what information and video is sent to them. Broadcasters and agencies alike typically argue that agencies provide only the raw material; that the meaning of stories is shaped by the broadcasters. Much of the literature supports this view (Gurevitch et al., 1991; Malik, 1992).

The culture of journalistic objectivity – the 'meaning-free product' – is deeply rooted in the television news agencies. From the company's inception, the motto of Visnews photographers reportedly was 'We don't take sides, we just take pictures' (Read, 1992). In their study of international television news images, Gurevitch et al. (1991), find considerable commonality in the images used by broadcasters worldwide, due to the pervasiveness of the few common sources discussed here, but cautiously favour this 'neutral image' thesis. However, there is a body of theory (reviewed below) suggesting that news images themselves convey meanings which cannot be, or routinely are not, substantially altered by the end-users of those images. It is for this reason that the images of the world distributed by television news agencies are crucial determinants of popular perceptions.

The impact of the television news agencies, if there is an impact, depends on the influence upon audiences of the portions of television newscasts to which the agencies contribute – primarily, then, the visual component of international stories. After decades of scholarship, there remains little consensus as to whether the messages conveyed by television news lie mostly in the auditory narrative or mostly in the visual (often agency-provided) story elements (Adams, 1982; Grabe, 1994; Graber, 1990; Grimes, 1990; Kozol, 1989). Kozol and Grabe describe the use of the visual component of television news to reinforce cultural myths about race and power in South Africa. Tuchman (1978: 107) observes that much of the literature of television news analysis, 'naively supposes that news film captures reality without imposing its own rules'.[7] We must recognize the potential of agency images, sounds and information to influence audience reception of a news story.

In his explanation of TV news agency WTN's objectives, its Managing Editor Lowndes Lipscomb, discerning no ideological conflict, makes clear the easy confluence of journalism and profit:

> We cover the world for the world. . . . On any given day we are responsible for covering all the stories . . . that we perceive to be of international interest and supply them to . . . all the world's broadcasters who subscribe to us and we always want that subscriber base to grow by making sure that the quality of our news coverage and the kinds of stories that we cover not only make our existing subscriber base happy but also attract new subscribers. (Interview with author, 1995)

The international television news agencies go to great lengths, and take great pride in their ability, to provide a 'balanced,' 'objective' view of the world in their newsfeeds. They generally admit, however, that their newsfeeds concentrate upon news of the industrialized world, but insist that the reason is that these countries established them and (mostly) pay for them. They also historically claim to provide 'raw' pictures and sounds which enable broadcasters to construct their own international news stories. The claim of balance and objectivity has historically served the agencies in the promotion of their product and their growth.

Some general characteristics of the output of the three video agencies are demonstrated in an ongoing content analysis of agency output and use of agency product undertaken by the author. This has involved the coding of international television news agency output for two days of September 1995, as part of a larger international news flow study, 'Foreign news and international news flow in the 1990s'. Agency stories averaged just over two minutes in length, ranging from 38 seconds to 5 minutes and 45 seconds. The main topic of the majority of stories (n = 42 of 256) was coded as international military, or defence, or conflict. The second most common topic (n = 38) was international politics, and the third (n = 33) was civil war or domestic conflict.

The focus on these topics is explained by the traditional news agency and Eurovision (Hjarvard, 1995a) focus on strife, in this case including the breaking story of riots in Tahiti, and the ongoing story of war in Bosnia. The countries deemed by coders to be the most important in an agency story were most frequently the United States and Bosnia, each accounting for 12% of stories. The dominant type of main actor in the coded news agency stories was a state official or 'nation'. A cross-tabulation demonstrated that each of the three agencies was giving roughly equal coverage to these major stories, yielding a statistically insignificant difference (.069) in their coverage. The causes of such a highly standardized television news agency agenda are explained by:

- the similarity of extra-media factors (Shoemaker and Reese, 1991) influencing news production
- the similarity of news production routines among agencies

- competitive pressure to duplicate coverage by other agencies
- universal focus on several standard frames or themes of news coverage.[8]

My preliminary comparative content analysis of newscasts from around the world during the study period suggests a heavier dependence upon television news agencies than the literature traditionally indicates, and a greater degree of influence upon the local newscast's visual text than some recent studies would suggest. For example, the Finnish state broadcaster, YLE, on 7 September 1996, did its first international story about rioting in Tahiti. Most of this 2 minute 26 second story contained footage from Reuters Television. What is especially noteworthy in the YLE story on the rioting is that large portions of the story, including fully 30 seconds' worth at the start, is the edited visual text provided by Reuters. YLE is allowing the news agency to tell the story in its own edit of its own pictures, rather than extensively re-editing agency material or adding images from other sources. The YLE narrative is therefore substantially dictated by the visual text created by Reuters. In our ongoing content analysis, we are finding the practice is common among broadcasters worldwide. A broadcaster choosing to rely so heavily upon a news agency's telling of an important international story contradicts the hypothesis of Gurevitch et al. (1991) that global stories are substantially localized, or 'domesticated', by local broadcasters; that there is no 'global' story.

Broadcasters and news agency personnel tend to see the role of the international television news agencies differently. Broadcasters, despite evidence to the contrary (Hjarvard, 1995a; Malik, 1992) continue to downplay the significance of the agencies, arguing that they only provide supplementary illustration to stories, sometimes derisively called 'video wallpaper', but that the agencies' contribution never constitutes the bulk of a story, nor does it determine the 'spin' of the story.

Agencies are often referred to as 'protection' or called 'insurance policies' by major broadcasters – allowing them to give their audience visual news coverage from anywhere without the prohibitive cost of having to be everywhere themselves. For example, according to former BBC Head of Newsgathering Chris Cramer, 'The BBC and major broadcasters buy agency pictures as fire insurance', compared to 'a lot of broadcasters who actually buy [them] as their entire news supply'.[9]

But, traditionally, major broadcasters like the BBC have a great deal of difficulty giving credit to international television news agencies, even when an agency-provided story is regarded as a major triumph for the broadcaster. As chronicled by Tetley (1988), such was the case with then Visnews videographer (later Reuters Nairobi Bureau Chief) Mohamed Amin's story of the 1984 famine in Ethiopia (which triggered a massive global fundraising drive). Amin (killed with biographer Tetley in a 1996 plane crash) discovered the story, arranged the access to it, and essentially produced, as well as photographed, the coverage of it, but the BBC, and NBC in the US, took the credit for it. Visnews, and Amin in particular, were especially incensed that while privately acknowledging that Amin was responsible for the story, the BBC continued publicly to accept credit for it. The situation was nearly identical to one in 1980, when Mohamed Amin tracked down and interviewed former Ugandan dictator Idi Amin in Saudi Arabia, but a BBC reporter accepted most of the international credit for the scoop (ibid.).

The notion that the agencies are everywhere when broadcasters cannot be must itself be problematized. Both Reuters Television and WTN once had more substantial coverage of the world than they do now, with stringers in virtually every country. The agencies are tight-lipped about the extent of their international coverage cutbacks, which paralleled cutbacks at major broadcasters worldwide during the late 1980s and early 1990s. In the 1980s many of these stringers were dropped when the agencies decided the cost of maintaining them was not justified by their very limited use. The agencies' ability to get a professional crew rapidly to a news event anywhere in the world had improved by that time, although some countries deliberately impeded their ability to practise this sort of 'parachute journalism' (Paterson, 1992).

The television news agencies attempt to obscure the decreases in the number of countries they cover by referring to a dramatic increase in 'bureaux', a term which is notoriously slippery. A lone stringer with an obsolete camera in 1985 might be called a bureau in the 1990s, and be charged with covering a wider area because other neighbouring stringers have been let go.[10] In the case of Associated Press and Reuters a 'television bureau' may be a staff correspondent for the wire service who has been provided with a Hi-8 camera to get video pictures of breaking news until a proper television crew can get to the scene. Neither company admits to how many of their television bureaux fit this description. The number of people agencies claim in their promotional literature to have in different parts of the world has declined over the last several years, while the amount of news each company produces has increased, suggesting a trend of providing more with less.

Television News Globalization

The growth of the agency sector of the television news industry is the result of many interconnected factors resulting from the globalization of television news. Several examples are evident. The BBC World Service Television and CNN International now broadcast globally around the clock, and Rupert Murdoch's News Corporation and General Electric and Microsoft's MSNBC are likely soon to join them. Some non-English language news programming is available to much of the world via the German-language Deutsche-Welle, Spanish-language Tele-Noticias and CNN International, and Japanese NHK services.

STAR TV (owned by News Corporation),[11] South Africa's M-Net, and other satellite services, with more soon to come, provide a wide range of these and other news channels in areas that previously had no television news at all. National public broadcasters are generally in decline worldwide, the result of many forces, including comparison by their audiences to these slick and timely international services (Dillenger, 1995; Helland, 1995; Hjarvard, 1995b). Television news has thus moved from being mostly a publicly owned service to being mostly a privately owned service. Regional television news channels in one or more languages have emerged, but the major global services still deliver the news in English, contributing to English becoming a global 'lingua franca', as put by Schiller (1995) (even a large amount of exported NHK and Deutsche-Welle news programming is in English).

The rapid spread of cable and satellite technologies has given rise to many fledgling news operations, most multinational in character. The process can be seen as but one aspect of the internationalization of television identified by Negrine and Papathanassopoulos (1991). Leading the way has been the US news network, CNN International. Following on the heels of CNN's growth in Europe was an attempt to provide a European flavour to news: Euronews. The problem has been defining European flavour. Euronews is owned by several European public broadcasting organizations and the French media conglomerate Générale Occidentale. It broadcasts news video only, without news anchors, narrated in five different languages. It has had several years of financial difficulty, and has been criticized for an inability to please its ideologically diverse audience and for its impersonal approach to news presentation. Euronews's principal source is Eurovision, which in turn takes international stories from WTN, Reuters and APTV. Euronews also takes direct feeds from the agencies.[12]

The third British newscaster, Sky News, has a European news service reaching 33 European countries,[13] and may be joined in offering a European news service by the BBC or ITN. But if these developments in pan-European news broadcasting exemplify internationalization, the 'counter-tendencies to the process of internationalization' which Negrine and Papathanassopoulos (1991: 13) hypothesize are also emerging. These are primarily the cultural and linguistic barriers to transnational broadcasting which abound in the European television market. The result has been the rapid development of several single-language news channels, aimed at specific regional or national audiences (also see Garitaonandia, 1993; Heinderyckx, 1994).

There are indications that Rupert Murdoch may pursue such a localizing strategy with television news, either instead of, or as a complement to, a global network.[14] Examples of regional non-English television news are the German-language channels VOX, owned by the Bertelsmann media group,[15] and N-TV, owned by Time-Warner and German investors. VOX takes its international news from Reuters.[16] N-TV's international news comes from Reuters[17] and from CNN, whose principal international source is WTN. Other single-language European news channels have been proposed.

Importantly, while these trends suggest substantial growth of television news channels at the local, regional and global levels, the sources for international television news – the television news agencies – remain a highly concentrated few. At the conclusion of their book on media concentration, Tunstall and Palmer (1991) allude to the significance of the dominance of these few sources in the provision of raw news (the sources analysed in this dissertation). Gurevitch et al. (1991) describe this phenomenon as 'the Global Newsroom', but fail to address the implications of a few homogeneous sources providing the raw material for newscasts worldwide. Malik, in his useful TV news agenda survey, demonstrated the worldwide congruence in international television news coverage: 'What our pages show is that the power of the exchange systems and the TV news agencies is much greater than the public generally feel or know' (1992: 37–41). His data showed the same video, of the same stories, from the same sources, running in roughly the same position in newscasts all over the world on the evening of his survey. The recent trends in European television news suggest further homogenization of international news, despite the increase in news channels. For example, with substantial cutbacks to their own news operation, in 1993 Britain's ITN began exclusively using the international footage of its new shareholder, Reuters. Thus Reuters was supplying international news to every major British television newscast (BBC, ITN and Sky) – virtually giving the British television viewer just one ideological window on much of the world.[18]

Alliance Capitalism

International business, as it has developed in the 20th century, has traditionally been based on Fordism and a capitalism based on hierarchies within corporations (Dunning, 1995). This is the 'ideal' form of international trade still preached to newly opening economies by US industry and government (in pursuit of markets), particularly in telecommunications and cultural industries (see, for instance, Paterson, 1993). However, this form does not represent the actual practices of contemporary transnational business in general and contemporary global information and entertainment industries in particular. In the latter arena, a few enormous multinational corporations and alliances of corporations dominate (Bagdikian, 1992; Duarte and Straubhaar, 1996; McAnany and Wilkinson, 1994; Miller, 1996; Schiller, 1991, 1995).

In this scenario there exist the complementary forces of both co-operation and competition, and both on a grand scale. Adam Smith viewed co-operation in international capitalism as a symptom of structural market failure, but in the current climate of international 'alliance capitalism', corporations building the strongest alliances are envied, and often, though not necessarily, are the most profitable (Dunning, 1995). It may be argued that no economic sector has more thoroughly discarded this traditional approach to capitalism than the global culture producers. Transnational alliances as a complement to horizontal and vertical integration have become routine.

An obvious advantage of alliance capitalism is the elimination of competition. This is the creation of oligopoly, whereby industry sectors are shared by just a few giants, or consensus monopoly, whereby industry sectors are, virtually in their entirety, co-operatively divvied out to participating TNCs. Such has long been the case in the international television news gathering sector. Visnews and UPITN, and their successors, maintained their duopolistic dominance of this industry sector through the consent of the largest corporations active in international journalism and broadcasting: the BBC, ITN (and its various owners), Reuters, NBC, ABC, CBS, CNN, Australia's Channel Nine Network, and others.

Such a concentration of control over an industry sector – largely by the consent of major players – is becoming the norm now for other sectors of global communications. Bagdikian (1992) identified 29 giant firms controlling over half the output of US newspapers, calling them a 'Private Ministry of Information and Culture'. The term even more aptly applies to the emerging television news alliances identified here, for they are fewer and larger than the companies Bagdikian surveyed, and reach into more aspects of information (political, financial and cultural, across all media) and entertainment (again, all genres, in all media). Major players in the globalization of television news (along with their holdings which impact upon international television news) are:

Reuters Holdings Plc
(Reuters Television, Reuters wire service, ITN, [currently] Tele-Noticias, global programme production, Polish and Russian commercial broadcasting)

Rupert Murdoch / News Corporation
(STAR TV, Sky, BSkyB, Fox network, global broadcasting and production)

BBC
(BBC, BBC-World)

Carlton
(UK programme producer and broadcaster, majority owner of ITN)

Disney / Capital Cities–ABC
(besides ABC in the US, majority shareholder in WTN, Scandinavian Broadcasting)

General Electric
(NBC, CNBC, NBC Super Channel, Asian Business Channel, MSNBC)

Time-Warner
(US production, broadcasting, and third largest US cable operator,

German-language regional news in Europe and now owner of Turner Broadcasting which includes CNN, CNN-International, specialized CNN TV and radio channels, Latin American CNN-International, German-language regional news in Europe, Russian broadcasting)

Bertelsmann
(European production and broadcasting, German-language regional news in Europe)[19]

Alliances between news gathering companies are important determinants of what information is distributed worldwide and how it is tailored. In 1992, Tunstall observed that, 'The loose Reuters–Visnews–BBC alliance constitutes the strongest single news entity on the world scene'. Now, the loose alliance between giants Reuters Holdings Plc (itself both global culture producer and broadcaster) and News Corporation (also both global culture producer and broadcaster, on a far larger scale) would qualify for that description.

The alliance Tunstall alludes to is disappearing. Visnews and Reuters are one and the same, and the Reuters alliance with the BBC is dwindling. Reuters currently maintains a very limited alliance with the BBC both as a supplier of international news, and as a partner in a Latin American television service, Tele-Noticias, but that service is being sold to Westinghouse.[20] Reuters is also allied with US network NBC as a news provider, and in a satellite business channel.[21] Thus the loose News Corporation–Reuters alliance may be gaining a third powerful partner: General Electric, which controls NBC, CNBC, and half of the emerging global news network MSNBC.

The alliance between transnational information giant Disney – through Capital Cities–ABC – with global broadcaster and international agenda setter the BBC – is also unprecedented and monumentally influential in global information flow.[22] For now, it seems these two giant alliances will at times compete with and at times supply and co-operate with the two other global information giants: General Electric, the world's largest corporation,[23] and Time-Warner, which owns the various CNN services.

In the case of News Corporation influence over Reuters and Associated Press, quantification is elusive. News Corporation does own and closely control major newspapers, particularly in the US and UK, which control shares and have directorial influence at Reuters and AP; both organizations claim to have safeguards in place to prevent takeover or editorial influence by any single force.[24] News Corp. also has an interest in Carlton Plc, an approximately three-billion-dollar British communications firm, which in turn has an interest in Reuters, as well as ITN.

Television news alliances also allow participants to increase news gathering capabilities while reducing costs to each partner. The resulting homogenization of the news is never mentioned within the industry. Tunstall (1992), Weiner (1992), and Bell (1995) all allude to the alliances that dominate television coverage of major international stories. My interviews confirm these accounts. The contracts between agency members and broadcaster members of each alliance make the sharing of news footage and news gathering resources in the field possible, and ensure that each member of each alliance, and all the clients of each agency in each alliance, get the best pictures and best interviews shot by any of several news crews covering the story. It was just such a set of alliances which allowed CNN and WTN to work together to dominate coverage from Iraq during the Gulf War, thereby not only shutting out the BBC, NBC and Visnews, but also bolstering the position of BBC rival ITN and NBC's rivals ABC and CBS (Bell, 1995; Waite, 1992; Weiner, 1992).[25]

The dramatic 1993 agreement developed by Chris Cramer of the BBC and Richard Wald of ABC, and others, which allied those two companies also destroyed the aforementioned alliances and began a chain reaction of realignments which continues today. ITN could no longer work closely with ABC or WTN (even though it continued to own 10% of WTN), since WTN had, through the ABC arrangement, become allied to the BBC. NBC lost the ability to work with the BBC and use large amounts of their material. Visnews (then transitioning to Reuters Television) was being shut out by the BBC, but soon formed new alliances with ITN and Sky. CNN and CBS probably gained from a strengthened WTN, a WTN which could now offer BBC stories.

But alliances in international broadcast news often have peculiar limitations. Examples abound. In southern Africa in the late 1980s the stringers for ITN and WTN would sometimes co-operate, but usually would compete for stories, although each would always compete with the single cameraman in Harare who served both the BBC and Visnews.[26] In London in 1995, ITN journalists began producing a programme for the BBC's Radio Five – an example of outsourcing for programming that would have been unimaginable in the early decades of intensive competition and non-co-operation between ITN and the BBC.[27] When the city of Knin in Bosnia fell to Croatian troops in August 1995, an important turning point in the war, ABC had the only footage thanks to an agreement with APTV, and refused to share it with WTN.

Characteristics of the TV News Agency Story

Mohamed Amin's description of his experience of trying to convince his London Visnews/Reuters editors to use his African stories over the years clearly illustrates the representational frames traditionally sought by those London agency editors:

> I have a lot of grievances with the decision makers. . . . I think they live in a different world. They live in a completely different environment. They don't understand Africa. All they want out of Africa is death, blood, famine, corruption, and all that. We've got plenty of that in Africa – there's no shortage of that. But we've

also got a hell of a lot of other stuff in Africa which is much more important to the continent than just the various wars that go on. I'm not suggesting for a second that these wars should not be covered – they have to be covered. They're quite crucial in terms of the news coverage, but we should look at other stories as well. (Interview with author, 1995)

The consequences of ethnocentric news priorities can be far more significant. Here I refer to the human life equation; the tendency to attach far greater value to loss of human life as the victims are geographically, ethnically, politically, and culturally more proximate to the news producer (see, for example, Larson, 1988; Rosenblum, 1993). The response of one WTN journalist to the question of the 'human life equation' suggests that the very tendency to focus upon the same kinds of stories from developing countries actually leads journalists to attach less value to the lives of people from such areas:

> When you think of, for example, a bus crash in Turkey or a bus crash in India, you know that the last twenty stories you've had from that part of the world, of India say, four or five of them would have been bus crashes with at least fifty killed or something like this and you say 'oh no, not another one'. . . . Third World stories tend to be massacres in Africa or bus crashes in India. (Interview with author, 1995)

This journalist acknowledges that 'what we need are a broader range of stories'. He claims there is not a 'broader range of stories' because the major WTN clients are not interested in stories from developing countries (a common assumption at agencies), so the agency cannot devote more resources to cover developing countries.

Herman and Chomsky (1988: 37) refer to 'worthy and unworthy' victims, empirically demonstrating the tendency of US media to provide far greater coverage of the deaths of people at the hands of 'enemy' states versus those killed by nations which the US government is supporting. For example, based on *New York Times* coverage, the death of '[Polish priest] Popieluszko is valued at somewhere between 137 and 179 times that of a victim in the US client states' (1988: 39). A Reuters editor of the day was unusually forthright about his decision process as he correlated the number of deaths to issues of proximity and ethnocentrism:

> It is a body count. . . . I would guess that you would say obviously a story in Rwanda has to have a lot more bodies in it than a story in a Western country, a lot more. . . . There is probably a relativity, an unfortunate relativity, which is an economic one, between certain countries in the world as to how many people, how many dead, before it becomes an international story, which is an ongoing debate that we have all the time – something that we fight against. But . . . if a ferry goes down in Bangladesh, Calcutta, something like that, we're there; we do it, but at the time of the Herald of Free Enterprise ferry disaster [off the Swedish coast] there were 180 people killed and we ran the immediate story, the funerals, absolutely every reaction.

News values are those particular characteristics of an event which make it more likely to be chosen for the news agenda (or 'newsworthy') (Galtung and Ruge, 1970; Gans, 1980). Providing that the vast intra-organizational and extra-organizational factors affecting news production are also considered (as I attempt to do through ethnographic and institutional analysis), a review of key news determination factors of international television news agency journalists from a news values perspective is useful. According to this approach, the more of these qualities a news story substantially exhibits, the more prominence it will be given by journalists.

How applicable are such news values to international television news agency news production? Based upon both my ethnographic research and the limited quantitative research I have conducted to date, I propose a few brief answers, but also suggest the question warrants further research. I attempt below to indicate (not quantify) their relevance to agency news production and suggest modifications to existing news value theory in the context of the unique TV news agency environment.[28]

Timeliness is the paramount value across nearly all categories of agency news story, with a notable exception: news from developing countries. In that case agencies are routinely content to send stories to London via scheduled airlines instead of satellite; or to allow a story to sit in the newsroom for a few days before feeding it to clients. *Proximity* is also an important consideration for television news agencies, but the concept requires a modification from its previous use in the literature. If we accept the agency journalist's 'imagined audience' (Ang, 1991) to be television stations around the world, we might expect the proximity value to lead to news coverage evenly dispersed across the planet. It is not, so it seems the proximity value applies only to a limited number of influential agency clients. An event's proximity to those clients will increase its chance of selection.

The same is true of the traditional news value of *consequence*. Stories must be consequent only for specific favoured agency clients. *Human interest*, or *emotional value*, is given great importance by news agency workers, but is often sacrificed for the perceived obligation to cover, or update, major stories with little human interest value. I have noted the frustration this causes agency news workers. There is tremendous satisfaction in the newsroom when the agency produces an emotional, human interest-filled story for clients. *Prominence*, or how well known story subjects are, is another highly applicable and basic agency news value. My analysis of news agency output found that 38% of the main story actors are government officials or representatives of nations. These are mostly the same recurring news elites whose comment is routinely sought on any of several international crisis the agencies are devoting most of their resources to.

Conflict is probably the most prominent agency news value. It would seem that the salience of this news value is correlated to another value: proximity, in this case, to favoured agency clients. Thus conflict in the Balkans is highly covered; conflict in southern Africa or East Timor is not. Further, conflict must involve more than one nation for extensive coverage by agencies – civil war on its own, no matter how brutal, does not get heavily covered (for example, Cambodia or Algeria). *Visual quality* is a major factor dictating news choices. Rarely are agency journalists willing to give their clients a story if the visual element is unsatisfactory. *Topicality* relates to the extent of existing audience interest, so again, taking the world's broadcasters as agency audience, we can say that their interest is a major determinant of agency coverage, with some provisos. The interest of a few favoured broadcasters – the BBC, CNN, ABC, etc., – reigns supreme.

Conclusion

The coverage decisions of the international television news agencies are based largely upon what their rival company is doing, the costs of allocating resources to areas from which it is expensive to provide coverage, and the will of the most powerful international broadcasters (even though this is often assumed). The dominance of a few powerful media alliances in the provision of international news product means that news, in both print and electronic form, from much of the world, is now determined and provided by what is essentially a single editorial perspective – that of a small number of culturally homogeneous news workers in a few very similar and often allied Anglo-American news organizations based in London.

My extended ethnographic research with television news agencies demonstrated that they are more inclined to treat major corporations and western governments as acceptable sources (of information or video images) than institutions from developing countries, and that management and news-processing structures are designed not to insulate journalists' decisions from commercial considerations but to ensure that such considerations prevail at all levels of news production. Gitlin observed the same in his study of how television news shapes political discourse in the United States. He notes that journalists 'tend to share the core hegemonic assumptions of their class: that is, of their managers as well as their major sources', while all the time being assured of, and assuring everyone else of, their journalistic autonomy (1980: 256).

The trend seems to be that television news coverage of the developing world is likely to diminish, and to become increasingly more homogeneous. Ungar and Gergen reached a similar conclusion, mostly in regard to print coverage of Africa, in their 1991 analysis. They argue that trends in world events are increasingly crowding Africa out of the 'news hole', that US news audiences seem to be becoming increasingly parochial, if not isolationist, and that there is a trend in journalism generally away from serious international coverage. Globally, TV news is also being seen less as a special case – a form of television which provides a needed socio-political function – than as just another transnational cultural commodity.

This change to the evaluation of the place of news is occurring in each of the three essential sectors of society delineated by Galtung (1994): the state, capital, and civil. To vastly simplify Galtung's argument, today state and civil society approximately balance each other, but capital 'is not challenged and made accountable'. Applying news to his model, capital has clearly appropriated an institution (television journalism) which was established, at least in part, to insulate and protect civil society from the state and from capital itself. And it does so now with the full support and acquiescence of states and to a large extent, apparently, the civil society. The increasing control of global news production and flow by a decreasing number of institutions suggests a variety of dangers, as posited by Smith (1990), Bagdikian (1992) and others. The cultural product of the international television news agencies serves to perpetuate a western hegemony hostile to developing nations. The diversity which the 'marketplace of ideas' news would ideally represent is diminished.

There are indications that through much of modern society, television news is playing an ever-increasing role as the vehicle for essential civil discourse: Habermas's public sphere. Habermas (1989: 231) summarized this as 'a domain of our social life in which such a thing as public opinion can be formed'. Hjarvard (1993) has theorized the potential development of a (useful) pan-European public sphere resulting from the increased influence of pan-European television news services and the decreasing influence of national news. There is no reason not to extend this argument globally. The globalization of television news is producing an international public sphere, but one dominated by mainstream Anglo-American ideologies conveyed in the texts of internationally distributed television news. A link can be seen to the 'ideoscapes' hypothesized by Appadurai. Hallin (1994: 161–7) raises the spectre of an 'international public sphere', but similarly notes that most countries are excluded from any political dialogues it entails (see also Venturelli, 1993).

The discourse of the New World Information and Communication Order (NWICO), and the specific demands it put upon international print and television news agencies, lingers in the consciousness of news agency journalists – and the international broadcasters whom they supply – like a sort of vaguely recalled bad dream involving totalitarian governments and annoying academics[29] trying to wrest control of the international news agenda. Minor efforts to address NWICO complaints were made by television news agencies then, and minor efforts are being made now[30] – in each case justified by wholly economic, not political or cultural, rationales. But substantial efforts have not been made, nor will they.

The perception of a single, valid, and globally appropriate view of news is so pervasive among international television news agency workers and among broadcast journalists worldwide that cultural relevance (Duarte and Straubhaar, 1996) has become a nil concept in global TV news distribution. And equality of information flow is similarly immaterial, for as long as the pictures of the world's news arrive each day from people with the shared understanding of news, its means of production and distribution are irrelevant technicalities.

The trend at the wholesale tier of international television news is to try to be a diversified, multi-media news agency cum all-purpose TV production company. Reuters and Associated Press have the backing of deep corporate pockets to continue in the marginally profitable field of television news gathering, providing they don't spend too much doing it. Disney Corporation's commitment to stepchild WTN's future is far from certain; but neither is Reuters Holdings' or Associated Press's commitment to television news a certainty.

The wholesale/retail distinction may become less significant as all players offer their news products directly to subscribing computer users, the form of (multi-)media consumption predicted to displace television eventually. In regard to the future of these companies, one may well ask if they will have any role at all when each individual news consumer in the world can put together their own newscast on their home media terminal, comprising only the news they want to see. The lifeblood of the television news agencies is the boring politics, the unending human tragedies, and the wartime carnage that the average viewer often would prefer to do without. Television news as we now know it may be in its final days.

Television coverage of the developing world is already deplorably infrequent and misleading. The developing world appears now to be more excluded from contribution to the global flow of television news than it has ever been. For now, the homogeneity of international television news sources is a concern. Despite the increasing number of news services, ownership is highly concentrated, and broadcasters are becoming increasingly dependent upon a few news providers to supply the international images they use on the air: the images which shape our global reality.

Notes

1. That Reuters Television is the largest international television news agency is the conventional wisdom in the industry, but since each agency keeps its client base and news revenues, and, to a considerable extent, its resources, as privileged information, it is difficult to test this assumption. One recent trade article pronounced WTN 'the largest and most mature of the three', but offers no evidence to demonstrate that it has eclipsed Reuters in any way (Fuller, 1995: 63). The difficulty is primarily in delineating the television news aspects of Reuters Television from its various other parts (a distinction the company does not report; the company's tradition of reporting revenues by geographic region further complicates the situation). By way of earlier comparison, in 1993 Reuters Television was little more than the sum of Visnews, which had 1990 revenues of $99.3 million compared to WTN's 1990 revenues of $35.8 million (Waite, 1992).

2. Disney owns Capital Cities, which owns ABC, which owns 80% of WTN. As of this writing, it seems Disney has yet fully to discover that it owns the second largest provider of international television news pictures; it has not announced any synergistic global television news strategy. Disney executives are being relocated to London to take charge of various ABC enterprises, including WTN (Disney press release, 25 June 1996, from PR Newswire via Lexis/Nexis).

3. 'APTV Signs up Four New Clients' (1995) UK Press Gazette, 16 October: 13.

4. My assertion that most of the television images from the fringes of international news flow are provided by several London-based news organizations and a few international news exchanges is based on still very limited analysis in the academic and trade literature and newspaper articles. There are virtually no empirical data on the amount of such material actually broadcast – even the television news agencies themselves do not generate such statistics. Nor do broadcasters generally do so, as confirmed by inquiries to ITN, CNN and ABC. This researcher is conducting a study designed to locate and quantify such use by broadcasters around the world.

5. Such a contention also assumes every client broadcaster uses some Visnews footage each day – something agencies have never actually bothered to find out. Agencies often deduce that the payment of a subscription fee equates to extensive use of their product.

6. Conus (derived from the satellite industry's term for Continental Untied States) is a commercial satellite news exchange between local stations in the US, and CNN and the US broadcast networks operate news exchanges for their affiliated stations. CNN is a global broadcaster and a global provider of news pictures. Its position confuses the industry, as evidenced even in a contractual document of the European Broadcasting Union, which refers to 'broadcasting organizations which at the same time operate like agencies (such as CNN)' (*sic*). Its pictures and finished stories may be used by broadcasters around the world with whom it has an exchange agreement, as most do. Such is common in the case of fast-breaking stories where CNN has the only exciting coverage (such was the case in the first days of the Gulf War). CNN also sells raw footage in competition with the three TV news agencies, but so far, this seems quite limited.

7. It would be useful for future research to relate existing detailed analysis of the visual grammar of television news to the output of the television news agencies. Literature addressing this grammar includes Graber (1990), Grimes (1990), Gunter (1987) and Tuchman (1978).

8. Detailed analysis of these factors is provided in my dissertation (Paterson, 1996).

9. In Steve Busfield (1994) 'Cramer vs. Cramer', *Broadcast*, 30 June: 20.

10. Paterson, 1992; based mostly on interviews with agency stringers in southern Africa, and witnessed by the author in these cases. A WTN manager denied my conclusion in correspondence, arguing that coverage budgets have doubled in the last decade (but he failed to provide evidence that agencies keep journalists in as many parts of the world as they once did). The word 'stringer' has various meanings and variations. In 1979 Visnews (in *A Visnews Newsroom Operating Handbook*) separated photographers into 'Staff Cameramen', 'Contract Cameramen' (local employees working for a Visnews bureau full-time), 'Retainers' (paid to work for Visnews for a few days each month), and 'Stringers' (paid only when assigned to a story). This system continues at each of the three agencies, with minor variations.

11. In 1993 Rupert Murdoch bought 63.6% of STAR from the Li family of Hong Kong. In 1995, Murdoch paid $299 million for the 36.4% of the STAR Group still owned by Richard Li and Hutchinson Whampoa. The five-channel STAR TV service is now beamed to 53 countries (Fuller, 1995) 'Murdoch tightens Asian grip', *Broadcast*, 21 July: 5.

12. Reuters' internal document, May 1993, and *Le Journal de Genève* (via Lexis/Nexis), 23 August 1993.

13. Satellite TV Finance (via Lexis/Nexis), 29 April 1993, and Reuters European Business Report (via Lexis/Nexis) 1 September 1993.

14. A recent trade magazine article noted that 'rather than a CNN-style service broadcast to the world, News International appears to be utilizing its Sky News resources, largely supplied by Reuters TV, to create localized news services' (Busfield, 1995: 20–1). For example, News Corporation is starting a DBS service with the

Brazilian Globo organization, to be carried by the Net Brasil satellite (*Broadcast*, 14 July 1995: 2–3). Like News Corporation, CNN is pursuing localizing strategies in tandem with its globalizing strategies. In 1995, the PAS4 satellite was launched to provide DBS for Africa. The satellite carries News Corporation's Sky News and Time-Warner's CNN-I, and negotiations were underway to add the BBC (*Broadcast*, 21 July 1995: 10). In a deal with Indian national broadcaster Doordarshan, CNN-I is leasing an Indian satellite transponder for an Indian CNN service which will incorporate between two and four hours daily of Doordarshan-produced material. CNN paid approximately $1.5 million to Doordarshan in the deal and promised to train Doordarshan journalists (*Broadcast*, 7 July 1995: 11).

15. Satellite TV Finance (via Lexis/Nexis), 8 July 1993.

16. Reuters' internal document, May 1993.

17. Reuters' internal document, May 1993.

18. *Broadcast*, 28 May 1993; Westcott (1995a: 22) confirms that 'Reuters now supplies news to all of the major UK broadcasters'. The BBC has continued to draw international coverage from its own extensive resources and WTN and has added APTV. ITN is in negotiations to return to WTN as supplier, and may end its relationship with Reuters due to unease about Reuters' close relationship with Sky.

19. Miller, 1996; Paterson, 1994; Auletta, 1993; Bagdikian, 1992; Tunstall and Palmer, 1991.

20. *Wall Street Journal*, 24 May 1996 via 'Shoptalk' on-line service.

21. *Broadcast*, 29 October 1993: 15.

22. The 1993 BBC alliance with ABC had numerous repercussions. NBC had an arrangement to share news pictures with the BBC from 1954. After the ABC deal, NBC executives declared, somewhat naively, that the relationship would continue. ABC had a prior relationship with ITN to share resources and footage for 'spot news', and ABC claimed that the relationship 'would continue, for now' (Ben Kubasik [1993] 'ABC, BBC forge a news partnership', *Newsday*, 26 March, II, 20). It is clear now that neither earlier arrangement continues in any significant way. At the end of 1995, the Reuters contract with the BBC ended, and ABC subsidiary WTN became the sole agency allowed to distribute BBC material. According to a WTN editor, the BBC's realignment (to the WTN camp) from its historical relationship with Visnews began when it got irked by Reuters for competing for the morning audience in Britain with 'GMTV'. BBC executives were probably already uncomfortable with the rapidly increasing collaboration between Rupert Murdoch's interests and Visnews, later Reuters. This was not just because Sky presented substantial competition to the BBC for news viewers in the UK and globally, or because Murdoch dropped the BBC World Service from STAR TV because it offended the Chinese government (Tefft, 1993). It was also probably because throughout the 1980s Murdoch's newspapers in London had a policy of writing articles intensely critical of the BBC in order to weaken the BBC as a political and cultural institution and steer viewers to Sky.

23. According to Miller (1996), GE is tied with General Motors for the number one position in the Forbes 500 listing.

24. The myth of the 'firewall' is often invoked by journalists in reference to the separation of editorial decisions in the newsroom from corporate priorities. For journalists who consider themselves independent thinkers to participate in the form of conglomerate journalism described herein, they must continue to believe in an almost magical firewall that will protect their higher motivations of journalism from the lower motivations of business and politics. The use of a television news agency as an ideological tool of a single group has historic precedent. In 1975, half of WTN predecessor UPITN was purchased by a US newspaper publisher financed by and representing the interests of the South African Information Ministry, in an effort to alter and improve international television representation of South Africa (detailed in the dissertation by this author; see also Boyd-Barrett, 1980; Fenby, 1986).

25. See Weiner (1992) for a detailed account of CNN's coverage from Iraq.

26. Based on my ethnographic research in Harare, Zimbabwe in 1990. Mohamed Amin of Visnews/Reuters (in Tetley, 1988) reports his frequent competition for stories with BBC or NBC crews, despite the close alliance and picture flow between Visnews and those broadcasters.

27. *Broadcast*, 21 July 1995: 6.

28. McManus (1994: 119–120) posited these and other news value categories, synthesizing news values suggested by previous researchers.

29. By all known accounts, until my research in 1995, one and a half decades after the height of the NWICO dialogue, UPITN/WTN and Visnews/Reuters had effectively barred academics from their newsrooms. Schlesinger (1980) notes this was not uncommon for television companies in the late 1970s, domestically in the UK, mostly the result of perceived negative portrayals of television journalists by the Glasgow Media Group.

30. Andrew Ailes, former Visnews managing editor, interview. For example, under Ailes in the late 1970s and early 1980s an (ultimately unsuccessful) newsfeed for Africa was established, considerable assistance (for profit) to developing country broadcasters by Visnews continued, and it appears that coverage resources in developing countries were increased. Ailes told me that editorial decisions during that period specifically addressed NWICO concerns, but this is all but impossible to verify. Reuters Television has recently established a commercially successful weekly news programme for African broadcasters. Associated Press Television is aggressively targeting Latin American and Asian broadcasters by giving well-connected regional editors, native to the region, considerable input on story choice.

References

Adams, W. (1982) *Television Coverage of International Affairs*, Norwood, NJ: Aldex.

Al-Hajji, M. and Ogan, C. (1996) 'How does Saudi ownership affect the content of UPI?: a qualitative analysis of selected coverage by the Associated Press and the United Press International', paper presented to the annual meeting of the International Communications Association, Chicago.

Alleyne, M.D. and Wagner, J. (1993) 'Stability and change at the 'Big Five' news agencies', *Journalism Quarterly* 70 (1): 40–50.

Altheide, D. (1976) *Creating Reality: How TV News Distorts Events*, Beverly Hills, CA: Sage.

Altschull, J. and Herbert, J. (1984) *Agents of Power: the Role of the News Media in Human Affairs*. New York: Longman.

Ang, I. (1991) *Desperately Seeking the Audience*, London: Routledge.

Appadurai, A. (1990) 'Disjuncture and difference in the global cultural economy', in M. Featherstone (ed.), *Global Culture: Nationalism, Globalization, and Modernity*, London: Sage.

Auletta, K. (1993) 'Raiding the global village', *New Yorker*, 2 August: 25–30.

Bagdikian, B. (1992) *The Media Monopoly*, 4th edn, Boston: Beacon Press.

Behr, R.L. and Iyengar, S. (1985) 'Television news, real-world cues, and Changes in the Public Agenda', *Public Opinion Quarterly*, 49: 38–57.

Bell, M. (1995) *In Harm's Way*, London: Hamish Hamilton.

Beltran, L.R. (1978) 'TV etchings in the minds of Latin Americans', *Gazette*, 61–85.

Berger, P.L. and Luckman, T. (1966) *The Social Construction of Reality: A Treatise in the Sociology of Knowledge*, Garden City, NY: Anchor Books.

Boyd-Barrett, O. (1980) *The International News Agencies*, London: Constable.

Boyd-Barrett, O. and Thussu, K. (1992) *Contra-Flow in Global News*, London: John Libbey.

Broadcasting and Cable (1993) *Special Report – News Services: Filling Changing Needs and Niches*, 31 May: 27–44.

Busfield, S. (1995) 'Bureaux de change', *Broadcast*, 10 November: 20–1.

Clarke, N. and Riddell, E. (1992) *The Sky Barons*, London: Methuen.

Clarke, S. (1995) 'London: international news capital', *Variety*, 18 December.

Claypool, S. (1995) 'The changing role of the news agencies', *EBU Review*, Autumn.

Cohen, A., Levy, M., Roeh, I. and Gurevitch, M. (1996) *Global Newsrooms, Local Audiences: A Study of the Eurovision News Exchange*, London: John Libbey.

Dahlgren, P. and Sparks, C. (eds) *Communications and Citizenship: Journalism and the Public Sphere in the New Media Age*, London: Routledge.

Dillenger, B. (1995) *'Finnish Views of CNN Television News: A Critical Cross-Cultural Analysis of the American Commercial Discourse Style'*, Ph.D. dissertation, University of Vaasa.

Dominick, J.R. (1988) 'The impact of budget cuts on CBS News', *Journalism Quarterly* 65 (2): 469–73.

Duarte, L.G. and Straubhaar, J. (1996) 'Cultural proximity, class and the emergence of satellite TV services in Latin America', paper presented to the International Communications Association annual meeting in Chicago.

Dunning, J.H. (1995) 'The eclectic paradigm in an age of alliance capitalism', *Journal of International Business Studies*, 26 (3): 461–87.

Epstein, E. (1974) *News from Nowhere*, New York: Vintage Books.

Featherstone, M. (ed.) (1990) *Global Culture: Nationalism, Globalization, and Modernity*, London: Sage.

Fenby, J. (1986) *The International News Services*, A Twentieth Century Fund Report, New York: Schocken Books.

Ferguson, M. (1992) 'The mythology about globalization', *European Journal of Communication*, 7: 69–93.

Fishman, M. (1980) *Manufacturing the News*, Austin: University of Texas Press.

Foote, J. (1995) 'Structure and marketing of global television news', *Journal of Broadcasting and Electronic Media*, 39 (1): 127–33.

Freedom Forum Media Studies Center (1993) 'The media and foreign policy in the post-cold war world', Briefing Paper, New York: Columbia University.

Friedland, L. (1992) *'Covering the World: International Television News Services'*, paper for the Twentieth Century Fund.

Fuller, C. (1995) 'Elbowing for news room', *TV World*, October: 63–6.

Galtung, J. (1994) 'State, capital, and the civil society: a problem of communication', paper presented to the *MacBride Round Table*, Honolulu.

Galtung, J. and Ruge, M. (1965, 1970) 'The structure of foreign news', in Jeremy Tunstall (ed.) *Media Sociology*, London: Constable.

Gans, H. (1980) *Deciding What's News*, New York: Vintage Books.

Garitaonandia, C. (1993) 'Regional television in Europe', *European Journal of Communication*, 8: 277–94.

Gitlin, T. (1980) *The Whole World is Watching: Mass Media in the Making and Unmaking of the New Left*, Berkeley, CA: University of California Press.

Golding, P. and Elliott, P. (1979) *Making the News*, New York: Longman.

Gonzenbach, W., Arant, M. and Stevenson, R. (1991) 'The world of U.S. network television news: eighteen years of foreign news coverage', paper presented to the Association for Education on Journalism and Mass Communications meeting in Boston.

Gowing, N. (1994) 'Real time television coverage of armed conflicts and diplomatic crises: does it pressure or distort foreign policy decisions?', Working Paper 94–1, Joan Shorenstein Barone Center, JFK School of Government, Harvard University.

Grabe, M. (1994) 'South African Broadcasting Corporation coverage of the 1987 and 1989 elections: the matter of visual bias', paper presented to the Association for Education on Journalism and Mass Communications meeting in Atlanta.

Graber, D. (1990) 'Seeing is remembering: how visuals contribute to learning from television news', *Journal of Communication*, 40 (3).

Grimes, T. (1990) 'Encoding TV news messages into memory', *Journalism Quarterly*, 67 (4): 757–66.

Gunter, B. (1987) *Poor Reception* Hillsdale, NJ: Lawrence Erlbaum Associates.

Gunther, M. (1994) *The House That Roone Built: The Inside Story of ABC News*, Boston: Little Brown.

Gurevitch, M., Levy, M. and Roeh, I. (1991) 'The global newsroom: convergences and diversities in the globalization of television news', in P. Dahlgren and C. Sparks (eds) *Communications and Citizenship: Journalism and the Public Sphere in the New Media Age*, London: Routledge.

Habermas, J. (1989) *On Society and Politics: A Reader*, S. Seidman (ed.) Boston: Beacon Press.

Hallin, D.C. (1994) *We Keep America on Top of the World: Television Journalism and the Public Sphere*, Routledge: London.

Harrison, P. and Palmer, R. (1986) *News out of Africa: Biafra to Band Aid*, London: Hilary Shipman.

Heinderyckx, F. (1993) 'Television news programmes in western Europe: a comparative study', *European Journal of Communication*, 8: 425–50.

Heinderyckx, F. (1994) 'Language as the irreducible impediment to transnational television programmes', paper presented to Turbulent Europe: Conflict, Identity and Culture Conference, British Film Institute, London.

Helland, K. (1995) *'Public Service and Commercial News'*, Ph.D. dissertation, University of Bergen.

Herman, E. and Chomsky, N. (1988) *Manufacturing Consent*, New York: Pantheon.

Hjarvard, S. (1993) 'Pan-European television news: towards a European political public sphere?', in P. Drummond, R. Paterson and J. Willis (eds) *National Identity and Europe. The Television Revolution*, London: British Film Institute.

Hjarvard, S. (1995a) *Internationale TV-nyheder. En historisk analyse af det europæiske system for udveksling af internationale TV-nyheder*, Ph.D. dissertation, Copenhagen.

Hjarvard, S. (1995b) 'Eurovision news in a competitive marketplace', *Diffusion*, Autumn, Geneva: EBU.

Hjarvard, S. (1995c) 'TV news flow studies revisited', *Electronic Journal of Communication*, 5 (2, 3): 24–38.

Johnston, C.B. (1995) *Winning the global TV news game*, Boston: Focal Press.

Kozol, W. (1989) 'Representations of race in network news coverage of South Africa', in G. Burns and R. Thompson (eds), *Television Studies: Textual Analysis*, New York: Praeger.

Larson, J. (1984) *Television's Window on the World: International Affairs Coverage on the US Networks*, Norwood, NJ: Ablex.

Larson, J. (1988) 'Global television and foreign policy', paper for the Foreign Policy Association.

McAnany, E. and Wilkinson, K. (1994) 'From cultural imperialists to takeover victims? Questions on Hollywoods buyouts from the critical tradition', *Communication Research*, 19 (6): 724–48.

McCombs, M.E. (1981) 'The agenda setting approach', in D. O. Nimmo and K. R. Sanders (eds), *Handbook of Political Communication*, Beverly Hills: Sage, pp. 121–40.

McCombs, M.E. (1988) 'Setting the agenda: the evolution of agenda-setting research', paper presented at SOMMATIE X, Veldhoven, The Netherlands.

McCombs, M.E., and Shaw, D.C. (1972) 'The agenda setting function of mass media', *Public Opinion Quarterly*, 36: 176–87.

McManus, J. (1994) *Market-Driven Journalism*, Thousand Oaks, CA: Sage.

Malik, R. (1992) 'The global news agenda', *Intermedia*, 20 (1).

Melnik, S. (1981) *Eurovision News and the International Flow of Information: History, Problems and Perspectives 1960–1980*, Bochum: Studienverlag Dr N. Brockmeyer.

Melody, W. (1993) 'On the political economy of communication in the information society', in J. Wasko, V. Mosco and M. Pendakur (eds), *Illuminating the Blind Spots: Essays Honoring Dallas W. Smythe*, Norwood, NJ: Ablex, pp. 63–81.

Miller, M. (1996) 'Free The Media', *Nation*, 3 June.

Mirabella, A. (1994) 'News explosion of '95', *Columbia Journalism Review*, 33 (4).

Molina, G.G. (1990) *The Production of Mexican Television News: The Supremacy of Corporate Rationale*, Ph.D. dissertation, Leicester.

Morales, W.Q. (1984) 'Latin America on network TV', *Journalism Quarterly*, 61 (1): 157–60.

Murdock, G. (1982) 'Large corporations and the control of the communications industries', in M. Gurevitch et al. (eds), *Culture, Society, and the Media*, London: Mcmillan.

Musa, M. (1990) 'News agencies, transnationalization and the new order', *Media, Culture and Society*, 12: 325–42.

Negrine, R. and Papathanassopoulos, S. (1991) 'The internationalization of television', *European Journal of Communication*, 6: 9–32.

Ogundimu, F. (1992) 'Media coverage, issue salience, and knowledge of Africa in a midwestern university', paper presented to the African Studies Association meeting in Seattle.

Paterson, C. (1992) 'Television News from the Frontline States', in B. Hawk, (ed.) *Africa's Media Image*. New York: Praeger.

Paterson, C. (1993) 'Remaking South African broadcasting: in America's image', *FAIR EXTRA*, January/February.

Paterson, C. (1994) 'More channels, fewer perspectives: international television news provider concentration', paper presented to Turbulent Europe: Conflict, Identity and Culture Conference, British Film Institute, London.

Paterson, C. (1996) *News Production at Worldwide Television News (WTN): An Analysis of Television News Agency Coverage of Developing Countries*, Ph.D. dissertation, University of Texas at Austin.

Ramaprasad, J. (1993) 'Content, geography, concentration, and consonance in foreign news coverage of ABC, NBC, and CBS', *International Communications Bulletin*, Spring.

Read, D. (1992) *The Power of News: The History of Reuters 1849–1989*, Oxford: Oxford University Press.

Rodriguez, A. (1996) 'Made in the USA: the production of the Noticiero Univision', *Critical Studies in Mass Communication*, 13 (1): 59–82.

Rosenblum, M. (1993) *Who Stole the News?* New York: John Wiley.

Schiff, F. (1996) 'The Associated Press: its worldwide bureaus and American interests', *International Communications Bulletin*, 31 (1–2), Spring: 7–13.

Schiller, H. (1990) 'The global commercialization of culture', *Directions* PCDS. (4) 1.

Schiller, H. (1991) 'Not yet the post-imperialist era', *Critical Studies in Mass Communication*, 8: 13–28.

Schiller, H. (1995) Lecture, University of Texas at Austin.

Schlesinger, P. (1980) 'Between sociology and journalism', in H. Christian (ed.), *Sociology of the Press and Journalism*, Keele: University of Keele.

Schlesinger, P. (1987) *Putting 'Reality' Together: BBC News* (2nd edn), London: Routledge.

Schudson, M. (1992) 'The sociology of news production revisited', in J. Curran and M. Gurevitch (eds), *Mass Media and Society*, New York: Routledge.

Shoemaker, P. and Reese, S. (1991) *Mediating the Message: Theories of Influence on Mass Media Content*, New York: Longman.

Shoemaker, P., Danielian, L. and Brendlinger, N. (1991) 'Deviant acts, risky business and U.S. interests: the newsworthiness of world events', *Journalism Quarterly*, Winter: 781–95.

Smith, A. (1990) 'Media globalism in the age of consumer sovereignty', *Gannett Center Journal*, 8 (4): 1–16.

Sreberny-Mohammadi, A., Stevenson, R., Nordenstreng, K. and Ugboajah, F. (1984) 'The world of news study', *Journal of Communications*, Winter: 120–42.

Struabhaar, J.D. (1991) 'Beyond media imperialism: asymmetrical interdependence and cultural proximity', *Critical Studies in Mass Communication* (8) 1: 39.

Taylor, J. (1991) 'Reuters Holdings PLC', in Adele Hast (ed.), *International Directory of Company Histories*, vol. IV, Chicago: St James Press.

Tefft, S. (1993) 'Satellite Broadcasts Create Stir Among Asian Regimes', *Christian Science Monitor*, 8 December.

Tetley, B. (1988) *The Story of Mohamed Amin: Front-line Cameraman*, London: Moonstone Books.

Tuchman, G. (1978) *Making News: A Study in the Construction of Reality*, New York: Free Press.

Tunstall, J. (1992) 'Europe as world news leader', *Journal of Communication*, 42 (3).

Tunstall, J. and Palmer, M. (1991) *Media Moguls*, London: Routledge.

Ungar, S.J. and Gergen, D. (1991) 'Africa and the American media', paper for the Freedom Forum Media Studies Center, New York: Columbia University.

Vanden Heuvel, J. (1993) 'For the media, a brave (and scary) new world', *Media Studies Journal*, 7 (4), Fall.

Venturelli, S. (1993) 'Democracy as fiction in the transnational public sphere', *Media Development*, 4.

Vidal-Beneyto, J. and Dahlgren, P. (eds) (1987) *The Focused Screen*, Strasbourg: AMELA.

Waite, T.L. (1992) 'As networks stay home, two agencies roam the world', *New York Times*, 8 March: 5.

Wallis, R. and Baran, S. (1990) *The Known World of Broadcast News*, London: Routledge.

Weiner, R. (1992) *Live from Baghdad: Gathering News at Ground Zero*, New York: Doubleday.

Westcott, T. (1995a) 'Getting mighty crowded', *Television Business International*, November.

Westcott, T. (1995b) 'War stories: the agencies', *Television Business International*, November.

Westerstahl, J. and Johansson, F. (1994) 'Foreign news: news values and ideologies', *European Journal of Communication*, 9: 71–89.

Winseck, D. (1992) 'Gulf War in the global village: CNN, democracy, and the information age', in J. Wasko and V. Mosco (eds), *Democratic Communication in the Information Age*, Norwood, NJ: Ablex.

Part II

NEWS AGENCIES IN THE FURNACE OF POLITICAL TRANSITION

Introduction

Oliver Boyd-Barrett and Terhi Rantanen

The first national news agencies were founded in the wake of nationalism in Europe to serve the territories of nation states in the latter part of the 19th century. The relationship between news agencies and the state has been a persistent theme ever since throughout most parts of the world. Each of the contributions to this section illustrates facets of the state–agency relationship, with particular reference to periods of dramatic political transition. Whether it was the nationalization of the Spanish agency in 1927 and in 1938, or of the Nazi agency in Germany in 1933, to mention the most extreme examples, the issue remains the same: the state has strong interests in news transmission, both domestically and internationally, and these become especially visible in times of national or international crisis which are a threat to the state itself. How do states and how do agencies behave in these circumstances, and with what consequences for the role of agencies in the construction and transmission of images of the state and nation? It is not only the relationship between state and national agency that counts, however, as very often a third partner in this relationship is the global agency: the choice of national partner by a global agency has implications for the survival of officially sanctioned national news agencies, and sometimes for the survival of the states which sanction them.

In the 19th century when the French Havas, British Reuters and German Wolff expanded their operations outside their national boundaries they were also to begin a process that would eventually provide a strong Spanish voice within the global news system. The account by Ingrid Schulze-Schneider, in chapter 7, of an agency that started life in 1866 as the Spanish private agency Fabra, is important for at least three reasons. In the first place, the extraordinary role played by the French agency, Havas, in control of the Spanish agency through many decades, is an extreme example of the power of global agencies to influence national destinies. Second, the history of the Spanish national news agency is replete with examples of the complex manoeuvrings of national agencies in their endeavours at various times to appease the dominant political establishment, or to distance themselves from it, or to work within it. Third, the recent expansion of EFE in South America illustrates how, in competitive global markets, a national agency can take on the mantle of a new, in this case Hispanic, voice in the development of major regional alliances within a neo-liberal globalized world order.

The 1859 agreement between Havas, Reuters and Wolff had defined Spain as Havas' territory. Fabra soon became Havas' branch office and lost its independence. This arrangement, however, was fully supported by the Spanish government with which the agency closely collaborated. After the death of the founder of the agency, Nilo Maria Fabra, in 1903, the French agency purchased the agency's name and all the rights from the family. After the military coup in 1923, leading to a regime which detested the francophilia of the former government, the agency was nationalized. When the dictatorship was overthrown, the agency received little attention and continued its close contacts with the French Havas. In 1936 after the outbreak of the Spanish Civil War, the Republicans nationalized the agency again. Later, the Nationalists took over the agency and Fabra became an official agency under the title EFE. The new state agency claimed to 'propagate the Spanish truth in the world and to supply Spain with international information' and was later transformed into a joint stock company heavily dependent on state subscriptions. In recent years, EFE has expanded to become an influential Hispanic voice throughout South America, to rival the influence there of the global agencies.

Chapter 8 deals with the transformations in eastern Europe. Many eastern European agencies face the consequences of their disentanglement from state structures following the collapse of communism. Terhi Rantanen observes that in the Czech Republic, Hungary and Poland, the process of disentanglement has reached the stage at which new legislation has been adopted. Laws in the Czech Republic and Hungary give the agencies a status that is to a certain extent similar to that of broadcasting companies. These agencies have become shareholding companies whose councils are elected by Parliament. Eastern Europe has thus witnessed the birth of a new kind of ownership of news agencies that comes close to the public ownership of broadcasting companies. However, in the Slovak Republic the agency has remained in state ownership. At the same time, the survival of these agencies is threatened by the liberalization of global trade which permits global news agencies such as Reuters to enter what were once tightly controlled domestic markets, to set up new national and financial news services and to form links with domestic media, which undermine the market prospects of the newly reformulated national news agencies.

In chapter 9, Kivikuru's analysis of the national news agency SHIHATA in the general media context of Tanzania, is further illustration within an African context of the implications for established national news agencies of the twin threats of political and economic liberalization to their continuing viability. What is at stake, however, here as in eastern Europe, is not simply which kind of organization survives, but what kind of news will be developed and, in the wake of this, what kind of image of the 'world', 'state', 'nation' and of the nation's 'regions' will be generated for domestic and international consumption.

Established in 1976, at the height of NWICO dialogue, the Tanzanian agency was for some time taken as *the* model of an alternative but national agency, envisaged as an editorially independent, solely responsible para-statal, public service agency for domestic and international news, the sole vehicle through which international agencies could distribute in Tanzania. Among other things it was charged with journalism training. Reality never matched the vision even in good years, and in the 1990s the original concept of SHIHATA has grown dangerously unfashionable. Associated with one-party states, and the government information services from which some of them emerged, such agencies still find it difficult to retain credibility in multi-party conditions. They find it hard to hold on to the support of yester-day's sponsors: aid has declined with the demise of the cold war, and what-ever aid is available is more likely to target private commercial media operations which are assumed – wrongly as it happens – to be more 'demo-cratic'. The agency is still dependent on state subsidy, but as the Tanzanian government struggles to meet World Bank conditions of prudence in public spending, SHIHATA is pushed towards consideration of other models, including privatization and commercialization. Sadly, the service is much weaker in the democratic 1990s than in the autocratic 1980s: less foreign news, less regional (political, policy, cultural) but more local ('car crash') news, less 'development' news, and less news overall. The connection with Reuters came to an end in 1996 (the inevitable response of the global agency to non-payment of local subscriptions) whose exit was even followed by that of the ideologically sympathetic IPS. SHIHATA's catalogue of woes include too few staff, abysmal shortages of equipment, dependence on government officers for regional news, civil service conditions of employment and pay – which motivate employees to work for private news groups – inadequate training, and a confused sense of mission in an era when people are even less inclined to agree on what exactly is 'development news'. While recog-nizing the problems, Kivikuru is at pains to point out that private or com-mercial sources of supply do not and probably cannot substitute for the public service functions envisaged for a national agency – resonances here with the experiences of eastern Europe described in chapter 8 – and that other solutions must be sought.

The analysis of South Africa, by Forbes in chapter 10, charts yet another kind of transition, also one with similar resonances to those of eastern Europe and Tanzania, raising yet again worrying concerns about the impact of a more liberal political and economic environment on the evolution and maintenance of an adequate infrastructure for national news gathering. In reviewing the history of news agencies in South Africa, Forbes recalls that this was part of Reuters' old empire, in collaboration with the local co-operative, SAPA, which Reuters had helped to establish. Under apartheid conditions, SAPA was hardly a candidate to offer an 'alternative' news agenda. The 'alternative' potential of the UNESCO-backed continental news agency, PANA, developed under the auspices of the OAU, had little impact either. Among other things, PANA suffered from inadequate resourcing, a surfeit of 'protocol news' and political compliance with member states. In the declining years of the apartheid epoch there emerged instead a number of radical news agencies, of which Forbes narrates the story of one, Ecna. Ecna developed a distinctive local, ethnic and political voice in the Eastern Cape. But its prospects were undermined, first, by the ending of apartheid itself, which reduced the demand for 'alternative' perspectives; second, by the decline in sources of aid (in the wake of the ending of the cold war) and, thirdly, the consequent need to 'go mainstream' where it ran into tough competition, fourthly, not just from SAPA but also from Reuters, which has now broken from SAPA, weakening SAPA's relationship with its most important client, the South Africa Broadcasting Corporation, while establishing its own, Reuters' domestic South African news service. This combined threat pushed Ecna (now ECN) further towards collaboration with SAPA. SAPA also must establish a new identity and strategy to compete against Reuters, and this may entail a closer alliance with Reuters' competitor, Associated Press, and/or with a reformulated and privatized version of PANA, which itself may forge closer links with IPS (see chapter 12) which had supplied much of its telecommunications infrastructure.

7   From Dictatorship to Democracy

Ingrid Schulze-Schneider

The historical relationship between the Spanish state and its most important news agency differs considerably from the links that bound the great international news enterprises of Havas, Reuter and Wolff to their respective governments. The reasons lie in the difficult political and social circumstances which marked Spanish history in the second half of the 19th century. A remarkable outcome of this history is that a country whose internal and international news gathering was once largely controlled by the major news agency of a foreign power (France) should now, in conditions of relatively secure democracy, boast an agency mainly owned by the state, yet which has become the first primarily Spanish-language global agency, possibly the most important source of news for Hispanic and South American clients

When Nilo Maria Fabra created the first so-called 'Correspondents' Centre' for the transmission of news in 1865, Spain was living through the last years of the turbulent reign of Queen Isabel, soon to be ended by the revolution of 1868 and followed by six years of instability until the restoration of the Bourbon Monarchy in 1874. At the time when Italy and Germany had confirmed their unity, playing thereafter an important role in international politics, Spain had to concentrate more and more on its internal problems. The Spanish colonial empire was now far from being an advantage, but only hampered the country's conversion into a modern state by draining it of substantial money and human resources.

Historians identify the following main reasons for this lack of development of Spain.

1. The incomplete accomplishment of the industrial revolution. Apart from the industrial centres in the north, Spain was still a rural country with almost three-quarters of its population illiterate. Though enormous efforts had been made to promote the construction of railways and to modernize agricultural production, the inadequate structures of land ownership, obsolete manufacture and low output hampered industrial progress. As a result, social misery afflicted large parts of the population, opening the way to an important workers' movement in the last decades of the century.
2. Though the Spanish Parliament approved a modern constitution in

1876, its application turned out to be very difficult, due to the lack of a moderate middle class willing to accept the rules of a two-party system. From both right and left, radicals did their best to torpedo the delicate balance of the reigns of Alfonso XII and Alfonso XIII, based on peaceful shifts of power between the conservatives, under the leadership of Cánovas del Castillo, and the liberals, headed by Sagasta.

3. At the end of the century, the dramatic loss of the last Spanish colonies – Cuba, Puerto Rico and the Philippines – threw the country into a profound political and intellectual crisis, accompanied by internal military and social conflicts that it was unable to surmount. The impossibility of finding a peaceful solution to fill the wide gap between the 'traditional' aristocratic and bourgeois elites and the anarchist- and socialist-led proletariat finally led to the civil war of 1936.

This brief historical summary makes it clear that while other European countries developed strong nationalistic feelings in the second half of the 19th century, climaxing in the first world war, Spain went the opposite way, retiring within her borders after losing the status of a world power. Thus, conservative as well as liberal governments withdrew from the international scene in order to keep the peace within the country and to defend their own – invariably weak – positions.

In those years the Spanish press was not yet a mass medium. Being split into numerous factions, it was fundamentally aimed at political and intellectual elites. While the most important members of the two dominant political parties maintained special relations – of different kinds – with one or more newspapers, the Spanish government as a whole never controlled a range of officious dailies as was the custom in Germany and most of the other European countries. Nor did the Spanish leaders value adequately the services that the press and, consequently, an efficient news agency with international contacts, might render them. So, while Havas, Reuter and Wolff served their governments as well as their own interests, receiving more or less adequate payment in cash or kind in return, Fabra was left alone in its efforts to connect with the developing flow of international news monopolized by the pool of the three European agencies.

Fabra, a Spanish Agency under French Control

The first Spanish news agency was created by Nilo Maria Fabra, son of a prosperous Catalan cloth merchant, who aimed to supply the demand for information which the Spanish dailies were unable to offer to their readers on account of their difficult financial situation. After a short and not very satisfactory career as a poet, playwright, author and journalist, Fabra opened in 1865 in Madrid a modest 'Correspondents' Centre'. He himself gathered the news, copied it and supplied it to different newspapers in the capital and the provinces. We know very little about the beginnings of

Fabra's business, as there are no documents which might shed light on those first years. The real history of the agency is supposed to have started after Fabra's encounter with Havas correspondents during the German–Austrian war in 1866. Though there is no complete evidence, historians suppose that the first contact between Fabra and Havas ended with some kind of agreement between them, as it is known that from then on Fabra offered a service of international news to his subscribers and also furnished the French agency with Spanish information. This collaboration seems very likely, because Spain belonged to the territories allocated to Havas by the agreement of 1859 between the French, the English and the German agencies. It is thought that international interest in the events of the Spanish revolution of 1868 moved Havas to fix the terms of a permanent exchange of news with the Spanish firm. Two years later, after the renewal of the pool's agreement in 1870, the French agency changed the contract with Fabra, in fact buying the whole enterprise, and leaving its former owner with a small share in the business and the post of director, together with a French agent. By this deal, the Spaniard in effect lost his independence, becoming a branch office of Havas-Paris, also closely linked from 1869 to 1876 to Reuter by a joint-purse agreement, according to which both firms shared common book-keeping, distributing benefits and losses on equal terms. Hence, Fabra would furnish his customers with a mixture of international news, sent directly from Havas-Paris, and national information collected by himself and his employees.

Though the Spanish government did not – as far as we know – intervene in the process, the enterprise was fully supported by the Spanish ambassador in Paris, Salustiano Olózaga. Some authors maintain that there was a close relationship between Havas and Olózaga, even to the point of alleging that both belonged to a secret society, and that the creation of the Spanish news agency had been the result of a conjunction of the political interests of the ambassador and the financial ones of Havas (Montero Rios, 1975: 9–10).

The restoration of the monarchy in 1874 and the consequent shifts in power between the conservative and liberal parties did not change the strategy of Nilo Fabra, though generally political changes in Spain have always had – and do today – important effects on people and enterprises more or less dependent on governmental decisions. Spain had isolated itself from international politics, and newspaper readers therefore paid very little attention to news about world affairs. It seems that Fabra found himself more at ease under conservative rule. He himself was a Member of Parliament from 1876 to 1878, when Cánovas was Prime Minister (Paz Rebollo, 1988: 101–2).

On the other hand, Havas always maintained excellent relations with the various governments in Madrid. Thanks to the diplomatic tact of the French company, the presidency of the Spanish Council in Paris subscribed to the Havas bulletin, while Fabra did not succeed in achieving the same distinction for his national newsletter. But the direct contact between the French agency and the Spanish authorities did not last very long, as there were always enough Spaniards resident in Paris to act as amateur informants using the channel of the Paris embassy to transmit their news. Finally, when Duke Fernán Nuñez was named ambassador, he himself took over relations with the press.

Fruitless Quests for Alternative News Channels

Although the exchange of news between France and Spain via Havas and Fabra was working perfectly, the big Spanish newspapers did not unanimously applaud the agreement. The Spanish press was hardly thriving under the first government of Cánovas (1874). In order to prevent the publishing of any information that might upset the difficult process he had just begun, the conservative leader suppressed all republican papers. Other dissenters were closely watched. A special licence was needed to start up any newspaper, and was only granted when the local authorities provided favourable reports about the applicant. In 1875 a special Court of Justice for press offences was established. Though most of the restrictions would be relaxed in the following years, the situation was only reversed after the elections of 1881 which gave victory to the liberals. In 1883, a new Press Law freed the profession from all chains, thus favouring the birth of an outstanding era in the history of the Spanish press which, though still addressed to an elite, contributed greatly to the modernization of Spanish society at the end of the century. The number of titles, substantially reduced in 1875, now started an important expansion, reaching its climax in 1886. The most important newspaper centre was Madrid, followed by Barcelona. The Spanish capital had in 1880 the same number of political newspapers as Paris (40–50) with only a fifth of the population of the French metropolis. There are no statistics about the exact number of copies printed, but the highest circulations, such as that of the *Imparcial*, fluctuated between 120,000 and 140,000 (Seoane and Sáiz, 1996: 291).

The big dailies of Madrid frequently complained about the information offered by Fabra–Havas, saying that it served French rather than Spanish interests, leaving too little space for specific topics such as, for instance, the visit of the Spanish Foreign Minister to Paris. But their protests never went very far. As their financial means were always very tight, no real efforts were made to change the dependence on Fabra–Havas. Between 1874 and 1879, various agencies tried to capture at least part of the news market. The most important were Centro Telegráfico Española, Agencia Española y Americana, Alcance Telegráfico Epistolar y Agencia Americana, but none of them lasted for more than two years, because they could not compete with their European colleagues, whose international net was secure (Paz Rebollo, 1989a: 71–2).

Fabra, on the other hand, received strict orders from Havas about the amount, selection and handling of the news. The French firm demanded specific information to meet the interest of its clients. The Spanish agency covered news from Spain, Morocco, Portugal and the West Indies. All information from these areas was gathered in Madrid and transmitted to Havas-Paris, the only permitted contact of Fabra in Europe.

We do not know exactly how many Spanish newspapers subscribed to the services of Fabra–Havas, as many agreements were made verbally and have left no traces. Furthermore, there was considerable piracy in the telegraph business. There were journalists who sent the news received from Fabra to dailies edited in the provinces without having permission to do so. Others stole the information when it reached the Central Telegraph Station or reproduced it from the newspapers in Madrid and Barcelona without naming the source (Paz Rebollo, 1989b: 136–7).

The few serious attempts to reduce the influence of Havas in Spain always arose from the personal interest of politicians or diplomats, as was the case of the Spanish Ambassador in Berlin, the Count of Benomar. Deeply impressed by Bismarck's Germany and the skill with which the Chancellor used the press for his own ends, he proposed to his superiors the creation of a direct telegraphic news service from Madrid to Berlin using the service of Wolff. In this way Benomar tried to improve the rather negative image of Spain promoted by most German newspapers. We learn from Benomar's diary that his idea was put into practice and worked well from 1879 to 1881. Afterwards, the fall of Cánovas and the rise to power of the liberals ended the deal. Though the arrangement interfered with Havas' information monopoly in Spain, Wolff did not violate the cartel's agreement of 1870 because it only reserved to Havas the sending of news *to* Spain, saying nothing about a prohibition on receiving direct information from Madrid (Schulze-Schneider, 1989: 375–80).

In the 1880s, multiple internal problems arose which preoccupied the Spanish government and opinion leaders. The unexpected death of King Alfonso XII at the age of only 28 threatened the precarious balance achieved by the restoration. Nevertheless, documents found in German archives reveal that there had been another attempt to lessen Havas' monopoly, just when Bismarck and the Italian Prime Minister Crispi were trying to adapt the international news flow to the interests of the Triple Alliance, to which Spain was linked by means of an agreement with Italy. A certain Mr Thompson, an English citizen, living permanently in Madrid, who had previously worked as a reporter for *The Times* and who maintained excellent contacts in New York, London, Berlin and Paris, proposed in 1889 to the Spanish Minister of the Interior, Moret, a plan to establish an independent news agency in Madrid, in order to free the Spanish press from the domination of Havas. Though the liberal Moret apparently favoured the project, he repeatedly delayed the final decision, until he lost his post. It seems that Moret – like most of the liberals – was much more francophile than he openly admitted, while the conservatives, especially Cánovas, had always been more inclined to strengthen the bonds with Germany, at least until the crisis over the Caroline Islands in 1885. The conservative leader even negotiated with the

German ambassador in Madrid a special news service from Berlin for his official daily *La Epoca* (Schulze-Schneider, 1987: 774).

In 1893, the liberal government revealed its latent sympathy for France by means of a coup in the information business. Moret, now Foreign Minister, made a direct deal with Havas-Paris – without the knowledge of Fabra – to transform the Spanish agency into 'La Agencia Española e Internacional'. Refused any official explanation, Fabra was dismissed and his remaining shares and rights were bought by Havas at the price of 7,500 francs. The leadership of the new firm was entrusted to a Frenchman, M. de Bourgade. This unusual procedure was unique in the history of the news agencies, and the only possible explanation for it is that it was political revenge. For nearly 20 years Fabra had received hardly any help from the Spanish governments, and when one finally decided to create a news enterprise of a national character, it entrusted its organization to a foreign firm and a foreign director. Though Fabra went to Paris to express his indignation to his former partners, he got only sympathetic words. Neither did a written complaint to the government achieve better results. The Spanish press seemed not to care either, and the Agencia Española e Internacional sought alternative suppliers. But under M. Bourgade the agency lost clients and money. Finally, after the return of the conservatives to power in 1895, Fabra regained his post as director of the firm, receiving a fixed annual salary for his work and a specific percentage of the profits, but no shares in the enterprise. In 1896, Cánovas annulled the treaty with Havas signed by Moret. With the agency under its old familiar name, Fabra took up the work in the same way as before, independent on a local basis and bound exclusively to Havas and – through it – to the international pool for foreign news (Paz Rebollo, 1988: 216–45).

During the following decades the French agency continued 'colonizing' Spain in the same way, now and then provoking the protest of the Spanish press against the one-sided news selection offered to Fabra, but finding only on two occasions serious difficulties in its relationship with the Spanish government. The first of these crises occurred during the Spanish–Cuban war in 1898. The agencies belonging to the cartel clearly took the side of Spain's enemies, offering distorted information about the development of the war and its origin. Probably for the first time, the Spanish government had become aware of the importance of being able to influence international news. Following the advice of its embassy in Paris, it severed all official links between Madrid and Havas-Paris. But the anger only lasted for a few months. Once Havas agreed to give 'universal distribution' to official statements from Madrid, a new agreement about the management of the exchange of news was signed. Something similar occurred during the negotiations over the status of Morocco where Spain and France acted as rival powers. But, in the end, Havas and Fabra were always the winners, as the French agency's worldwide connections made it difficult to replace.

Some of the biggest Spanish newspapers were forced to the same conclusion after failing in their revolt against Fabra and Havas in 1900–1901. In order to create alternative channels of information, *El Liberal, El Impar-cial, La Correspondencia* and *El Heraldo* sent their own correspondents to Paris. But the dailies were not able to obtain the international news sub-mitted to Havas from the allied agencies. So, sooner or later, all of them had to come to new terms with the French firm. A further rebellion of the Spanish press in 1905 ended in the same way. Havas always maintained its role as the main supplier of foreign news to Spain. After the death of Nilo Maria Fabra in 1903, the French agency even purchased the Spanish name and all the rights from the family.

Matters did not change during the first world war. Spanish neutrality in the conflict favoured the expansion of allied and German propaganda on Spanish soil. Fabra had, of course, no choice and defended the French point of view, though sometimes giving the opposite impression in public, just to disguise its real sympathies. The increasing volume of news caused by the war and rising Catalan nationalism made it necessary for Havas to create a bigger branch agency in Barcelona. It did so in 1918 by transforming the small bureau that had been opened in the Catalan capital in 1910. The ser-vices of the agency were in great demand by the big Barcelona newspapers, which were glad to establish a direct line with Europe via Paris, first because they always distrusted the 'centralism' supposedly practised by all insti-tutions and enterprises in Madrid, and second because they thought that they would find in the new channel a better way to promote Catalan inter-ests in Europe. But, as it turned out later, these expectations were not ful-filled, because on the one hand Havas's clients were not at all interested in the domestic troubles of Spain, and on the other, Havas-Paris was very careful not to misrepresent the Spanish government and acted very cau-tiously in all political matters. That is one of the reasons why the French firm was never in collision with the authorities in Madrid.

Havas' success in Barcelona was not only due to the Catalan newspapers but also to financial speculation in the years after the war on the inter-national stock exchanges. Bankers, merchants and private investors apprec-iated the agency's excellent economic service, which transmitted at very frequent intervals the latest news of the global market (Paz Rebollo, 1988: 494–515).

The autonomy of the Barcelona office did not last very long. In spring 1919 Fabra was converted into a limited company and, at the same time, the management of the Catalan branch service was transferred from Havas-Paris to Fabra-Madrid. The reasons for this reorganization are not clear, as there are no documents explaining the transaction. We must suppose that revenue facilities and the political need to conceal the French dependence on Fabra moved Havas to take this decision.

The fact is that on 3 April 1919 Havas and Fabra officially constituted the Agencia Telegráfica Fabra. According to the protocol, Havas-Paris gave to the company its property (Fabra-Madrid), receiving in return 180 shares out of a total of 200, at a price of 500 pesetas per share. Maximino Esteban Nuñez and Luis Amato e Ibarrola, director and deputy director of Fabra, each received 10 of the remaining shares. A few days later, the former was elected president and the latter secretary-councillor of the new firm. Though the Agencia Telegráfica reorganized the handling of its news services, especially with Barcelona, on the whole there were few changes in the management and control of Havas-Paris over the volume and contents of international information from and to Spain.

In the 1920s, various international agencies established themselves in Barcelona and Madrid and tried to compete with Fabra, but none could really damage it (Paz Rebollo, 1989b: 206–14).

Problems of Nationalization

A real change in the life of the Spanish agency came about at the end of the restoration era. The lost war in Morocco and repeated attempts at revolt in Catalonia moved King Alfonso XIII to support the military *coup d'état* of Miguel Primo de Rivera in 1923. The dictator did not share the francophilia of the former government and personally took on the control of the press. He reintroduced censorship, among other measures, and in 1927 nationalized Fabra in order to prevent Havas from spreading 'false and tendentious news' as the agency had done – in the opinion of Primo de Rivera – during the negotiations of the Tanger protocol. Following government instructions, various Spanish Banks (Banco de Bilbao, Central Hispano-Americano, Urquijo and Vizcaya) purchased Havas' shares in the company. At the same time, the Barcelona office was put under the orders of Fabra-Madrid. The relations between Havas and Fabra were stipulated in a special agreement signed on 15 February 1927. The different articles reflected basically the same principles that governed the worldwide co-operation of the cartel: exchange of news between the two countries; inviolability of the contents of official news; exclusivity in the territories covered by the contract – Spain, her colonies and protectorates in the case of Fabra, and countries assigned by the cartel in the case of Havas – and exclusivity in each partner's respective areas, as well as common defence against intruders from competing firms.

Prior to this arrangement, the Spanish government had also set up an office in Paris in order to propagate Spanish culture in France and South America. But as it would take some time for this propaganda department to become operative, Fabra should meanwhile act as a substitute (Paz Rebollo, 1989b: 212).

The idea of increasing the Spanish presence in South America to exploit the common cultural links with the former colonies was not new. The national newspapers in Madrid had been demanding it for years. For example, *El Sol* asked the government, in an article published on 29 April 1922, to install communication cables from the Canary Islands to Argentina and to Cuba, and from there to Mexico, Venezuela and Colombia. Furthermore, the daily urged the government to create a special news agency which would be in charge of linking all Spanish-speaking countries in the New

World so that they might receive information other than that of the North American companies (Paz Rebollo, 1988: 689–90).

Havas-Paris tried to weather the storm, reorganizing all services to Latin America and to Fabra, with which it continued co-operating in the transmission of international news. But the establishment of other agencies in the north of Spain and in Madrid would make its task much more difficult than before. The agency Franco–Española (Frañola) was created in 1927 in Irun, located on the French border, by a right-wing nationalist and former member of the Spanish Parliament named Arazadi. The organization was concerned with the exchange of news with the French daily *La Liberté*, and the sale of it to Spanish newspapers. Another competitor, much more dangerous than Frañola, was the agency Argos, also located near the French border in San Sebastián. By means of a correspondent in Hendaya this enterprise had arranged an exchange of information with the French newspaper *La Gazette de Biarritz*. The cheap way of gathering news and transmitting it simply by telephone to the border-delegate, enabled Argos to supply French and international news to an important number of provincial newspapers in northern Spain and also on a national scale. Argos maintained an office in Madrid with three journalists who prepared the material they received from San Sebastián, as well as the news gathered by themselves. Among its customers there were even international dailies such as the English *Manchester Guardian* and *La Prensa* from Buenos Aires (Argentina).

Fabra had to face another national competitor, the agency Mencheta, created by the journalist Francisco Peris Mencheta in Madrid in 1883. This enterprise served mainly Spanish news both to most papers in Madrid, which paid for all information they bought, and to about 25 publications in the provinces which signed a monthly contract. Mencheta also occasionally purchased messages from the French agency Fournier – which did not belong to the cartel – offering Spanish news in return (Paz Rebollo, 1989a: 75).

At the same time, the advent of an increasing number of American enterprises in Madrid, headed by the National Telephone Company which disposed of the monopoly for the instalment of national and international connections, was accompanied by the arrival of American news agencies in Madrid. The first was United Press followed by International News Service, Associated Press and Internews. All of them rivalled Fabra in offering Spanish newspapers information from the United States and also from Berlin, London, Moscow, Rome and the Balkans, avoiding only the area dominated by Havas. During the following years the American firms won a considerable share of the market. In order to stop the expansion of United Press and Internews, Fabra came to terms with Associated Press whose entry in Spain had been allowed by Havas. After a visit by Kent Cooper to Madrid in January 1928, Fabra and AP signed an agreement establishing the limits of their activities. But very shortly after, the American firm tried to free itself from its arrangement with the European cartel, finally obtaining – at the Conference of the allied agencies in Budapest in 1931 – the right to sell its news directly to papers in France, Portugal, Great Britain and Germany. In answer to Fabra's protest, AP was forced to maintain the status quo in Spain for a few more years, but the reality was that the American agency would repeatedly try to break these constraints (Paz Rebollo, 1988: 767–84).

The international financial crisis of 1929 damaged the news business severely. Fabra's situation worsened after the fall of Primo de Rivera in the same year. Its official status would not protect it in the turmoil that was about to shake Spanish society. With the agency's links to the hated dictator, nobody cared what might happen to it. As a safeguard, Havas opened its own office in Madrid, in case Fabra did not survive the political chaos. In the long run, nationalization had not favoured the agency, though that status had been little more than theoretical. In fact, the collaboration with Havas had never been interrupted, but this relationship damaged Fabra's prestige in the eyes of the new government that followed Primo de Rivera.

The political crisis did not end in 1931 after the abdication of Alfonso XIII and the transition of Spain to a republic. On the contrary, during the following years, governments of both the left and the right were unable to calm their respective radicals, leading to the final confrontation in the terrible civil war, which raged on the peninsula from 1936 to 1939.

The fate of Fabra during these years, as well as that of most Spanish newspapers, was not very pleasant. Nobody wanted to take any responsibility in a company that had been sanctioned by Primo de Rivera. The economic crisis of the Spanish state even caused the Ministry of the Interior to cancel its subscription to the Fabra newsletter which it had been receiving for more than 60 years. Other departments, such as the Board of Directors of the Colonies and Morocco did the same. All efforts by Fabra to renew its status and become the official organ of the republic were in vain.

1934 would be a year of important changes in the relations of all the international news agencies. Due to the rise of the Hitler regime in Germany, Wolff now required the same rights as Reuter and Havas. Associated Press also demanded complete freedom to sell its information without restriction. The 'barriers' in the international flow of news, which had been denounced decades ago by Kent Cooper, were now removed. The European news agency cartel had come to an end, opening the way to internal and external competition. Havas had foreseen this situation and established timely and direct connections with the Spanish newspapers without using the channel of its Spanish partner. Fabra lacked sufficient capital to face the new situation. Amidst increasing German and French propaganda campaigns, Fabra would be accused abroad as a tool of government and in Madrid as francophile (Paz Rebollo, 1989b: 214–16)

The fact is, that in 1935 five international agencies (Fabra, UP, AP and the German Cosmos and Transocean) were competing to sell their news to the 10 Spanish newspapers capable of paying the normal price for that kind of service.

Thus, Fabra was in a very bad way when civil war broke out on 18 July

1936. The director Luis Amato and other members of the staff, accused by the republicans of favouring the rebellion, escaped to France. As a consequence, Havas cancelled its correspondence with Madrid. On 29 October, the republican authorities ordered the nationalization of Fabra, already left without any management. Though Amato was summoned to Madrid he did not return. Instead he sent a circular to all allied agencies asking them to break off relations with the company in Madrid as it had been nationalized by 'marxists'. Amato's letter split the staff of Fabra into two factions. The international agencies supported Franco, but all Fabra's technical equipment had remained in the office of Madrid under republican management.

Once again, Amato tried to win the support of the authorities – this time the nationalists – for his plan to transform Fabra into an official agency, but its 'French' reputation kept the Falangists from accepting his proposal. Nevertheless, in 1938, nearing the end of the war, Fabra would be absorbed by Franco's government, when the nationalists realized the need to own a news agency for propaganda and information services. After buying all the shares and rights from Amato, including the international agreements, Fabra became – at last – a truly official enterprise, though not under its own name, but as EFE. The origin of the name is not clear. Some historians say that the F stands for the initials of two small Spanish agencies, Febus and Faro, absorbed by the Franco regime. The first had been created in the 1920s and was taken over by the nationalists after the occupation of Madrid. Faro operated in nationalist territory during the war and was also taken over by the new regime, though it is not known if the enterprise received any compensation. Others attribute the F to the political organization Falange, main supporter of Franco during the first years of his government. The latter explanation seems much more logical, though the staff of modern EFE like it much less.

EFE – The State's Agency

EFE was born on 3 January 1939, three months before the end of the war. From the very first moment, the agency proclaimed its intention to 'propagate the Spanish truth in the world and to supply Spain with international information'. The new director Vicente Gallego made it clear that for him 'national news agencies are powerful instruments in the task of the distribution of news and influence abroad', being at the same time real representatives of the national feelings of which they are essential servants. The character of EFE, therefore, could only be 'fundamentally and inalienably' official with respect to both state and government.

Gallego explained that so far Spain had never been able to defend its spiritual and economic interests against those of other countries, because it had always lived with its back turned to international realities. On the other hand, foreign affairs are matters of interest only to peoples and governments who have already succeeded in forming a national consciousness.

According to Gallego, though Spanish roots can be found in numerous countries, especially in Latin America, where the Spaniards left indestructible religious, cultural and linguistic ties, the early loss of the colonies and the political disasters suffered by the peninsula in the previous 100 years, had separated the Spaniards into two warring factions, making any emergence of true national unity impossible. Moreover, the lack of external enemies led to permanent internal confrontation, especially after the disaster of 1898 (Paz Rebollo, 1988: vol. 1, 114–21).

This meant that EFE would be the appropriate instrument to amend past errors, a messenger of the New Spain, made up by the intimate fusion of government, army and the people. Though the mission of the company was in the first place a spiritual one, its foundations had to be much more practical. EFE adopted the form of a private limited company with full powers to create and exploit branch offices in the information business. The official relationship with the Spanish state would consist of a financial arrangement by which the latter demanded from the agency the service of special information transmissions which would be paid for accordingly. EFE disposed of an initial capital of 10 million pesetas, divided into 10,000 shares of 1,000 pesetas, which were bought by most of the Spanish dailies, banks and commercial enterprises and by some individuals. But as most of the post-war newspapers belonged to the Falange movement, they were as good as state property. Until 1978 EFE's information services were divided into four departments: EFE (international), CIFRA (national), ALFIL (sports) and GRAFICA (photographs). After that date the name EFE covered all services.

The first real national news agency was thus created in order to fortify Franco's regime and to make it respectable in the eyes of the international community. Vicente Gallego tried to eliminate the last two national agencies which were still active after the war – Logos, founded in 1929 by the Editorial Católica and dedicated especially to serve news to Catholic newspapers in the provinces; and, above all, the old rival Mencheta. Though Gallego managed to obtain the order to close Mencheta from the Ministry of the Interior, the lack of charges enabled the agency to reopen in November 1939. In order to obstruct the expansion of both competitors, EFE established an obligatory canon for its clients, who were forced to subscribe to the package of news offered by EFE, CIFRA and ALFIL, not being allowed to buy them separately. Furthermore, the Ministry of the Interior had virtually reserved for EFE a monopoly in international information by prohibiting Spaniards from listening to foreign radio stations, and international agencies from establishing contacts with any organization other than EFE. Thus, no other Spanish agency could offer foreign news. As a result, most of the Spanish newspapers had to accept EFE's conditions, as their financial means did not allow them to send correspondents abroad. Though Mencheta and Logos survived the attack, their market share was considerably reduced. The increasing difficulties led Mencheta in 1978 to change to a specialized agency for sports news, while Logos maintained its religious profile, forming part of

Editorial Católica. In 1966 EFE's monopoly in international news was officially sanctioned by the new Press Law of the Minister of Communications, Fraga Iribarne (Paz Rebollo, 1989c: 349–56). This order would not be revoked until May 1978, granting EFE – for nearly 40 years – the absolute domination of foreign news in Spain, and giving the company time to prepare to face international competition (Paz Rebollo, 1989c: 349–50).

The beginning of the cold war had helped EFE consolidate its hegemony in the Spanish market, expanding its geographic coverage slowly but surely and adopting modern information technologies. In 1946 EFE and Reuters founded the agency COMTELSA for the special transmission of economic news, each of them owning 50% of the capital. In the years from 1963 to 1965 EFE's initial capital of 10 million pesetas was doubled and the agency opened the first delegation abroad (1965). Very soon others followed in all European capitals, and from 1966 on the agency began its expansion in South America. The first office was created in Buenos Aires. In 1973 EFE took part in the creation of the Agencia Centroamericana de Noticias (ACAN), located in Panama, alongside leading media of Central America. In fact, EFE contributed to the new enterprise by supplying most of the financial capital and modern technology.

In 1977, two years after Franco's death, EFE moved to a modern building fully equipped with up-to-date technical facilities, from that moment embarking on an astonishing international career, which would soon turn it into the first Spanish-language worldwide agency and – according to EFE's own sources – the fifth among the big western enterprises. The statistics of that year list more than 2,000 professionals working for EFE in numerous countries, and 24 new international branch-offices as the beginning of a continuing global expansion.

In 1979, EFE's nominal capital was again increased four-fold, the state buying two-thirds of the shares, and various communication and banking enterprises the remainder. This transaction confers on the government the right to choose the president of the board of directors.

Given that the Spanish state is the real proprietor of EFE, it is not surprising that the firm strives not only for professional success but also to obtain political achievements. The directors of the agency are changed according to the political party in power, as has always been the deplorable custom in Spain, where political commitment is more important than professional expertise. Every year, in his inaugural speech to the shareholders, each newly appointed executive faithfully reiterates the ultimate aim of the company: to serve the Spanish state in its national and international projects. On a national scale, EFE's task is to coordinate the information flow between the different Spanish autonomous regions, especially Catalonia, the Basque Country and Galicia, all of them very reluctant to accept the guiding 'centralism' of Madrid. With regard to the European and overseas services, the recovery of influence in Latin America has been its prime goal. President Alfonso Sobrado Palomares, appointed by the socialist government, expressed this once again very clearly in 1986:

It has been said that no other European nation owns something similar to our common historical roots with Latin America and the possession of the same language. But while our neighbours and friends of the European Community use the gifts they receive, or create stepping-stones for themselves in foreign countries, we Spaniards have not been able to organize a cultural multinational in Ibero America. This is the challenge our agency must win before 1992. (EFE, 1986: 1)

The year 1992, the 500th anniversary of Columbus' discovery of America, was the date fixed for the new conquest of a land from which the Spaniards had been expelled in the 19th century, a conquest to be achieved this time by more peaceful means.

In 1989, on the occasion of the celebration of the 50th anniversary of EFE, the same director recalled the firm determination of the company, shown during the last 25 years, to ensure 'informational autonomy in the Spanish-speaking world'. The way to fulfil this desire had been the expansion of the international communication web, with EFE at that time connected directly to more than 80 countries. 'EFE is the first international agency of Spanish origin and language and has voluntarily linked its reason for existing to the ambitious aim to become the agency which more than 300 million Spanish-speaking people scattered around the world may feel is their own.'

In 1993 – according to data researched by Fernando Reyes Matta, Professor of the University Andrés Bello in Chile – EFE's dream had come true. With a 28.76% share of the news published during that year, the Spanish agency had displaced Associated Press (18.37%), Agence France-Presse (13.22%) and Reuters (12.85%), climbing to the first rank in Latin America. The rise of EFE had been continuous, moving from a share of only 8% in 1976 (UPI, 39%; AP, 21%; AFP, 10% and Latin Reuters, 9%) to 12.32% in 1983 (AP, 26.85%; UPI, 15.12%; AFP, 7.91%, ANSA, 5.62%; DPA, 3.47% and Reuters, 0.61%) (EFE, 1994: 12–15).

This progress was due not only to the professional skill of EFE's staff and to the advanced technology used, but also to other external factors. On the one hand, the introduction of democracy after Franco's death gave Spanish politics a new credibility, and the transition period attracted considerable interest from the rest of the world, which favoured the demand for Spanish news. About a decade later, the Latin American countries, which had also advanced towards democracy, began to discover a new identity, approaching each other and trying to put aside past resentments. EFE seized the opportunity to assume the role of Spanish-speaking global agency, closer in world outlook and sensibility to Latin America, and more attentive to the foreign interests of these countries, especially outside the Spanish area. The Chilean researcher Reyes Matta has described the achievement of EFE in the following words:

> EFE has built the Latin American identity in the international information space and has marked our differences inside global society. It brings to a continent that speaks, reads and writes in Spanish the news of other continents and regions, seen from a nearer and more proper cultural point of view. (EFE, 1994: 14)

Reyes Matta asserts that his investigations confirm that EFE not only has become the most important trans-oceanic news agency in South America, but is also the main source of domestic news in the South American continent, displacing, thanks to a new cultural strategy of enormous success, North American enterprises which had dominated the market for nearly a century. According to these data, 18 Latin American countries primarily use EFE's news about their neighbour states.

In the last two years EFE has been busy trying to further its multinational expansion, extending its English-speaking services, inaugurated in 1979, and also beginning transmissions in Arabic. On 29 January 1995 in the Alhambra of Granada, the most famous symbol of the splendour of the Moorish presence in Spain, the Spanish King Juan Carlos I inaugurated EFE's new international services in the Arabic language. Juan Carlos expressed his satisfaction about the links between the Spanish and Arabic communities, referring to North Africa as 'a world which has many similarities with ours and an old history bound and intertwined with ours' (EFE, 1995: 38).

In 1995, the enormous efforts of the Spanish news agency were recognized officially, being awarded the so-called Nobel Prize of the Latin American world, the 'Premio Principe de Asturias'. In his last eulogistic speech before his replacement by the conservative Miguel Angel Gonzalo in 1996, EFE's president Alfonso S. Palomares again summarized the core of the agency's politics since its inception: EFE has always been a 'necessary project' of the Spanish state.

- Today, EFE maintains 44 international bureaux in the most important cities of the world, covering a further 50 centres by means of correspondents.
- In Spain the agency has 20 offices, located primarily in the capitals of the autonomous communities.
- Apart from EFE's national and international news services, the agency also recently initiated multi-media programmes. EFE-Television has created an audiovisual information service which is distributed mainly to the channels of the Latin American countries and the Hispanic broadcasting stations in the United States. Furthermore, EFE delivers weekly to 18 South American clients a programme called 'Línea America'.
- The service 'Teletexto' provides television audiences with all kinds of information ranging from international to local, sports, advertisements, etc. In 1994, Princess Elena de Borbón inaugurated in the Philippines a cable television channel in Spanish which also offers a news service called EFETEX.
- In the last two years, EFE has also taken part in the creation of two specialized agencies: EFECOM and EFEAGRO. The first distributes economic information on an international scale, especially in Latin America. The latter produces information about agricultural and food topics.

* Since March 1994, EFE has broadcast a special programme about the activities of the European Union, called EUROEFE. It addresses mainly professionals, public organizations, mass media and enterprises operating on the European market.

This list of EFE's present activities is far from complete, but may serve as an illustration of the dynamism the agency has been displaying latterly in order to be able to compete in national and international markets.

Epilogue and Summary

Lack of space prevents me adding more details about the fascinating history of the most important Spanish news agency Fabra–EFE. In recent years, because of the general economic crisis and the need to cut expenses in order to fulfil all requirements of the Maastricht Treaty, the Madrid government has substantially reduced its financial support. That means a significant deficit for EFE which – according to the 1995 annual accounts – supplied services to the state at a cost of 7,975 million pesetas, yet received in payment only 4,840 million pesetas. The total losses of the firm amounted in 1995 to 1,146,906 pesetas. Nevertheless, the new director is confident that the company will overcome this handicap without any problem.

According to EFE's own data, it has, during the last year, moved up another step in the international ranking of global news agencies, and now occupies fourth place. Despite this record, Miguel Angel Gonzalo admitted, in an interview published in the Gazette of the University Complutense, that the basic aims of the company remain the same as those announced in Burgos in 1938: 'EFE is not a commercial enterprise, at least not in the first place, it could be one, it even should be one, but this is not its final mission. . . .We remain outside political conflicts, being at the service of the people but not of governments'. The reporter clearly did not believe this last comment and asked if Gonzalo would try to loosen the ties that bound EFE to the government. The answer was: 'I am very much bound to the government, because it named me President of EFE. But this agency is non-political. . . .We do not belong to the government, we belong to the state, and that we cannot deny. Really, we love it that the state takes care of us' (*Gazeta Complutense*, 27 November 1996: 4–5).

This statement speaks for itself. It does not leave any room for doubt that EFE's work, however efficient and trustworthy, must in the final analysis take into account the guidelines fixed for its existence. The particular circumstances of the Spanish company keep it virtually out of the current discussion about the problems caused by the two main political and economic tendencies which clash on the international stage: globalization versus nationalization. For EFE there is no contradiction in these opposites. On the peninsula its news services try to smooth over controversies between different autonomous regions, supplying objective and comparative data about any topic in dispute, in order to create a sense of national identity that is above domestic quarrels. In the rest of the world, mainly in South America, the globalization of EFE's selection of news aims at strengthening cultural bonds, not with a particular state but with the Spanish-speaking community, whose perspective on life is different from that of Anglo-Saxons, who are spreading their culture worldwide by means of a dominant media and entertainment industry. The Spanish tongue, rather than special marketing techniques, is the instrument with which Latin countries try to fight the global information battle. The faster-growing Spanish-speaking population might tip the balance in their favour in the next century.

References

Alvarez, Jesús Timoteo (1981) *Restauración y Prensa de Masas. Los engranajes de un sistema (1875–1883)*, Pamplona: EUNSA.

Cooper, Kent (1959) *Kent Cooper and the Associated Press*, New York: Random House.

EFE (1986–1995 incl.) *Memorias* and *Informes anuales*, Madrid: EFE.

Jover, José Maria (1969) 'España. Edad contemporánea', in *España Moderna y Contemporánea*, Barcelona: Teide, pp. 157–407.

López Escobar, Estéban (1978) *Análisis del 'nuevo orden' internacional de la información*, Pamplona: EUNSA.

Mattelart, Armand (1993) *La comunicación-mundo*, Madrid: Fundesco.

Montero Rios y Rodriguez, Juan (1975) 'De Fabra a Efe, pasando por Santa Ana', *Gaceta de la Prensa Española*, 112.

Paz Rebollo, Maria Antonia (1988) *El colonialismo informativo de la Agencia Havas en España (1870–1940)*. Dissertation. Madrid: University Complutense.

Paz Rebollo, Maria Antonia (1989a) 'Las agencias: España en el flujo internacional', in J.T. Alvarez et al., *Historia de los medios de comunicación en España*, Barcelona: Ariel, pp. 71–80.

Paz Rebollo, Maria Antonia (1989b) 'La batalla de las agencias', in J.T. Alvarez et al., *Historia de los medios de comunicación en España*, Barcelona: Ariel, pp. 206–18.

Paz Rebollo, Maria Antonia (1989c) 'El predominio matizado de EFE', in J.T. Alvarez et al., *Historia de los medios de comunicación en España*, Barcelona: Ariel, pp. 347–62.

Schulze-Schneider, Ingrid (ed.) (1987) *El sistema informativo de Bismarck: Su proyección sobre la política y prensa españolas*, dissertation, Madrid: University Complutense.

Schulze-Schneider, Ingrid (ed.) (1989) 'El Conde Benomar, agente informativo' in *Haciendo Historia: Homenaje al Prof. Carlos Seco*, Madrid: University Complutense, pp. 375–80.

Seoane, María Cruz and Sáiz, Maria Dolores (1996) *Historia del periodismo en España. 3. El siglo XX: 1898–1936*. Madrid: Alianza Textos.

8   From Communism to Capitalism

Terhi Rantanen

According to Slavko Splichal, before the 1980s media policy throughout eastern Europe was rather simple. State responsibility for print and broadcast media was legitimized in terms of the political, educational and cultural importance of the media to society and especially to the state (Splichal, 1994: 27). Karol Jakubowicz writes that eastern Europe is now the setting for a scene of the process which took place in most other European countries a long time ago, namely the disentanglement of the media from the structures of state and political identities (Jakubowicz, 1995a: 75). Both authors consider the demonopolization of the press and reregulation of broadcasting key issues in the process of media's democratization.

The disentanglement of the media from state structures is central to all sections of the media market. Still, most scholarly work concentrates on television broadcasting (see, for example, Sparks and Reading, 1994; Splichal, 1994; Jakubowitz, 1995a, 1995b). When Sparks and Reading (Sparks and Reading, 1994: 244–5) write about the importance of television broadcasting in the transition from communist totalitarianism to capitalist democracy, the same emphasis could be applied to news agencies. Despite the importance of news agencies, they have received the least attention, although they stand at the crossroads of all forms of media. It is the news agencies that combine both printed and electronic media by providing both of them with material. The invisibility of news agencies operating behind the media and thus never reaching the audience directly as other media do, does not reduce their significance as the key institutions in any media system. They are the only intermediary institution to reach every kind of media, from print to electronic, from large to small, from capital to provincial.

News agencies are also the oldest national electronic media institutions in Europe to be founded in the wake of nationalism in the 19th and early 20th centuries. And the fact that they still exist proves their importance not only to the media but to governments as well. Most of the national news agencies in eastern Europe have been very closely affiliated with the state. This tradition originated in the 19th century and as such precedes the era of state socialism. For example, the government-owned Austro-Hungarian Korrespondenz-Bureau (founded in 1860) dominated the central eastern European news market until the first world war. The Romanian, Serbian and Bulgarian agencies were all government agencies from the beginning of their operations in the 1880s and 1890s. In some of the eastern European countries the news agencies experienced a period of private ownership between the two world wars, but were taken over by the communist governments after the second world war.

The countries under consideration here are the so-called Visegrad Group. There were three original members of the group (Poland, Hungary and the Czechoslovak Federal Republic), but the number has increased to four with the division of Czechoslovakia into the separate Czech and Slovak Republics. Brezinski distinguishes four groups of countries in eastern Europe. The countries where transformation into pluralist, free-market democracies is already under way and is unlikely to be turned back, include Poland, the Czech Republic and Hungary, while Slovakia still belongs to the second group – those having optimistic prospects for the future, but being still politically and economically vulnerable. And as Sparks and Reading note, these countries are examples of relatively peaceful transition (Sparks and Reading, 1994: 244). Brezinski's two remaining groups are countries whose political and economic future will remain undecided for at least a decade (Russia, Ukraine, Belarus, Georgia and Armenia) and those with a less than optimistic outlook for the future (Serbia, Macedonia, Bosnia, Moldova) (see Jakubowicz, 1995a: 82).

Several authors have identified processes which they consider fundamental to media change in central and eastern Europe. Sparks, for example, writes about the different aspects of the overall development of broadcasting which include: (a) the collapse of the old system; (b) the passage of new broadcasting laws; (c) the struggle over the political control of broadcasters; and (d) the licensing and operation of new commercial franchises (Sparks, 1995: 12–13). Jakubowicz writes that the transition takes place in different phases and includes demonopolization, deregulation and differentiation (Jakubowicz, 1995b: 67).

I find their concepts useful in analysing news agencies as well. However, the process of disentanglement of news agencies has not necessarily preceded the actual changes that have taken place within news agencies. It has not been a direct and fast lane: on the contrary, most news agencies in eastern Europe have not been able to disentangle themselves completely from state structures. The process within news agencies takes different forms compared to broadcasting. Still, the processes that have touched the development of other media in eastern Europe are crucial for news agencies as well. And, more importantly, the disentanglement of news agencies from the structures of the state is a crucial but neglected factor in studying the democratization of media systems in eastern Europe.

The Options of the Agencies

In principle, there are four possibilities for the institutional arrangements of news agencies. The first alternative is the private ownership of the agency. In eastern Europe this would mean that the former state agency would be sold to private shareholders, and the government would no longer subsidize it or have any control over it. The model has its origins in the early history of news agencies, although most agencies that started as private enterprises have become shareholding companies. Some of the first European agencies were founded as private enterprises in the 19th century and still carry the name of their founders, such as Reuter, Ritzau or Havas. The second is co-operative ownership. Co-operatives are a form of association for the purpose of directly operating a service in which the associates have a common interest, with a view not to making a profit on capital but to improving the service and making it less costly. However, many co-operative agencies have adopted the form of a commercial company controlled by the media (*News Agencies*, 1953: 26–7). The first co-operative agency in the world was the US Associated Press begun in the 1840s, but the model also became common in Europe after the first world war when, for example, Scandinavian agencies were turned into co-operative agencies.

The third alternative is the government/state agency that is owned, financed and controlled by the government. The news agencies in the former socialist countries in eastern Europe are typical examples of this category. Because of their importance to the dominant political systems under the period of socialism in eastern Europe, news agencies have had the closest possible ties with both governments and the Communist Party. The state news agencies in eastern Europe enjoyed a total monopoly inside the borders of their home countries. The general managers of these agencies were appointed by the government, and these agencies were fully subsidized by the state. Their main task was not only the delivery of news, because they served other functions as well. News agencies operated not just as gatekeepers of news, but as vanguards of the dominant ideology. This task was executed in three different ways. First, they operated as mouthpieces for their governments and the Communist Party by spreading any information the government or the Party considered necessary. Second, they controlled the import of foreign news into their respective countries and the export of their domestic news abroad. The majority of the foreign news originated from TASS and other eastern European agencies. Third, news agencies actively promoted the distribution of a positive image by distributing positive news ('All is well in the country') or producing propagandist literature (most agencies owned publishing houses). The distribution of negative news (for example the views of the political opposition, social problems and accidents) was either prevented or delayed.

Traditionally, the ownership of news agencies has been divided into private, co-operative and government (*News Agencies*, 1953): involvement of the state varies considerably within news agencies. For example, the French agency AFP is a public body which has legal status and is responsible for its own finances. Although AFP's council is made up of media representatives, the government still has a direct channel of influence in AFP's policy-making by playing a major role in its financing and in appointing three members of the agency's board of directors. It is difficult, though, for the director general to hold his job without a good 'working relationship' with the representatives of government ministries, who also sit on the board (Tunstall and Palmer, 1991: 70–82). So, it would be unfair to place AFP in the same category as the agencies that are completely state-owned and controlled. As I shall later demonstrate, the French model has been adopted in some form or another in many eastern European countries.

What is needed here is a new category between the state-owned and co-operative agencies that would combine features of both. And this is where the concept of public service is particularly useful. Although news agencies do not reach the public directly, their task is to provide domestic and foreign news to every medium in a given national territory. They serve all media, regardless of their size or location, in their own national language(s). The state subsidies to the agency indirectly support those media that would otherwise be unable to subscribe to the agency's services. The argument can be taken even further: the public has right of access through the media to the information provided by national news agencies. In this way, it is the government's duty to subsidize such public institutions as news agencies so as to provide the media with news. In the meantime, however, it should not exercise its political power over the agency, but let it operate as an independent news organization.

So far none of the state agencies in eastern Europe, except the Lithuanian agency, has been turned into a private or co-operative agency. There are two main reasons for this. The first has been a lack of revenue. Secure funding is a necessary condition for both private and co-operative agencies. Their economic success is directly dependent on their owners, on the enterprises that invest in them. If the media have economic difficulties or are not eager to invest their money in a co-operative venture in a competitive situation, the founding of a private or a co-operative agency becomes difficult, if not impossible. The second reason is the role of national news agencies in the process of nation-building. Despite the acceptance of the disentanglement policy, governments, especially new ones, still need news agencies to spread their information. The most obvious example comes from the Slovak Republic which was left without a national agency after the splitting of Czechoslovakia into two separate countries and had to create a new national agency as soon as possible.

Because of the instability of media systems and the needs of the governments, all the news agencies in eastern Europe have remained somehow affiliated to the state. The degree of government dependence varies considerably from one country to another. The most radical changes in the ownership form of the agencies have taken place in the Czech Republic in which a new law to change the former state agency into a public agency has been accepted.

The Reregulation of News Agencies

Splichal writes that in all post-socialist countries, new broadcasting laws are working their way slowly through the legislative process (Splichal, 1994: 45). A broadcasting law providing demonopolization and the introduction of the private sector has already been adopted in the Czech and Slovak Republics, Romania, Latvia, Poland, Estonia, Slovenia, Ukraine and Croatia (Jakubowicz, 1995a: 84), and in Hungary in 1996. As far as news agencies in central and east Europe are concerned, the legislative process has also been slow. As expected, the adopted laws reflect the variations in the process of disentanglement from state structures in different countries. It is the Czech law that gives most autonomy to the agency in its relation to the state, while the Slovak law leaves the agency under government influence. The Hungarian and Polish laws stand between these two.

As in broadcasting (Sparks and Reading, 1994: 263), the Czech and Slovak Republics were the quickest to adopt new laws on news agencies. The Czech national council passed a law on the Czech News Agency (ČTK) in October 1992. So far the Czech news agency law is the most ambitious attempt to change a former strictly state-controlled agency into a public news agency. According to the law, the agency is a public organization directed by a supervisory council which elects a chairperson and a general manager. Moreover, Parliament and not the government, elects this council which consists of seven members. These members are not allowed to be members of any political party, political movement, or have any financial interests in the mass media which would impair their objectivity. The aim of the law is to make ČTK financially independent. The agency owns its property (for example, its premises), but the state is no longer responsible for the agency's liabilities. The Czech agency is entitled to a special grant from the state budget which cannot be used to cover the agency's losses.

The Hungarian news agency law was adopted in December 1996, paving the way for the foundation of the Hungarian News Agency Corporation, a public service agency that is controlled by Parliament. Section 2 of the act guarantees access to all news stories and reports which the public needs for asserting appropriately individual and collective rights and interests.

The agency is also obliged to transmit to print and electronic media statements that are in the public interest from the state and other organizations and individuals. The agency transmits information on Hungarian communities living abroad and provides them with a news service.

There is, however, one article that clearly differs from its equivalent in Czech law. According to section 6 of the Hungarian National News Agency Act, the President of the Republic, at the behest of the Prime Minister, appoints and dismisses the President of the Corporation. This enables a new government to change the president of the news agency if it so wishes. Moreover, the act prohibits the appointment of currently active politicians or high-ranking government officials to the position.

The law has a clear aim of balancing power between the government and the opposition. As a result, the agency has two boards. One half of the Owner's Advisory Board consists of members nominated by the governing parties, while the opposition parties nominate the other half. The governing parties nominate the chairperson and the opposition parties a deputy chairperson. A five-member Supervisory Board consists of a chairperson nominated by the opposition parties, and a member elected by Parliament, a member elected by the Owner's Advisory Board and two members elected by the company employees.

The legislation process in Poland has been slow and has taken several years. The PAP (Polska Agencja Prasowa) has been operating under the 1983 law that has given it a full monopoly in Poland. Any other agency (including Reuters) must pay commissions to the PAP to be able to operate in Poland. Although the PAP has been able to take some advantage of the situation both politically and financially, the reform was considered necessary to cut costs and increase revenues. After a vote of 368 to 11, with three abstentions, Poland's lower house of Parliament, the Sejm, passed a bill in July 1997 to transform the national agency PAP into a treasury-owned joint stock company from the beginning of 1998. Its character will be 'of a public press agency, which, among other things, is obliged to publicize Poland's Sejm, Senate, President and government'. The PAP will be managed in line with the commercial code, except that its first president and board will be chosen by the Treasury minister. The government will reduce its stake to 51%, with the rest of the stock to be sold to private investors. The PAP received a subsidy of PLN 6.4 million which accounted for 25% of the agency's budget in 1996, but it is expected to survive without subsidies. It will expand its activities into specialized economic news services to business circles and into promoting local business, promoting books, films, and home videos on the PAP's Internet pages ('Poland: PAP to be commercialized, 1997; 'Poland: Polish MPs pass bill on PAP news agency sell-off', 1997).

If the Czech, Hungarian and Polish news agency laws demonstrate the attempt to disentangle the agency from the state, the Slovak agency (TASR) law is the opposite and has left many features of the old state agency untouched. First, the agency is still financed by the state. Although the law itself is very vague, it defines TASR as the agency of the Slovak Republic which is financed from the state budget. Second, the agency has the obligation to transmit government news. According to the law, it is obliged to publish information concerning the central state authorities at their request. And third, the government still nominates and dismisses the general director of the agency.

The Differentiation of the Agencies

Jakubowicz argues that differentiation may be a consequence of deregulation, but it can also mean the medium's own efforts to win autonomy by rejecting the ownership and control by the state or some other non-media structure, as well as by severing links to political forces and adopting a stance of impartiality and non-partisanship (Jakubowicz, 1995b: 73). In the case of news agencies where regulation has been much slower than was generally expected, they were forced to act before new laws were established. It is, however, important to bear in mind Sparks' and Reading's (1994: 266) observation on broadcasting companies. According to them, the broadcasters have operated under the framework inherited from the old regimes, except in the very important respect that censorship has been abolished. The framework for the news agencies also remained the same, except in the Slovak Republic where a new national agency was founded.

A new law on news agencies was adopted in Czechoslovakia in April 1992. It separated the new Slovakian news agency TASR from the Czech-Slovakian agency ČSTK. The former Czechoslovakian agency had its headquarters in Prague and in Bratislava. The news agency headquarters in Bratislava, together with other offices in Slovakia, were given to the Slovakian Republic while the rest of the agency's property remained in the Czech Republic. When Czechoslovakia was split into the Czech and Slovak Republics in January 1993, the newly born Slovakia faced a situation in which it had to create its own national media institutions. In this situation the Slovakian government decided to establish a state-owned news agency (TASR) on 1 January 1993. According to the agency, there was no time to consider any other options.

In the case of the Hungarian, Czech and Polish agencies, the first measure, as in broadcasting (see Sparks, 1995: 11), was the dismissal of the top managers who had closely collaborated with the former communist governments, and their replacement with the representatives of the former opposition. For example, since 1990 the Polish PAP has had five general managers. This reorganization only touched the surface of the organization, while most of the employees remained in their jobs. Even in the Slovak Republic where a new agency was founded, it inherited a staff of 300 people from the branch offices of the former Czechoslovakian agency in Slovakia who remained in their jobs.

The economic difficulties that hit the agencies were enormous, including the rapid rise in prices, high inflation and the lack of investment potential and foreign currency. For example, the Hungarian agency MTI's deficit rose from 500 million forints in 1994 to 600 million forints in 1995. Receipts were 20 million forints in 1995 while costs rose 160 million florints ('Hungary: MTI news agency faces reorganization 1995'). The easiest way to reduce costs had been the reduction of employees. For example, the Hungarian MTI had 1,400 staff members in 1990 compared to 500, of whom 300 were reporters, in 1995. The Czech agency had 1,100 employees in 1990 compared to 385 in 1995, while the Polish agency had 856 in 1989 and 560 (of whom 230 were journalists) in 1996. The agencies have also tried to sell their most unprofitable operations such as printing and publishing houses.

One of the most expensive operations is the maintenance of an international network of correspondents. Of the MTI's total budget of 1.2 million florints, about one-sixth (200,000 florints) goes in expenses relating to the network. To cut its expenses, the agency decided to reduce the number of its foreign correspondents from 27 to 14. Most of the reductions have been in former socialist and non-European countries. The agency closed down its bureaux in such cities as Prague, Hanoi, Ulan Bator, Beijing, Havana, Tokyo and Cairo. The Czech CSTK used to have 20 correspondents but has closed down six foreign bureaux in 1995 and now has correspondents in nine countries. As in the case of the MTI, most of the closed bureaux were located in the capitals of former socialist countries and non-European countries. The Polish agency PAP had 27 correspondents in 1990 compared to the 11 it had in 1996. Even the state-owned Slovakian agency reduced its number of foreign correspondents by two in 1995 and has now six foreign correspondents. Although the number of the agencies' correspondents is still relatively high compared to most western European agencies, the agencies have become much less self-reliant in their foreign news coverage and much more dependent on the global agencies.

The disentanglement from state structures also meant that the agencies that had previously been completely financed by the state faced a situation in which their subsidies had been reduced and they had to find new sources of revenue. At present, the Hungarian agency MTI receives 35% of its budget in the form of state subsidies while the Polish PAP receives 20%. In 1995 the Czech agency was still receiving a subsidy that represented 7–8% of its budget, but since the beginning of 1996 it has become financially completely independent of the state. The most subsidized agency is the Slovakian agency which still receives 60% of its budget as state subsidies.

In contrast to broadcasting, which can always turn to advertisers (see Sparks and Reading, 1994: 264), news agencies had to find alternative sources of funding. In practice, this has turned out to be very difficult. First, they have been unable to recover costs directly from their customers. In some cases, for example in the Czech Republic, competition with another agency prevents the agencies from raising subscription fees. In other cases, for example in the Slovak Republic, the media just cannot afford to pay higher fees. Second, foreign ownership or foreign shareholding, which has become so common in the press, has so far been resented because the idea of a national news agency has been so much based on domestic ownership.

Despite the slow-moving legislation, the agencies have been able to set up companies that are under state ownership but operate as business enterprises allowing them to reach the market directly. For example, the Hungarian MTI has set up three different firms. The Czech news agency offers 12 different news services by satellite. Following Reuters' business ideas on economic news transmission, all agencies have sought to attract non-media clients as well. The Slovakian agency has 60% media and 40% non-media customers. Fifty per cent of the revenues of the Czech agency CTK come from other sources including non-media clients while the Polish agency PAP receives 25%. The Hungarian agency receives 15% of its revenues from non-media customers.

The Consequences of Demonopolization

As a result of the liberalization of the market, the agencies now also face competition in their domestic market. The Slovakian agency (TASR) has no domestic rivals so far but competes with the Czech agency (CTK) in Slovakia. The Czech and Slovakian languages are so close to each other that although the CTK provides its service in Czech, Slovakian customers are able to use it. For the Czech agency Slovakia is a secondary market because only 2–3% of its revenues come from there. And yet the Czech agency is able to sell its service at a lower price than the Slovakian agency and thus to compete successfully with the newly established national agency. The situation has reached the point where the CTK and TASR have no relations, but instead the Slovakian agency co-operates with the private Czech agency CTA which in turn competes with the CTK.

The Czech CTK has faced serious competition from the new private agency CTA that was founded in the autumn of 1994. The major owners of the CTA are stockbrokers and one newspaper. Because of the competition, neither of the agencies can raise their subscription fees. According to the most recent information, the CTA faces closure after accumulating more than $1 million in liabilities (Konviser, 1996: 25). A new company CTI was formed in 1996 to discharge the liabilities.

The Hungarian MTI has no serious domestic rivals in its own home market, but there are a number of smaller press agencies such as Ferenczy-Europress, Graffiti, Atlantisz and Karpatia. Ferenczy is the largest, with a staff of 25 and several freelancers. As a member of the Springer Group, Ferenczy employees have exclusive access in Hungary to the Springerpress service ('Hungary: MTI news agency faces reorganization', 1995).

The most serious competition comes from global agencies, especially from Reuters in the economic news service. Even in the late 1980s, as banks and commerce broke away from the control of central planning authorities and needed information and access to global financial markets, Reuters was active and has established its economic news service all over eastern Europe. Reuters estimates that 25% of its annual revenue will come from eastern Europe and the Commonwealth of Independent States (CIS)' ('Reuters changing face in CIS and eastern Europe', 1992: 11).

National news agencies in eastern Europe were already subscribing to all major news services such as Reuters, AP, AFP and DPA in the era of state socialism. Of course, the use of western agencies was restricted, and TASS together with other eastern European agencies dominated as the major foreign news source. When there were no ideological reasons left to use them, their position collapsed rapidly and gave way to western agencies (see Rantanen and Vartanova, 1995). With the demonopolization of the news market it also became possible for global agencies to sell their services directly to clients without the intermediary role of national agencies. Of course, only the biggest and wealthiest media can afford to subscribe to their services. The majority of the media are dependent on national agencies for their reception of foreign news.

As part of the increasing news coverage from eastern Europe, Reuters opened new offices in Budapest 1988 and in Prague in 1990 (10 years after closing its former bureau) and in Warsaw and Bratislava in 1993. By 1992 Reuters already had 61 full-time staff in eastern Europe and the CIS of which 23 were correspondents (12 in Russia). A further landmark in this transition came in 1992 when Reuters officially launched its first eastern European subsidiary, Reuters Magyarorszag (Hungary Ltd) Kft, providing news, photo and graphic services. Reuters had been using the communication networks of the Hungarian news agency, but now it set up its own network ('Reuter Foundation holds first media workshop in central Europe', 1992: 13; 'Hungary: MTI news agency faces reorganization', 1995). Reuters also established a Polish service in 1996. This marks a major change in Reuters' policy. It now delivers its news service in over 20 national languages and is likely to extend a similar service to eastern European countries as well. Although Reuters says that it does not compete with national agencies in the general news service, it does in the financial news service. Hence, indirectly Reuters' presence in eastern Europe prevents national agencies from expanding their activities into a financial news service and thus find new sources of revenue.

Conclusion

Although the process of disentanglement of the media from the state structure can be seen as a fundamental prerequisite for the emergence of democracy (Jakubowicz, 1995a: 75), it does take different forms in different countries and sections of the media system. The pace also varies from one country to another, even from one medium to another.

Jakubowicz also describes how the old broadcasting systems which had previously been controlled by the Communist Party are in some cases being 're-nationalized and turned into a government agency or, at best, a national, politicized and quasi-commercial public broadcasting system' (Jakubowicz, 1995a: 86). This is, of course, a danger that national news agencies encounter as well. As we have seen, the degree of disentanglement varies considerably from one agency to the next. Furthermore, the existing legislation and plans for future legislation do not guarantee that agencies can operate free from their governments' influence. How this comes about remains to be seen and will be a matter of political struggle.

According to Sparks (1995: 16), it is possible that the development of a global media market will render the idea of national media systems obsolete. However, he considers the globalization of national media markets possible only in the long run because there is little evidence that the forces of commercialization and globalization will be either strong or pervasive enough to negate the features of media systems which he considers European. Still, there is strong evidence that national agencies, not only in eastern Europe, but perhaps especially there, will face serious competition from global news agencies. In eastern Europe the strongest global agency is without doubt Reuters.

If national news agencies are considered institutions worth protecting, then there is the question of whose responsibility this is. One answer is that it is the state's. It is difficult to imagine that the media with diverse, clashing and possibly foreign interests would assume the responsibility of maintaining a national news service in any eastern European country in view of the vulnerability of the media market. Moreover, even if a group of firms could afford to invest in a news service they would be likely to invest in a private agency. For the interests of privately owned firms are in profit: not in a so-called common or national interest. But when the state assumes the responsibility, it can also increase its control, especially over news agencies, because there is no direct public control (in the sense of the public consisting of people) over their actions.

As Splichal (1994: 87–8) has noted, western observers have considered privatization of ownership and foreign capital as the only way to modernize the economies of the media in the former socialist countries. Splichal himself questions whether the developmental tendencies of privatization will result in genuine democratization. Whether all media institutions should be privatized remains, of course, an important question. Broadcasting companies have adopted the policy of public service more easily than news agencies, and the state's subsidizing for broadcasting has not been rejected. If news agencies are considered public service, they should be subsidized in the same way as broadcasting companies, but given an independent position in relation to governments. Failing this, the national news agencies in central and eastern Europe will remain under state control or simply become an endangered species.

Interviews

Mr Michal Broniatowski, Business Manager, Reuters, Warsaw, 25 April 1996.
Dr Wlodzimierz Gogolek, President and Editor-in-Chief, Polish Press Agency, 25 April 1996.
Mr Dezsö Kopreda, Deputy General Director, Magyar Tavirati Iroda, Budapest, 27 October 1995.
Dr Peter Marianyi, Manager for International Relations, Tlačova Agentura Slovenskej Republiky, Bratislava, 25 October 1995.
Mr Milan Stibral, Director General, Czech News Agency, Prague, 24 October 1995.

References

Act CXXVII of 1996 on the National News Agency (1996) Budapest: MTI.

'Hungary: MTI news agency faces reorganization' (1995) *Reuters Business Briefing* Figyelo, 27 July.

Jakubowicz, K. (1995a) 'Lovebirds? The media, the state and politics in central and eastern Europe', *The Public*, 2 (1): 75–93.

Jakubowicz, K. (1995b) 'Poland television: what mix of continuity and change?' *The Public*, 2 (3): 61–80.

News Agencies. Their Structure and Operation (1953) Paris: Unesco.

Konviser, B. (1996) 'Time Running out for Czech news agency', *European*, 9–15 (May): 8.

Law passed by the Czech National Council on 21 October 1992 concerning the Czech News Agency (1992).

'Perestroika brings windfall for Reuters' (1989) *Reuters World*, 63 (July): 6–7.

'Poland: Cabinet office argues for government-prepared bill on PAP press agency' (1994) *Reuters Business Briefing/BBC Monitoring Service*, 11 October.

'Poland: PAP news agency to remain state-owned' (1994) *Reuters Business Briefing/Rzeczpospolit*, 6 October.

'Poland: Polish government adopts draft on PAP news agency' (1994) *Reuters Business Briefing/Reuters News Service*, 7 November.

'Poland: Polish MPs pass bill on PAP news agency sell-off' (1997) *Reuters Business Briefing/ Reuters News Service*, 31 July.

'Poland: PAP to be commercialized' (1997) *Reuters Business Briefing/Polish News Bulletin of British and American Embassies*, 19 August.

Rantanen, T. and Vartanova, E. (1995) 'Post-communist Russia. From state monopoly to state dominance', *European Journal of Communication*, 10 (2): 207–20.

'Reuters business takes off in east Europe' (1990) *Reuters World*, 68 (February): 12.

'Reuter Foundation holds first media workshop in central Europe' (1992) *Reuters World*, 86, May: 24.

'Reuters changing face in CIS and eastern Europe' (1992) *Reuters World*, 86 (May): 10–14.

Sparks, C. (1995) 'Introduction to emerging media systems of post-communism', *The Public*, 2 (3): 7–17.

Sparks, C. and Reading, A. (1994) 'Understanding media change in East Central Europe', *Media, Culture and Society*, 16: 243–70.

Splichal, S. (1994) *Media beyond Socialism. Theory and Practice in East-Central Europe*, Boulder: Westview Press.

Tunstall, J. and Palmer, M. (1991) *Media Moguls*, London: Routledge.

Zakon Slovesnkej narodnej rady z 30. januara o Cesko-slovenskej tlacovej kancelarii Slovenskej republiki.

9 From State Socialism to Deregulation

Ullamaija Kivikuru

New information technology, together with increased commercialization has changed the mediascape of Africa radically in recent years. However, the most drastic changes are man-made, not technological. The mediascape has altered because of political changes, but news agencies are as they have always been: poorly resourced, badly run, and commanding little respect. As we see in a number of chapters in this volume, the overall progress towards liberalization of the media in countries where they were once heavily state-controlled poses significant difficulties of survival for the particular species of medium which is the news agency and the particular species of national news which they carry.

If the 1960s was the decade of political struggle for liberation in sub-Saharan Africa, the 1970s was the decade of the 'second struggle' (Nordenstreng and Ng'wanakilala, 1985), this time a struggle for cultural decolonization, manifest not only in the familiar international debate over the new information order but also in the new media institutions mushrooming in the newly independent countries; most African news agencies were established then. The following decade was a period of multiple frustrations in Africa, reflected not least in the gradual deterioration of the media institutions established amidst such high hopes only a decade before. And in the 1990s, once again, the African cultural sphere has experienced radical changes; this time the media have been considered the flagbearers of enhanced democracy and participation, a 'new' polyphonic choir of 'independent' African media gaining attention also in the North.

Some accounts of the complex character of African media freedom which have been published suggest that, whether free or controlled, African media reflect an attitude that authority represents the embodiment of a people (Bourgault, 1993). Meanwhile, Northern sponsors have enthusiastically witnessed the emergence of private forms of media, offering support in the form of concrete assistance, not just with rhetoric. A vulgar equation has been made between so-called independent and democratic media, while all public media seem to carry the legacy of the previous one-party states, now condemned as undemocratic. Notwithstanding such an equation, all African news agencies are still without exception publicly owned.

The categories commonly used to characterize news agency ownership have been 'private' or 'government'. For the latter, the term 'public' would seem preferable, because many African news agencies are in fact parastatals – public companies which, like their European broadcasting counterparts, are responsible to parliaments, not governments. In Africa, cultural parastatals such as news agencies formally have greater room for manoeuvre than broadcasting companies which are frequently regulated directly by governments.

Most African news agencies have a background as government information services; many a national news agency was established in the 1970s simply by changing the name of the institution. They continued to utilize the existing network of information gathering and, along with it, the old institutional climate, which they transferred to the new institution. If it was hard for the recently established agencies to convince their clients of their credibility as news agencies in the 1970s, today they appear more suspect than ever because of their government legacy. Most African news agencies still receive some subsidies, though the sums have reduced considerably in recent years. Even so, it is easy to label their dispatches 'government information' and, accordingly, some independent media refuse to pay anything for what they consider to be propaganda. At the same time the value of their claim to practise so-called 'developmental communication' has been undermined because recent changes in African journalism seem to favour, on the one hand, political debate and, on the other, news of automobile crashes from major cities. With all the social changes taking place in eastern Europe, it has been questioned whether the concept of 'development communication' should apply only to social and cultural changes in the South although it is only in the South that such a journalistic mode has been established. Development news covers regular reporting on social processes, and it attempts to address the basic needs of the majority of population (for example, Mowlana and Wilson, 1990: 127–49, 203–13; Musa, 1997: 131–7). But while the new wave of media freedom has strengthened political as well as sensational traits in African journalism, the slower social processes which are the stuff of development reporting have been forced to the fringes of journalistic attention.

In what follows, my point of departure is slightly different from that of most of the chapters in this book. I shall not focus solely on the news agency. Instead I shall try to determine the status and role of a news agency in the changed African mediascape, as a partner in a highly capricious and risky process of transformation. In part this stand reflects my own understanding of the role of a news agency in any mediascape; it is the whole media industry and environment that matters for society as a whole, not individual institutions as such. The focus is also partly conditioned by the present sub-Saharan situation. The difficulties and prospects for any news agency in that region cannot be explained without a more extensive perspective. Moreover, the treatment seeks credibility amidst a dearth of printed sources, for the simple reason that so few exist (Musa, 1997; UNESCO, 1994). Much of what follows originated in interviews with media professionals, predominantly carried out in June 1994 and June 1996.

The Giant that Never Existed

Though Tanzania is poor, since the early 1970s it has deliberately developed media policies which offer a balance between urban centres and the rural areas where up to 80% of the population lives. First of all was the nationalization of the major media in the late 1960s; in the early 1970s a series of seminars was organized to develop a coherent media policy emphasizing the public service role of all media, two-way communication, commitment to truth, encouragement of free debate and constructive criticism of the socialist policies which the media were expected to reflect (for details, see Nordenstreng, 1986: 180–8).

Tanzania has been strongly supported by development assistance for decades. In recent years, however, aid funds have been radically reduced. Meanwhile, the government has agreed to carry out a structural adjustment programme imposed by the World Bank. The allocation of funds for education, health and all 'soft' aspects of life has been cut. Hence a public news agency is also both politically and financially worse off than ever, with little prospect of assistance from abroad. The Tanzanian news agency SHIHATA (Shirika la Habari la Tanzania) was established in 1976, and was first supported by a News Agency Act, considered the most powerful in the world because it enabled the agency to operate as the sole collector and distributor of news, as well as the body for registration of journalists and foreign correspondents in the country. In practice SHIHATA never operated as such a gatekeeper, because right from the beginning it had very scarce resources. It 'inherited' part of the regional and district services from the Tanzania Information Services (Maelezo) which was obliged to give up news-gathering activities and to focus entirely on documentation and government information. This division of labour has never been clear in practice. Maelezo still reports from the regions, and because its own two papers appear irregularly, its regional and district-level information officers send their stories either to headquarters to be distributed free to the Dar es Salaam media, or the poorly paid upcountry professionals are tempted to earn extra by selling their features to the media directly.

Though the leglislation enabled the national news agency to act as the sole distributor of news to and from the country, it took a long time before SHIHATA was even capable of establishing a foreign desk, let alone controlling the incoming news. Some of its clients have over the years received Reuters' services directly, because SHIHATA has been slow. According to the Act, the agency was also made responsible for educating journalists, but the Tanzania School of Journalism has been fully independent of SHIHATA.

So the Act remained largely unimplemented. And yet, the Tanzanian News Agency Act was frequently cited during the Great Media Debate in the 1970s as an example of how the developing countries sought to eliminate international news agencies and replace them with Southern ones. The Tanzanian News Agency Act was revised in 1984 and totally altered in 1993, permitting the establishment of private media. With the exception of its early years under direct government control, the mode of ownership has remained unchanged; SHIHATA is a parastatal.

Policies and Reality Still Apart

A gap between policy and practice has characterized media affairs in Tanzania throughout the years of independence. The media have been weak and urban-centred. Yet nation-building has been more successful than in many other African countries; indeed Tanzania is today a coherent nation. However, as part of the nation-building process, regional newspapers written in vernacular languages were abolished. Later attempts to re-establish regional media have been largely futile. Rural papers, an integral part of massive literacy campaigns, flourished in the 1970s, but died soon after foreign financing ceased.

Up to the late 1980s, two dailies served the Tanzanian population of 30 million: the government-owned English-language *Daily/Sunday News* with its clear white-collar orientation, and the more popular, Swahili-language mouthpiece of the ruling party, CCM – *Uhuru/Mzalendo*. Total circulation of the two dailies, at its best, was 200,000 copies. Radio Tanzania Dar es Salaam (RTD) covered 85–90% of the population with its two Swahili channels and one English channel, and some 20–30 private journals were published irregularly. The island of Zanzibar had, and still has, its own media policies and structures; no newspapers, but a radio station (Sauti ya Tanzania Zanzibar, STZ) and colour television channel (Zanzibar Television, ZTV). Presently there are seven daily papers – two in English, the rest in Swahili – in the country, but their combined circulation is considerably less than 200,000. The biggest in circulation seems to be the private, popular *Majira* (Business Care Group), followed by *Mtanzania* (Rai Co-operative) with somewhat more elitist tendencies, and *Uhuru*, still a CCM mouthpiece, each having a circulation of roughly 30,000 copies. No baseline data of media consumption are collected. At least in the early 1990s, the issue of multi-partyism remained a distinctly urban phenomenon, while many in the rural communities feared the rapid changes. Radio is still by far the most important mass medium in rural communities (Kivikuru et al., 1994: 25–30, 64–86; Nthenge, 1997).

The period of most radical change in the media seems to be over in Tanzania. In the early 1990s, scandalmongering papers and those strongly biased towards Islamic fundamentalism were predominant; today both are practically gone. In 1995, there were more than 100 newspapers in the country, but since the parliamentary elections of October 1995, the figure has declined to 38 (Nthenge, 1997). Newsprint and printing are still expensive and advertising is still concentrated in the public media and the most established private media.

The present Tanzanian media, operating primarily in Swahili, have gradually shown interest in the regions, fearing that saturation point will soon be reached in towns and especially in the Dar es Salaam area with its population of roughly three million. So far, the 'media revolution' remains a highly urban phenomenon centred on Dar es Salaam. All Dar papers arrive on the same day in two major political and commercial centres, Arusha in the north and the new capital Dodoma in the Central Highlands, but not in other towns. Only the CCM paper *Uhuru* is distributed – via party channels – to districts and occasionally also villages, while copies of other papers are rarely distributed outside the major towns.

The public media have become much weaker since multi-partyism, but they seem set to stay. Printing remains a bottleneck. In earlier times, a government-owned printing plant had a monopoly; now the same position is enjoyed by a private company. With no competition, the quality of work remains poor and the prices are high.

The media are concentrated into three groups: there is the strong Independent Press Pool (IPP) owned by a local businessman, Reginald Mengi; there is another strong though smaller Business Care Group, also owned by a local businessman, Rashidi Mbuguni; and there are the public media. Outside these there is quite a variety of private papers, but they come out irregularly, the only exception being the Rai Co-operative with its three papers and fairly ambitious journalistic objectives.

Dar es Salaam is practically the only place where radio and television compete for audiences. Radio One (IPP Group) is favoured by the young, because it plays a lot of foreign disco music. A few insubstantial private radio stations have been launched in bigger towns at Lake Victoria and on the slopes of Kilimanjaro. In fact, the competitor for the public RTD is the equally public Zanzibari STZ, which plays a lot of taarab-music.

Roughly three million Tanzanians are now within reach of television, but there are fewer than 100,000 television sets in the country (Nthenge, 1997). Four private television stations (ITV, DTV, CTN, CEN) are on air in Dar es Salaam, although the official figure is higher. The Tanzania Broadcasting Commission (TBC) distributes TV licences and provides sporadic regulation of the quality. Two companies (ITV, DTV) issue daily Swahili-laguage news bulletins and some Swahili entertainment. ITV relays BBC newscasts, DTV relays Sky News. Most documentaries and serial films are bought from abroad; all TV stations are strongly oriented towards entertainment.

There are roughly 20 newsrooms in Dar es Salaam now, but none as large as the news agency SHIHATA or Radio Tanzania from some 10 years back. In the early 1980s, SHIHATA had a professional staff of 150; presently it has 30–35 professionals, half of them in the regions. However, the agency newsroom still remains among the largest four in the country.

In general, media still favour nationwide news and current affairs. Regional news coverage is scarce, and most local news covers major cities, focusing on crime, traffic, housing, and labour disputes. In the English-language media, some 25–30% of the journalistic output focuses on international or foreign issues, predominantly African, while the Swahili media are much more domestically oriented. The RTD used to have substantial regional coverage, but nowadays it concentrates on national and international news, with only one or two dispatches per bulletin from the regions. Practically all of these are either accidents or items of bureaucratic news, provided by various government offices, because the radio company does not have resources for news gathering in the regions.

Though media developments in Tanzania have been erratic and contradictory, the significance of the recent changes should not be underestimated. The professional integrity of journalists has undoubtedly grown, and interest in information occupations has increased accordingly; earlier, journalism was not considered a lucrative profession. Furthermore, calls for greater transparency in public life are far more frequent than ever before. Among the most radical changes is the fact that the most interesting media operate in the language spoken by the majority, that is Swahili. On the other hand, finely crafted policy papers do not seem to help much in the new situation. Almost anything seems to be up for grabs; the government has hinted that it could hand the school of journalism over to the media, and discussions about either the privatization or closing down of the news agency SHIHATA were frequent up to the summer of 1996 when the government announced that SHIHATA would remain in public hands. However, government support for the agency remains very modest. In order to operate, the agency must generate other sources of income.

A News Agency without Telephones and Transport

SHIHATA has operated on slender resources throughout the mid-1990s. For example, in June 1996 it had practically no operations at all. Reuters interrupted its services in March 1996 because of unpaid fees; only one telephone in the headquarters was in operation, and none in the regional bureaux. Fax and telex lines were also cut. The reason was the same: unpaid bills. The editor was not willing to release any statistics about the agency's performance in May or June 1996. Instead, she provided records for December 1995, when the regional bureaux were still operating. The professional staff numbered 34 in June 1996, 19 of these in the regions. In principle, 16 SHIHATA regional bureaux were operating in June. However, it was practically impossible for the regional staff to file any dispatches. The editor emphasized, however, that many regional officers in the public service gladly offered their telephones and telex lines for SHIHATA regional staff, because these civil servants wanted to get their material published. The editor did not reflect on the dangers of using sources which frequently operate both as sources and as gatekeepers for information from other sources. At least in principle, regional government offices could refuse to send sensitive material from the regions to Dar es Salaam. Some SHIHATA clients claim that this has indeed happened.

No other media in the country have regional services, with the exception of a few correspondents in the capital, Dodoma, and the big financial centre, Arusha in northern Tanzania. With multiple but weak independent media, the situation is hardly likely to change fast, because regional services are expensive. Thus, in principle, SHIHATA still commands the regional arena.

In 1987, SHIHATA filed some 180 stories per day, one-third of these foreign news and some 40% national, the rest regional (Kivikuru, 1990: 295–308). Some 5,300–5,500 dispatches were filed each month. Based on information given by the agency in June 1996, SHIHATA's 'diet' of regional news during the week of 10–16 June comprised 14 stories. At headquarters, 10–13 stories per day and two features per week were produced. In addition, two to three dispatches were said to be transferred from the Pan-African News Agency (PANA). The rest were domestic stories. Thus the daily diet offered by SHIHATA seemed to be 10–15 stories, the only foreign material being a few stories by PANA. A majority of SHIHATA regional dispatches from the week under study had local administrators, development agencies, or political bodies as sources. Most regional stories were statements by public officials; it was rare for there to be multiple sources in these dispatches.

Ten to fifteen stories per day might be an overestimate because many clients claimed that they received only three to five daily dispatches from SHIHATA. They also said that PANA stories were offered extremely rarely. My content analysis of the Dar es Salaam media for the week 10–17 June 1997 supported this claim, though bylines were missing and it was thus difficult to determine the origin of some stories.

In December 1995, the agency was in a slightly better financial situation; most telephones were in operation and at least some vehicles were mobile. In this month, regional bureaux filed 227 stories and the headquarters 226. The week of 10–17 June is representative of the end of the budget year, and production had dropped to some 300 dispatches per month, roughly half the December 1995 level. If compared with figures from April 1987, the change appears far more dramatic. The total for December 1995 (453 dispatches) was less than one-tenth of the monthly total 10 years earlier (5,360 dispatches), but naturally much more than the estimate for June 1996 (SHIHATA figure: *c.* 400; clients: *c.* 150) (Kivikuru, 1990: 182–90, appendices, interviews, content analysis).

According to several media professionals, such a downslide in SHIHATA activities, plus annual variation based on the course of the fiscal year, have been familiar throughout the 1990s, but the curves have become more dramatic with each year. As expected, later in the summer of 1996 SHIHATA improved its performance slightly, because the agency received part of its annual subsidy from the government, enabling payment of telephone bills, etc.

In principle, SHIHATA operates both in English and in Swahili, but in practice Swahili dominates. This means that English-language clients cannot use SHIHATA services as easily. On the other hand, more and more media also use the national language; thus this cannot be considered a severe limitation. In 1987, English was the dominant language used, and the Swahili service was then much slower than the English one (Kivikuru, 1990: 293–300).

In the 1995/96 government budget, the agency received a government subsidy of 140 million shillings (roughly US $300,000), out of which salaries alone comprised 100 million shillings, leaving only a minimal sum (US $85,000) for the running of the agency. Thus the operational costs must be almost totally covered by client payments.

The salary scales still follow those confirmed for government civil servants, though small incentives are available. This means that the pay level at the agency is considerably lower than in the other media, private or public, with the exception of the RTD, which follows a similar policy. This means that the agency tends to lose its most capable staff to other media, especially those in the private sector.

SHIHATA has three categories of clients. The big full-service clients pay more than the rest. These six big clients are: *Daily/Sunday News*, Radio Tanzania Dar es Salaam (RTD), *Uhuru*, *Mtanzania*, DTV and the IPP Group (Press Service Tanzania, ITV, Radio One, seven newspapers). Two small papers have cancelled SHIHATA services because of financial problems; the Business Care Group (for example *Majira)* has cancelled as a matter of principle. The agency has not revealed the price of its services, but a representative of a big client said that they pay SHIHATA US $6,000 per year. Therefore, the agency gathers some US $50,000–60,000 per year in client fees, the total budget thus amassed reaching US $350,000–360,000. Of this, only some US $135,000–140,000 can be devoted to operational costs, the rest covering salaries. By international standards, this is an extremely modest sum for running a news agency. Most probably SHIHATA will encounter difficulties even in collecting the present level of client fees without Reuters' services. PANA services are extremely haphazard and hardly interesting to the clients. If no other monitoring services are arranged, there is no foreign news supply.

A highly innovative reuse or misuse – depending on one's perspective – of SHIHATA personnel is that of the IPP Group-owned Press Service Tanzania (PST) agency, which serves all nine of the IPP Group media. The agency focuses entirely on the regions. It has a staff of only three full-time journalists, but it has altogether 25 regular stringers in 10 locations up-country. Some of these stringers ('correspondents') work full-time in a totally different field, while the majority are professional journalists, predominantly SHIHATA and *Maelezo* regional journalists, frustrated over non-existent telephone and telex lines, and eager to earn some extra money. The media outside the IPP Group condemn the PST activity as 'poaching', as not respectable and transitional, while the agency itself considers that it is offering a service to these journalists and enhancing their professionalism.

PST pays all the transmission costs of stories from up-country. For the future, PST is counting on the early retirement of civil servants in Tanzania, which will have a strong impact on SHIHATA in the late 1990s: after retirement, it is expected that former SHIHATA employees, aged 55–60, will be willing to work for PST, headed by a former SHIHATA editor whom they know well and respect. The agency files 12–13 stories (12,800 words) a day, with the exception of the rainy months, which cause problems with telephones in the regions. In June 1996, the supply by PST was on the same scale – if not larger – than that of SHIHATA. In principle and in practice, PST operates in both languages. The coverage is similar to that of SHIHATA; the sources are local authorities and the style remains formal.

Confusingly, the IPP Group has chosen a policy of co-operation with SHIHATA, while representatives of the other private media group, Business Care, have been far more radical in pronouncing the 'uselessness' of SHIHATA. Some aspects of PST operations may suggest that the IPP Group does not fully deploy the specialist expertise required to run a news agency. Hence, it might be the case that the PST has been established simply as a 'refinery tool' for a media company which has been very slow to hire people on a regular basis; naturally people working for the PST have a different picture of the future.

Since 1994 the IPP Group has subscribed to Reuters' services directly, and the *Daily/Sunday News* has had direct links with Reuters for more than 20 years, though they have been mediated by SHIHATA. After leaving SHIHATA, the Business Care Group has not had any regular foreign sources. Of the big SHIHATA clients the national radio station, the party paper *Uhuru* and the co-operative-based *Mtanzania* received Reuters' material via SHIHATA. Of these, both papers are in trouble after the Reuters' decision to pull out, because neither can afford the services alone. RTD radio newsroom has never used Reuters extensively thanks to its own monitoring system (BBC, Deutsche-Welle, Voice of America). Instead, the RTD would be eager to receive much more regional news than it presently gets. Working for a public medium in an equally desperate situation, the RTD staff well understand the problems involved, but the scarce supply of the national news agency is reflected in the material transmitted in radio news bulletins, still the main national news medium in the country. In the survey week, only one to two items out of 13–15 supplied in each bulletin were regional, the majority focusing on the government and the parliament.

Of international foreign services, Inter Press Service (IPS), Reuters, Xinhua, and the BBC have their correspondents in Dar es Salaam. The IPS used to collaborate with SHIHATA. The IPS daily services have declined considerably in recent years because of financial problems. Still, evaluated as alternative and pro-South its credibility remains high. Almost all interviewees in June 1996 noted that the IPS has left; for SHIHATA this was considered a serious blow.

SHIHATA does not monitor the use of its dispatches. Staff maintain that the greatest users of SHIHATA material are the national radio RTD, the television company DTV and *Uhuru*, while *Daily/Sunday News* traditionally uses SHIHATA material only to a minor extent, one reason presently being the domination of Swahili in SHIHATA supply. Most stories are translated, but they are transmitted late, while the Swahili versions are available hours before. Based on the one-week survey sample of Dar es Salaam media, the estimates given by the agency staff seemed justified.

Besides news agencies proper, various feature agencies are active in the country (Reuters, IPS, Gemini, Panos, Third World Features, Southern Africa News Features, African News Afrique, WREN, etc.). Feature material is easily available, and prices are reasonable. For the private media, the Media Institute of Southern Africa (MISA) regularly offers many supply options, and the IPS material is presently transmitted via MISA. The Rai Co-operative in particular makes considerable use of this channel.

If features are not a problem for the media, news pictures are. There is now a much greater appetite for pictures. SHIHATA offers a daily package of 5–10 domestic picture items. By contrast, no foreign news pictures are transmitted. The IPP Group subscribes to the full Reuters' picture services on-line, while *Mtanzania*, for example, subscribes to a package of Reuters' pictures, relayed via Nairobi and sent to Dar es Salaam by air mail on a daily basis. This service is considerably cheaper. When interviewed in June 1996, media professionals gave credit to SHIHATA's domestic picture services, though they were considered somewhat slow. Based on the analysis of a one-week sample, some 30–40% of the domestic pictures in the papers seemed to originate from SHIHATA, though many bylines were missing.

The television companies receive newsreel services from the international sources they are co-operating with, but there is a great need for domestic stories, pictures as well as text. For example the DTV broadcasts practically everything that SHIHATA provides.

The tragic Lake Victoria ferry accident in May 1996 revealed the inefficiency of the national news agency compared with Reuters or the BBC. Only in picture services was SHIHATA able to serve its clients, while in text Reuters was far faster than the domestic agency. In part this reflects lack of equipment, but perhaps to a larger extent, a lack of practice in handling breaking news. Regional journalists are accustomed to a slower pace of work. The Mwanza region SHIHATA photographer sent his rolls by air to Dar es Salaam with captions; the rolls were developed first in Dar and thus SHIHATA pictures of the accident were already available 2–3 hours after the accident was discovered, but SHIHATA dispatches came 6–7 hours later and did not offer any more details than the dispatches filed by the Reuters' correspondent, who travelled from Dar es Salaam to Mwanza but still filed his piece hours earlier than SHIHATA correspondents based in Mwanza.

Operation Downslide

In analyses of the substance of Tanzanian news media between 1967 and 1996 (Condon, 1967; Kivikuru, 1990, survey 1996), certain trends are distinguishable which reflect the news agency's performance. The figures are approximate and should be treated accordingly; they simply indicate trends. All figures are based on frequency of stories in a one-week sample. In June 1996, a total of 17 media was analysed. The journalistic material produced in eight days in June 1996 was scrutinized. Based on this content analysis, there seem to be three news media groups: first, the big English-language papers and the RTD radio newsroom with its national orientation; second the large popular Swahili-language media, the TV stations and a private radio station with a far more popular orientation; and third, small Swahili papers with markedly sensational tendencies, typified by news of road accidents. The differences between these groups were not dramatic but were none the less distinct. During the period under study, SHIHATA supplied only some 70–80 dispatches to its clients – only a dozen of them from the regions. However, the utilization of SHIHATA material was high. Though full documentation was impossible to gather, it seems that practically the whole SHIHATA supply was used by the major media, while the smallest media seemed to run without any agency material.

In a crude analysis of the material, three trends emerged: first, the proportion of foreign news (averaging 23%) had decreased considerably from 1987 (average 44%). Second, the average volume of news from the regions (11%) had dropped radically from 1987 (31%), even below the level of the 1960s (25%). However, another category of news had grown considerably: local news (average 22%), or perhaps it would be more justified to talk about 'city news', because the locality of these dispatches was limited to major towns. Third, news somehow linked with development (average 18%) seemed to have decreased also, though this drop is not as dramatic as for regional news. The precise definition of development affects the figures strongly; here, as in most other similar studies (for example, Musa, 1997) the category was inclusive of anything from news of campaigns to political statements. The fact that the proportion of foreign news has decreased in 10 years does not necessarily reflect the scarcity of direct foreign news sources, because the 'media revolution' in Tanzania quite naturally turned attention towards domestic phenomena and processes. The fact that bigger media and English-language media had considerably higher proportions (30–40%) of foreign news than the Swahili media (7–10%, mostly sports material) implies that the former do have foreign news sources which the small Swahili media lack. In the foreign material, there was still a clear focus on African issues, though the proportion of European material had grown somewhat; however, the European football cup in June 1996 could have affected the figures, because even small Swahili papers covered the games.

A factor affecting the decline of regional material besides poor SHIHATA performance is probably the fact that the new media go for the markets: their readership is in Dar es Salaam, and Dar es Salaam they cover. On the other hand, material on local accidents and political disputes is also easy to acquire. Many professionals said that the local bias was more a matter of convenience than of principle. They claimed to be willing to publish far more stories from the regions, if such material was available.

The present capital Dodoma received some coverage in the media studied, because the parliament had its session there; similarly, Zanzibar was covered due to political tensions there. However, the 'core' of the tensions, namely the island of Pemba, remained beyond the scope of coverage. The media were content to report on the political scenery from the Zanzibar Stonetown. Furthermore, only some 5–7% of the daily journalistic content of the media was devoted to the remaining 16 regions, while in 1987, with a better-run SHIHATA, the corresponding proportion approached 25%. Instead, in 1996, even minor incidents and accidents in Dar es Salaam were covered intensively, especially by the Swahili media.

Content analysis suggests that the Tanzanian media in the 1960s reflected the (then entirely foreign) agency scene quite directly, while the 1970s was the period when nation-making in all sectors of life was emphasized. In the 1980s, the proportion of developmental material was considerably higher than in the 1990s. In the 1996 material, there were two parallel tendencies: one stressing conventional agency-style news, though agency material as such was limited; the other putting emphasis on local novelty/oddity material. Quite interestingly, the proportion of material expressing opinions was limited; with some dramatic exceptions, editorials analysed backgrounds rather than expressing opinions. Most Tanzanian journalism respects the demarcation between news and opinion. There are more features in the Tanzanian media today than before, but the news bias is still distinct. Softer genres – accidents, oddities, crossword puzzles, clairvoyant 'professors', Swahili poetry and narratives – are tolerated by media professionals in greater numbers because of the hunt for mass audiences and for generating discussion and debate. All 'serious information' is still distributed via the genre of hard news.

The changes in African media have sometimes been called a well-marketed revolution that has not yet taken place. According to the content analysis of June 1996, a revolution in news criteria seems to have taken place in Tanzania, indicating decreased interest in foreign issues, development, and regional planning and increased coverage of political debate, city news, and superficial traditionalism as it appears in urban areas. Village news and features were rare in the old system, and they are even more so now. Media professionals claim, however, that these criteria are partly a choice dictated by necessity.

In all this then, the challenges for SHIHATA would seem to be gigantic.

Plans for the Future: a Co-operative with Mobile Units

Some members of the IPP Group claim that the PST is going to expand and perhaps gradually replace SHIHATA. Some members of the Business Care Group oppose the parastatal SHIHATA on ideological ('press freedom') grounds. But most media professionals still seem to share the opinion that no new media institutions are needed; rather, SHIHATA should operate more efficiently. The agency staff also share this opinion. The agency recently prepared a review of its future, to be presented to the government and the president, who enjoys great credibility among media professionals because of his journalistic background.

According to the SHIHATA revision plan, the agency should be small, mobile, well-equipped and financially independent of the state. Some regional bureaux could be closed down, while others should be strengthened considerably. A reporter can easily drive from Mwanza to Shinyanga whenever needed, if he has a vehicle and fuel. Furthermore, there should be a small number of reporters at headquarters ready to travel to wherever they are needed.

A news agency requires considerable funds to meet running costs. Hence, according to its development plan, SHIHATA should be self-sustaining and commercially minded. There are several options for SHIHATA's future administration and relationship to the state. The agency could continue as a parastatal and, in this case, the government should give the agency considerable support, though the agency should also generate funds independently. The tie to the government could also be far looser than in the parastatal mode, in which case funds should be acquired entirely through projects and services. A co-operative mode combining both public and private media could be a solution. An extreme option is to dissolve the agency totally – according to the review, even that is better than the current situation of being without resources to do what a news agency should do.

The SHIHATA development plan is a reminder that a development-minded news agency could be a precious resource for the government, itself geared to a development bias. A purely commercial agency would hardly show much interest in covering development projects.

Self-sustainability could be achieved via various projects. Somewhat surprisingly, the SHIHATA plan suggests seeking sources for income not from special services or their equivalent but primarily from outside news agency activities: from construction, real estate, or education.

The SHIHATA review also returns to the old disputed division of labour between the news agency and the Tanzania Information Services, currently better off with transport and equipment. *Maelezo*'s regional information officers still cover journalistic events and send their features to *Maelezo* headquarters which distribute them freely. Why would a medium pay for a SHIHATA feature if it is able to get a feature on the same event from *Maelezo*, free of charge? The division of labour works well in Dar es Salaam, but in the regions double coverage is more often the rule than an exception. A modern government and its agencies do require more PR and information services; hence *Maelezo* should be tailored accordingly.

The idea of a news agency co-operative is gathering support among media professionals. Though critical of SHIHATA's present performance, journalists representing the public as well as the private sectors assessed

SHIHATA to be valuable in two areas: in the provision of foreign material and in the regular coverage of the regions. Journalists from medium-sized media also suggested that SHIHATA should pay special attention to the coverage of parliamentary proceedings in Dodoma, because most media cannot send more than one reporter there. Media with limited personnel would be happy to pay extra for supplementary services. The quality of SHIHATA material was found to be satisfactory, but the agency was judged slow. Not too many professionals from the private sector mentioned SHIHATA's link to the government as a limitation, though there were some vocal exceptions, representing in particular the big private media group, Business Care.

Thus SHIHATA personnel as well as most other media professionals agree upon the basic line of future developments, though they emphasize slightly different matters. SHIHATA staff, perhaps because of exhaustion and desperation, want to develop new sources of income outside the news production field, while other professionals demand the improvement of professional competence and the development of special services. All view a news agency as a necessity for the Tanzanian mass media, and the majority see SHIHATA as the best choice for a new start.

Development News, Generation of Images, or Public Journalism?

A mass press with a form of news–entertainment–advertising mix and middle-market orientation (Boyd-Barrett, 1977: 120–1) appeared in Tanzania for the first time in the 1990s. The shape of broadcasting is still unclear. The public service orientation is a legacy from the colonial period, with a bias to development communication, while commercialization is still a novelty. The role of advertising will grow in the future. This affects public media too, who must increasingly earn their way through financing from advertisers, street sales and subscriptions.

The media industry is still undergoing transition, and it is difficult to apply to it any established modes of media economics. The media in a developing country follow economic rationale to a lesser degree than in industrialized countries. It is perhaps more fruitful to seek assistance from the concept of 'ideoscape' (Appadurai, 1990). An ideoscape provides a 'preferred reading' code for the mediascape in the country. The mystique surrounding media and democracy has led some observers to over-estimate the significance of the changes of the early 1990s in Africa. These changes did not, for example, do away with the ideoscape of authority which Louise Bourgault (1993) discusses.

Tanzanian media are still bound to an ideoscape biased towards development; the whole society is based on this 'national ideology', and not even the most commercially oriented media can abandon it totally. However, it is clear that the phase of strong social marketing of development is over; the promotion of development thinking will be more mediated and subtle in the future. No doubt a rapid expansion in entertainment will take place in Tanzania in the near future; such a development has less to do with democracy or freedom of expression than market logic. The shape given to television in its initial stage reflects that of other media also, because television consumes material fast, and a constant flow of television programme imports will have implications for the consumption of the media in general.

On the other hand, media policies reflect general politics. The political system in Tanzania has had a relatively low level of involvement in media – for better or worse, decision-makers have not been interested in the media. This *laissez-faire* stance might change, if competition between a plurality of political parties threatens to weaken the key status of the leading party, CCM. In this event, the significance of publicity will only grow and demands to regulate the media might intensify in periods when various political players try to consolidate their power. This kind of process will hasten a change from a 'development' to an 'image' orientation.

As contradictory as it might sound, the future for a nationwide news agency is perhaps more stable than that of many other media. In whatever way the news media develop, they cannot do so in a rural and development-biased country, without a joint news-gathering institution covering the regions. It remains to be seen whether this agency is going to be SHIHATA.

Specialized feature and news agencies will soon begin to sprout. Most likely, these agencies will be private or co-operatives, and there might be more space for South–South co-operation in this sector than in other news channels. Small enterprises can sometimes be more flexible, less bound to the tyranny of the deadline, and less difficult to establish. Such specialist enterprises, dedicated to such topics as the environment, the economy, sports, gender or development might improve the overall news system. However, specialized agencies of limited scope do not reduce the need for a stable, smoothly operating general news agency; rather the opposite. Some specialized services like news picture transmission can undoubtedly develop as branches of a general news agency, better able to develop contacts with a wide variety of foreign text and picture services for the benefit of client media. Although the largest of these may prefer to subscribe directly to international news and picture services – as a matter of prestige – most cannot afford such a luxury, either now or in the future.

An efficient general news agency requires major investments in technology, infrastructure, professional expertise, and marketing. In Tanzania, it is hard to imagine any other partner getting involved in such a demanding exercise than the state – and perhaps expatriate sponsors, through the state. A link to the state must remain, though the time of direct government control is definitely over; a 'public service' ideology, exercised by a co-operative covering both the public and the private media could perhaps suit the circumstances. However, there are problems. First, the co-operative mode has not proved successful when applied to news agencies in most other countries. And, in the Tanzanian ideoscape, public service carries a different connotation from the presently ever so fashionable debate on 'public sphere', 'public space' and 'public arena'. So far, media professionals and politicians alike tend simply to equate public service with government interference. In principle, the 'vernacularization' of Tanzanian journalism could pave the way for a genuine, popular approach – less news on elites and bureaucracy, more on rural villagers and their needs. A news agency with a nationwide news-gathering network stands in an unique position here; in theory it could act as a harbinger of journalistic change. So far, however, popular journalism has simply been equated with oddities and human interest material, easily collected from sports fields and market-places in big cities.

No 'alliances with ordinary citizens' suggested by the fashionable notion of public journalism (for example, Rosen, 1991) can be found in Tanzanian journalism. The basic ideology of 'not informing the public, but forming publics' fits well in Tanzania, known for its self-reliance ideology and its tradition of extended family. But this only tends to highlight the tragic contradiction between high ideals of democracy and almost non-existent resources.

The shallowness of the acclaimed media revolution in Tanzania has not yet instigated discussion and debate. Instead of elaboration and analysis of the issue, a 'contamination theme' (Jensen, 1990: 164–7) of government as an oppressive mass communicator has been introduced. It has been found perhaps safer to emphasize demarcation rather than blur boundaries. Unfortunately, the reality is extremely complex. Scarcity of resources is undoubtedly a severe limitation for rational development of news gathering and transmission in Tanzania, but the conditions are made even more difficult by a superficial understanding of professionalism, simplifying the notion of professional integrity into a simplistic demarcation between the state and journalism. A true professional anticipates the dangers of such a simplistic opposition: in the end, the emphasis on the integrity of the professional only serves to alienate journalism from the citizens.

One of the dangers of such a deeply dualist approach is that, because of limited resources and minimal media criticism, professional values are adopted from abroad at an accelerating pace. Media professionals too easily take for granted the valuable elements in their own journalistic conventions and cultural traditions. For example, the popularity of Swahili poetry and narratives could open up a totally new path in Tanzanian journalism, but for now they are just interpreted as marketing gimmicks.

A general news agency stands at the crossroads of media criticism and professional analysis; its daily storage of dispatches is a manifestation of dominant professional values and practices in any journalistic environment. Perhaps it is exactly this characteristic that leads Tanzanian journalism to reject or under-rate rather than elaborate on the analysis of the national news agency and its desperate situation. It is not easy for professionals to accept their own reflection in the mirror if the image differs markedly from the image which those holding the mirror have of themselves.

References

Appadurai, A. (1990) 'Disjuncture and difference in the global cultural economy', in M. Featherstone (ed.), *Global Culture: Nationalism, Globalization and Modernity*, A *Theory, Culture and Society* special issue, London/Newbury Park/New Delhi: Sage.

Bourgault, L. (1993) 'Press freedom in Africa: a cultural analysis', *Journal of Communication Inquiry*, 17 (2): 69–92.

Boyd-Barrett, O. (1977) 'Media imperialism: towards an international framework for the analysis of media systems', in J. Curran, M. Gurevitch and J. Woollacott (eds), *Mass Communication and Society*, London: Edward Arnold.

Condon, J. (1967) 'National building in the Tanzanian press', *Journal of Modern African Studies*, 5: 3.

Jensen, J. (1990) *Redeeming Modernity. Contradictions in Media Criticism*, Newbury Park/London/New Delhi: Sage.

Kivikuru, U. (1990) *Tinned Novelties or Creative Culture? A Study on the Role of Mass Communication in Peripheral Nations*, University of Helsinki, Department of Communication, Publication No 1 F/10.

Kivikuru, U. in collaboration with W. Lobulu and G. Moshiro (1994) *Changing Mediascapes? A Case Study in Nine Tanzanian Villages*, University of Helsinki, Institute of Development Studies, Report B 28.

Mowlana, H. and Wilson, L. (1990) *The Passing of Modernity. Communication and the Transformation of Society*, New York and London: Longman.

Musa, M. (1997) 'From optimism to reality: an overview of third world news agencies', in P. Golding and P. Harris (eds), *Beyond Cultural Imperialism. Globalization, Communication and the New International Order*, London, Thousand Oaks and New Delhi: Sage.

Nordenstreng, K. (1986) 'Tanzania and the new information order: a study of Africa's second struggle', in J. Becker, G. Hedebro and L. Paldan (eds), *Communication and Domination: Essays to Honor Herbert I. Schiller*, Norwood, NJ: Ablex.

Nordenstreng, K. and Ng'wanakilala, N. (1985) *Tanzania and the New Information Order: A Study of Africa's Second Struggle*, Dar es Salaam: Printpack.

Nthenge, D. (1997) 'Country Report Tanzania. Tanzania Media Freedom', *MISA-News*, 11 February.

Rosen, J. (1991) 'Making public journalism more public', *Communication*, 12.

UNESCO (1994) Intergovernmental Council of the International Programme for the Development of Communication, *Final Report*, Paris, 14–21 November.

10 From Apartheid to Pluralism

Derek Forbes (with the collaboration of Mustapha Malam and Oliver Boyd-Barrett)

Periods of major political transition since the late 1980s have occasioned a considerable loosening up in news agency markets in many parts of the world. This reflects a trend towards pluralistic political regimes, and the introduction by those regimes of neo-liberal economic policies designed to reduce the stake of the state in the economy, and to open up markets, both domestically and internationally. In some cases these tendencies have undermined the role of older state-controlled or monopolistic national news agencies, creating new spaces for oppositional or alternative news agencies, and fresh opportunities for international agencies. The importance of this account of developments in South Africa in the period 1986–1997 lies not so much in its timeliness (the situation is volatile and is bound to change), but in its demonstration of the following principles:

- In times of considerable political change, news agencies can still be regarded as significant vehicles for introducing fresh news agendas or for reinforcing the agendas of new power coalitions.

- In order to survive in the medium to long term as independent ventures, alternative news agencies have increasingly to take account of the needs of mainstream media, and serving these needs can be difficult to reconcile with the radicalism which inspired the alternative ventures in the first place.

- Liberal markets make it easier for international players to operate, and may lead to a more intensive presence of global agencies on national markets, threatening the markets of mainstream and alternative domestic players alike, possibly requiring greater collaboration between these latter in defence against the former, at the possible expense of alternative or developmental news.

Reuters and SAPA

Reuters – which is described by Lord Layton (Storey, 1951, foreword) as a 'unique' international institution which developed an 'international control'

– played an important role in the development of a national news service in South Africa. Set up primarily to serve British imperial interests, Reuters' news from South Africa developed into a regular service around 1861 (Read, 1992: 84–5). Soon after, gold was discovered (1885), and the agency expanded significantly, dominating the news exchange between Britain and South Africa. It gained control of the internal news supply with Reuters South African Press Agency (60% Reuters, 40% local) thus fulfilling the role of national news agency of South Africa: in this way it overcame a local South African attempt to drive Reuters from the country, its world resources proving too powerful for a rival syndicate (Storey, 1951: 136–7).[1] It was only in the 1930s that Reuters relinquished its handling of internal general news, giving way to the creation of the first indigenous agency when the South African Press Association (SAPA) was set up in 1938 (Storey, 1951: 200; Read, 1992: 118). Under the new partnership Reuters retained exclusive rights as supplier of world news (Read, 1992: 165). It was not until the 1990s that Reuters was to make another attempt to control news supply in South Africa.

SAPA, a co-operative, non-profit agency, was built around its members – the Afrikaans and English press. The agency has a history of serving the interests of its newspaper members – owned by both Afrikaaners and English whites but predominantly the latter. In the 1930s, guidelines for stringers – mostly school teachers and postmasters – included an instruction to ignore news involving 'natives' unless it was an attack by a black on a white. 'That was a specific instruction to ignore black people who make news' (Mark van der Velden, Editor, SAPA). While SAPA news is distributed in English, the rates for Afrikaans newspapers take account of their need to translate. It is an autonomous non-profit making news agency owned by four major groups and independent newspapers. Under their agreement with SAPA, members are required to supply SAPA with news in their area – an arrangement that today (1997) cannot be sustained (see below).

Changes and a New Demand for News in Africa

While Reuters was revitalizing its global business primarily through the development of its financial news services, calls were made from within UNESCO and the developing countries during the 1970s for a more balanced international news flow. The creation of a Non-Aligned News Agencies Pool (NANAP) to improve information exchange between developing countries was one response; other attempts to supplement the main transnational flow of news included Inter Press Service (IPS) a co-operative of independent journalists established in 1964, and the Pan-African News Agency (PANA) established in 1979 and starting operations in 1983. At best, these have been only partially successful. In some ways all of these initiatives may be seen as a response to the problems of immediate post-colonialism and the disillusionment which set in with the realization that political independence had not bought independence from the global economic system.

PANA, Africa's alternative news agency, was set up by the Organization for African Unity, involving the co-operation of 42 African national news services with assistance from UNESCO's International Programme for the Development of Communications (IPDC) and various international donor organizations, with headquarters in Dakar. In addition to its functioning as a news-pool operation, PANA has operated as a standard news agency with its own editorial staff (about 20, in 1990) (see Malam, 1992 for details of the history of PANA). But it has struggled to get off the ground as member countries failed to contribute financially; in 1991 only five countries out of 52 paid in full their contributions; not even the oil-rich members could be counted on. The agency almost always operated at half or even less than half of its projected annual budgetary requirement. It is possible that foreign international organizations had contributed to the agency's sustenance more that the African countries themselves. Even so, there were times when the agency's own staff went unpaid for prolonged periods of time.

The agency's impact on African media was dependent on the variable and sometimes negligible extent to which mainstream client media used its news services. Its definition of news was similar to that found in standard western journalist textbooks so that, unlike IPS, it could not claim to offer a radically different conception of news, although it gave emphasis to stories which it judged would help reinforce 'African unity' and 'co-operation', and was heavily dependent on the feed of stories from African national news agencies, reflecting the interests of the power groups in their respective societies. Indeed the agency's constitution requires it to seek permission before reporting 'domestic' events. Collection and distribution of news was hampered by poor telecommunications, high tariff rates and poor transmission equipment. Computerization of the newsroom (with the aid of IPS) in 1990 put the agency somewhat ahead of many of its clients who were unable to take advantage of the agency's direct transmission of news and features.

In an attempt to solve its financial problems PANA has recently followed a global trend, setting out to 'orient Africa within the framework of the prevailing transition and liberalisation mode'.[2] PANA chief, Bascar Fall, reported that the agency was too dependent on foreign funding, particularly UN agencies.[3] Although PANA was not intended to be a replacement of the international agencies operating in Africa but to provide 'alternative' news for the media of African countries, it sometimes sees itself as in 'competition' with Reuters and Associated Press. To avoid dependency on foreign countries, it is likely that PANA's future transmissions will use existing African telecommunication facilities.[4] Under the 'Recovery Plan' endorsed by OAU Heads of State (July 1992), PANA was to have been privatized by 1996, after three years under transitional management.[5] In 1994 efforts were made to revive the agency, with a workforce of between 30 and 40 correspondents and stringers, cutting translator posts, and expanding its distribution via electronic mail/Internet and satellite systems.[6] PANA's operating budget for 1994–1996 was 4.3 million dollars.[7] By the end of 1996 the agency had 48 permanent correspondents and 48 national news agencies affiliated to it, but governments still held 40% of PANA.[8] Part of the reason given was that where PANA correspondents are not available, such as in remote areas of Tanzania, the national agency is used.[9]

Alternative News in Southern Africa: the Case of Ecna

The great movements of political transition – characteristic of the late 1980s and early 1990s – from communist to capitalist systems in eastern Europe and from military or one-party dictatorships to more pluralistic regimes in parts of Africa and South America, and, in South Africa, from apartheid to a non-racialist democracy – may have opened up new and somewhat different spaces in the organization of global news, with the disappearance or restructuring of some state news agencies and the appearance of competition in previously controlled domestic markets. In South Africa a new form of alternative provision emerged with the establishment of the East Cape News Agencies (Ecna) in the 1980s.

Alternative news played a crucial role in South Africa's fight against apartheid. The 'progressive' news agencies emerged in the 1980s essentially to cover news ignored by the white-dominated commercial press. Mainstream media coverage of the Eastern Cape has been poor and the region – one of South Africa's poorest provinces – was looked upon by mainstream journalists as a 'black hole'. Coverage was left to the local newspapers, mostly urban-based, white-oriented newspapers, with little interest in the black community.[10]

Traditionally, the national news agency, SAPA, has relied on the regional press (the *Dispatch* and the *Eastern Province Herald*) for its stories. Thus SAPA had no flexibility in dealing with specific requests from clients and had to rely on stringers. This formed the incentive for the establishment of Ecna – originally in the form of four local agencies, Pen, Albany News Agency, Veritas and Elnews, which were set up separately in the mid-1980s as independent initiatives.[11] At that time, Ecna was a forum, with the different agencies meeting occasionally to discuss common problems. Although joint ventures were pursued at times, the agencies operated separately. Journalists aimed at consciously opposing the apartheid government and its restrictions on news reporting. They also saw their role as trainers of the underprivileged community and as promoting media development in the black community. During the 1989 state of emergency, Ecna was under much pressure – members were detained, offices burgled – and the agencies nearly closed down. At a time of extreme pressure a decision was taken to set up a central administration and news desk. Reorganization over

1990–1991 led to one organization being created (Ecna) with four branch offices.[12] The centralization process resulted in greater efficiency, increased income, and improved routine. In the early 1990s, Ecna news output consisted of only one cast of the stories on offer for a flat fee. By 1996 the feeling was that the system of sending out news to clients was outdated and a new deal was struck, for the first time, with the national agency, SAPA (see below).

Today Ecna staff members are committed to the ideal of independent and strong, critical news reporting and the agency continues to play a key role in the media with a supply of hard news. Ecna has managed to cultivate a particular niche in the market with its own style of independent news reporting. The alternative agency is not yet a fully fledged commercial organization. With an annual budget of between R600,000–700,000[13] it was until recently dependent on aid organizations for a substantial amount of its income. Over the period 1990–1991 (June) income rose three-fold and has continued to rise. In 1992 the income from the news service was estimated to be a total of R243,784, rising to a total of R345,812 in 1993 and R417,007 in 1994.[14] Ecna produced over 40,000 words per month during the period 1992–1993. The average word length per story is 250.[15] Since 1990 the agency has achieved recognition as a reliable supplier of progressive news to the market. Yet it remains limited financially (small budget), by the size of its workforce, and in terms of production (the volume of stories it can deliver). Like other independent media organizations in South Africa, it has had to come to terms with the drying up of international aid. But it is one of the few independent media organizations that has survived. The agency aims at self-sufficiency while marketing and selling progressive news. Financial income was boosted with the decision of Argus Newspapers (now Independent Newspapers) to take the Ecna news service in 1993. The new client became the biggest subscriber to the news service, while the number of alternative newspaper subscribers declined. Ecna's oldest allies in the alternative press were regular subscribers.[16] The agency also supplies the local press in the Eastern Province region, for example, the *Daily Dispatch* (35,940 readership) and *Eastern Province Herald* (29,767 readership).[17] But with the Argus (Independent) Newspapers accepting the news service and the South African Broadcasting Corporation (SABC) coming on line in 1996, a shift towards the major media organizations and away from smaller clients with different interests (and who pay Ecna less) continues. As Ecna meets the demands of its new mainstream clients, tension is growing among smaller subscribers. It is not clear what 'progressive news' can mean in the post-apartheid era.

Progressive News Reporting: the Goniwe Inquest

As an alternative news agency, Ecna aimed to probe a little further. It sought to reveal stories neglected by the mainstream press or stories which fell outside their concept of news (that is, mainstream newspapers and the national wire service, SAPA). Ecna can offer significantly different stories. It also has a strong background source. An example is the Goniwe inquest, a running story and one of the important stories covered by the agency. The long inquest was consistently on the news diary in 1993 and 1994. To Ecna the Goniwe story was essentially about apartheid security force 'dirty tricks'.[18] The agency covered the story from its inception in true investigative style – something the mainstream media had not done. However, *The Star*, a Johannesburg-based daily which had taken Ecna reports in the past, relied on the international news agency, Reuters, for this story. And only when the story reached its climax in 1997, did the national agency, SAPA, file a report from Port Elizabeth.[19] But daily diaries do not always include stories such as the Goniwe inquest. As mainstream demands are met, a greater variety of stories is supplied. The independent agency is being slowly moulded into providing what the commercial media demand as 'news'. Whether it can continue challenging the new Government of National Unity, which came to power in May 1994, remains to be seen.

Changing Perspectives: Organization Structure and Goals

How long the independent agency can promote its own idea of news and investigative reporting is uncertain. As the organization tries to meet clients' needs it is moving away from the original base it was built on (protest journalism of the 1980s) into open competition in the media market. Mainstream journalists have joined the agency. The working environment is also changing as South Africa moves towards democracy with the distinction between the independent press and the mainstream press becoming more blurred. This is acknowledged by Ecna:

> The fact that we deal so much with mainstream papers now has made a difference to the way we write and what we write about. That is a financial situation. Funding is not going to go on forever. The commercial press links your credibility with your financial situation. (Ecna group manager)

As Ecna deals more with mainstream media, meeting the demands of the commercial market, the organization's goals are shifting. Its definition of 'news' falls more in line with that of the mainstream press. Group editor:

> Many of the stories we do are indifferent – they don't matter much, they are light stories. In term of our positioning we have to do these stories. That is a commercial argument. In terms of credibility, long-term survival, we have to do those stories. We have to establish ourselves as a credible and comprehensive news service.

The essential difference between Ecna and the mainstream press lies in the type of treatment given to a specific news story. The independent agency looks for an interesting angle to the story and for those stories not covered by the mainstream press. The purpose is to get regional issues picked up by the national newspapers. Feeding through stories of local community issues and social concern to the mainstream media can only be successful once Ecna has achieved full credibility. Such credibility entails not only providing regular stories but including stories acceptable to clients (for example, the 'light stories'). 'It is at moments like that that our continued relevance becomes visible' says Ecna group editor, Franz Kruger (now with South African Broadcasting Corporation Radio). This approach appears to conflict with earlier Ecna objectives of being 'responsive to what people saw as important'.[20] But according to the group editor the move from protest journalism to a more commercially centred operation has not meant the agency dropping its investigative principles. Franz Kruger argues: 'Our job is to take the issues we care about and make them usable by mainstream papers'. Ecna argues that its approach makes for better journalists with better contacts and a better understanding of developments. However, news gathering to Ecna is now a commercial operation planned with competition and profit in mind.

Democratization – Undermining Ecna

As South Africa entered a new phase of democratization – the first free general election took place in 1994 – Ecna was faced with mounting problems. Production was held back by bad administration and insufficient use of resources. A lack of clarity as to its future role weakened the organization further, with low morale among its workers. Ecna's turnover of staff remains high. Shifting patterns of ownership in the press added to the pressure.[21] The climax was reached in 1995 when the agency was faced with maladministration, personality clashes, and a funding loss of R400,000 – a situation described as 'chaotic' by the new group editor, Mike Loewe, in conversation with the author in 1996. The agency's Veritas branch closed down in mid-1995. Ecna now has no office in Bisho, the capital of the Eastern Cape and the seat of local government, while some mainstream newspapers are now reporting directly from Bisho. However it has since established a new office at Umatata, Transkei.

Ecna's survival attempts included broadening its client base and stimulating more commercially driven, urban-centred news. The agency increasingly relied more on the output of stringers for news gathering. But the budget forecast for 1995 predicted a shortfall of R500,000. It needed to more than double its income over 12 months. The agency opted to double the subscription rate for the standard news service. It also embarked on a major retrenchment while intensifying its drive for further income from the news service. The organization suffered a severe loss through the movement of most of its black journalists into the mainstream media. This weakened its links with the black community. By 1996 it now had a mostly white, male-dominated workforce, as many of its reporters, especially black reporters, had been attracted to better paid jobs in mainstream media or in government offices and jobs of conscience such as the Truth and Reconciliation Commission and Human Rights Commission. Ecna's workforce dropped from 16 in 1993 to 11 in 1996. Whereas in 1993 there were seven women employees, by 1996 there were only three. In 1993, out of eight reporters, seven had been black. In 1996 only one black reporter remained on the staff. Although the number of Ecna trainees had doubled, from five in 1994 to 10 in 1995, the training scheme was no longer a long-term goal given cuts in foreign funding and other financial problems.

Structurally, the agency moved away from a system of 'working committees' towards a vertical top-down decision-making organization. Political change in the country also impacted on Ecna's news supply. Prior to South Africa's general election in 1994 stories were written on the problems of the separate Ciskei and Transkei, skulduggery, and on the 'Third Force'. After the election the Bantustans were incorporated into the greater Eastern Cape. Thus there was a shift in news emphasis from hard political stories to a new local government with new problems. The agency's investigative work continued, with a contribution to the Truth and Reconciliation Commission. Following on the takeover of Argus by Independent Newspapers, a further shake-up in the print industry has occurred, with deals being struck between previously politically opposed groups and an increasing number of black consortiums and trade unions acquiring media interests.

The latest changes are aimed at creating a commercially viable organization but are bad news for development journalism. According to group manager Loewe, it is 'hard to find a paying market for that [investigative] kind of report'. So the general trend continues: as the agency broadens its client base it is forced to cover more news events covered by local mainstream media and SAPA. Ecna now provides news for investors. And with the ANC now in power, Ecna has lost its exclusive access to its source. It must now compete with the general media. It is not clear how long Ecna will retain its niche in the market for its news service.

SAPA Undermined

As Ecna tried to come to terms with its radically changing environment, the morale of SAPA staff suffered considerably, and complaints within the organization over the running of the national agency added to calls for a new structure. Increased pressures led to threats of closure (in early 1995, SAPA's board issued a denial that closure of the agency was imminent). As SAPA's member newspapers experienced increasing financial difficulty, board members insisted that the agency spend less on staff, keep operational costs down, close foreign bureaux in order to achieve large savings (SAPA's London bureau closed after 53 years in 1991) and cut staff in the former homelands of South Africa.[22] Requests to the board for more extensive provincial coverage were rejected: SAPA remains in a weak position for coverage of provincial affairs. Arguably, SAPA's organization may be at fault – national agency coverage deteriorated because individual newspaper members of SAPA withheld their copy from it.[23]

As the country entered a new phase of democracy, the powerful global agency Reuters took advantage of the changing situation. In 1995 Reuters shocked the national agency SAPA when it relinquished its partnership with the domestic agency.[24] The global agency expanded its operations in the domestic South African market, improving its Johannesburg base to cover Southern Africa. Operating from its main bureau in Johannesburg – the 'hub' of Southern Africa – the international agency now had the most advanced infrastructure available on the African continent (Reuters celebrated 100 years in Johannesburg, South Africa, in November 1995). Up to June 1995 SAPA continued to distribute incoming general news, but Reuters was able to sell its economic news wire directly to banks and other financial houses. Reuters' strategy was to build up a new domestic wire service in South Africa, while it continued to receive the SAPA wire. While Harare is the main Reuters office in the region of Southern Africa, Johannesburg accounts for over 50% of the revenue from the region.[25] The advantage of the Johannesburg location is good communication infrastructure.[26] None of the other international news agencies has a domestic economic service in South Africa to match that of Reuters.[27] The domestic news agency, SAPA, cannot compare with the business and financial scope of information offered by Reuters. Competitors such as AFP and AP in South Africa do not have an integrated television system with bureaux whereas Reuters' main office in Johannesburg is closely integrated with its bureaux. While Reuters aims to provide clients in South Africa and other clients particularly interested in events in South Africa (for example financial institutions in London, New York, Frankfurt, Paris, Tokyo) with quick, accurate, real-time business information on that country, there are few Reuters clients in Africa because, it is argued, there are few big investment funds that have money to risk in an emerging market.[28]

The implications of Reuters' expansion in Southern Africa are serious for the South African national agency, SAPA. First, the loss of clients: SAPA's annual contract with SABC – described by the editor as 'substantial income' of R1.7 million – ended at the end of 1995 (that is September, the end of SABC's financial year). SABC decided to renegotiate the SAPA contract for one year and repeated the arrangement in 1996. Despite drawn-out negotiation the two organizations failed to reach an agreement and in April 1997 SAPA ended its service to SABC.[29] Second, a firmer and longer arrangement is crucial to SAPA's fight to strengthen its position against Reuters in the domestic market. Losing the SABC contract could severely affect SAPA. Although it may be renewed in the short term, it is clear that Reuters is now available as an alternative domestic source and will also aim at the emerging new radio stations in South Africa and the sub-Saharan region. Third, Reuters' control of the African market adds to the competitive threat domestically and limits SAPA's export potential. Fourth, the survival of SAPA in its own country is directly threatened. Reuters' main international competitor in South Africa is Associated Press, which has now grown closer to SAPA, as the two agencies have mutual interests in beating Reuters. The American agency's television news was set up in South Africa in 1994, luring Reuters' television staffers to join the opposing side. Both agencies have established global video news services.[30]

SAPA is an 'African' agency selling a new type of news to its neighbouring states. With the end of apartheid, South Africa is looked upon by those states as more accessible, a hope, and an identity for the continent's future. SAPA sees itself as the only independent – not government owned or controlled – national news agency in Africa. It has arrangements with other African agencies: a co-operation agreement with Botswana's agency, BOPA, an exchange agreement with ZIANA (Zimbabwe), it is negotiating with NAMPA (Namibia), ANGOP (Angola) and PANA on future deals. It serves SAPA's longer-term interests to develop relationships with these agencies.[31] How the state-controlled agencies like ANGOP are going to respond to the new situation developing in Africa remains to be seen.[32] Given the new demand for development news, SAPA could also shift its stance. Whether SAPA will retain its independence is too early to say. SAPA, as it stands at present, is hamstrung – it is the South African newspapers that will determine future agency policy. Recent changes in the Argus Group (now Independent Newspapers) indicate a leaner, possibly profit-making company as opposed to the trust company of today. SAPA is interested in PANA's new satellite distribution system for Africa, in contributing to the African service and providing South African subscribers with African news, and because it has the potential for regional pooling of news. Given PANA's poor record, such development is likely to take some time before the South African national agency is prepared to commit itself to PANA. What are the possibilities of a future Southern African pool system of news developing? On SAPA's side it feels it would not gain financially – that in fact it has more to lose: Von Gils, SAPA manager, says, 'people think South Africa is the economic powerhouse of the continent, that SAPA is a rich news agency. It is very much the contrary. In fact we are a poor news agency, financially speaking'.[33]

As South Africa goes through an overhaul of apartheid structures, there is on-going debate about the continued existence of the national agency. Coupled with that are the current statements of various government spokesmen/women, criticizing the press for misinforming the public about government progress on the post-apartheid Reconstruction and Development Plan (upliftment of social/economic standards and black empowerment).[34] They also claim that the government body, South African Communication Service (SACS), should be overhauled and possibly be turned into a government news agency to address the imbalance of news reports and to turn out 'quality government news'.[35] According to Sol Kotane, head of SACS, 'news' is not a means of control – it is 'a service'.[36] He questions whether the current national agency SAPA 'is enough'.[37] At the time of writing, further criticism of the national agency is being considered by Parliament where there are complaints that there is a 'poor news flow' from and to regions and that SAPA, although seen as 'neutral', has limited resources.[38]

Southern Africa's Future Prospects for Alternative News

Bearing in mind PANA's history, it is not surprising that many observers hold a sceptical view of its future outcome. Persistent problems include:

Finance: The agency has been 'severely hampered'[39] by non-payment of dues, and calls are still made for member states to fulfil their financial obligations to PANA and pay their arrears.[40] And a grim warning is given if the recovery scheme should fail: 'The repercussions would not only reflect on Africa, but will also affect its image and credibility'.[41] PANA chief, Bascar Fall, reported that at least three top officials were not paid by the agency but received remuneration from a UN agency and the European Community.[42] Two years later, journalists at PANA's headquarters in Dakar, Senegal, went on strike over non-payment of wage arrears and whether the agency 'had a future'.[43] Recently, Fall appealed to OAU and UNESCO to 'make a final decision' on whether to continue PANA, noting that member countries owed contribution arrears of up to US $31 million.[44]

Identity: Will the privatization of PANA lead to a loss of its African identity? African heads of state believe that the privatization of PANA 'would not in any way affect its African identity'. At the African ministers of information meeting in South Africa, one full day was spent debating PANA's effectiveness 'as an ideological tool to further the aims of a united Africa'.[45]

Political: Do member states have the political will to support the new scheme and to what extent do they identify with liberalization/pluralistic concepts? Of 48 least-developed countries (LCDs) about a third, mostly African, are afflicted by political turmoil.[46] It should also be noted that the Thatcher government exported pluralist democracy to developing countries – British government offices during the 1980s campaigned/advised developing countries to adopt pluralist values and privatization.

Economic: Are African member states capable of backing the revamped PANA financially? According to Unctad 48, LCDs – 33 of which are in Africa – are fighting a losing battle for survival. Despite a 2.2% increase in 1995 of the aggregate gross domestic product of African LCDs, economic growth is hampered by rising debts.[47] The total outstanding external debt of the 48 LCDs amounted to US $127 billion at the end of 1993, compared with 117 billion in 1990.[48]

Organization: Through privatization the goals of PANA are altered – from being state-run with goals serving African governments, to being a privatized company aiming at profits and serving the needs of a variety of shareholders. Some African states have expressed concern with the privatization process, particularly with regard to the 'right of participation' of voluntary organizations.

Given the powerful position of Reuters in South Africa, the apparent increase in local newspaper usage of Reuters' domestic wire copy, SAPA's financial burdens, and the fact that Ecna is struggling to adjust under new conditions, it seems the prospects of alternative/community media are not strong. Despite the expansion of IPS (Inter Press Service) into Africa and its attempts to bolster alternative news operations through improvement of telecommunication infrastructure and a drive to democratize communications, there is still a long way to go before alternative news is able to penetrate the formal markets.[49] There is no doubt *potential* for growth in alternative news. But how quickly and how far alternative news will develop is not clear. Larger, established organizations are likely to exploit the emerging market. For example, with the new dawn of community radio in South Africa, SAPA recently set up its National Radio Service (NRS) as an independent operating division in June 1995 aimed in the long term at increasing SAPA's overall income.[50] A new radio desk was established in Grahamstown (February 1996) and a contract signed with the SABC.[51] A year later it closed down – Ecna's radio coordinator was 'bought off' by a private station.[52] Community radio stations in the Eastern Cape lack funds and cannot afford to pay for voice pieces.[53] And they will take some time to become established as reliable stations. Little infrastructure exists to distribute community news – Ecna struggled with its own news service, trying to get news out quickly to clients.[54] Realizing that there was a need for community news in the changing environment, negotiations held between Ecna and the Independent Development Trust led to the creation of the Development News Agency (DNA).[55] Its purpose is to deal specifically with development issues for community papers nationwide. Set up under the auspices of Ecna, the DNA had its own funding base and was therefore not a financial drain on Ecna resources.[56] Although separate from Ecna, DNA was not an independent entity – it used the same trustees as Ecna. It saw itself more as an NGO than a news agency, but efforts were made to make DNA more self-sustainable – to have a commercial function, selling development stories to subscribers. The drying up of donor funds has led to increased efforts to make the organization more commercially viable. It will now concentrate on schemes to make money.[57] Community Business Initiative, aimed at supplying news to broadcasting and print sectors in the Eastern Cape, is run by DNA (six community radio stations and six community newspapers): through various training projects it aims to build the news network 'through business strategies', providing business skills which include advertising.

Meanwhile, under pressure for a speedier service, Ecna has signed an agreement with the national agency SAPA (1996). This agreement involves co-operation leading to an improvement in Ecna's distribution. There is to be speedier delivery of news, wider promotion of the regional agency, and a potentially wider market available to Ecna via SAPA. However, the advantages to SAPA outweigh those of Ecna: the national agency now is able to monitor freely events in the Eastern Cape put out by Ecna wire (SAPA only pays if it uses Ecna stories); Ecna is now dependent on the national agency for distribution. It is a compromise situation, particularly in terms of news values and newsworthiness. SAPA may use Ecna reporters as stringers; there is a possibility that Ecna could be absorbed by the national agency with its superior resources; Ecna's style and approach to stories could move closer to the SAPA style. In the long term SAPA hopes to circumvent its news-gathering problem in the Eastern Cape by drawing Ecna closer to its general operational network, which would be a 'good investment'.

Conclusion

The forces of globalization and liberalization on the one hand may promote a more diverse media system but not necessarily enhance democracy and a freer flow of information. The main flow of news is still driven by the big players despite the efforts of the alternative agencies such as IPS and Ecna.

It is clear that there are major difficulties in ensuring a more equitable supply of news in Southern Africa: first, PANA has a significant challenge in developing a workable and efficient organization supplying news; second, South Africa's domestic agency SAPA suffers from a broken relationship with the global agency Reuters, poor resources, and is adjusting not only to a new government but internally as ownership in the press changes; and third, Ecna/ECN (see below) appears to be a serious attempt at alternative news provision with a niche market for news – yet it faces stiffer and more direct competition as it expands into the broader market, and is already compromising through new demands of news and its new deals with SAPA. Whether Ecna/ECN and SAPA will manage to turn changes to their advantage is too early to say.

Postscript

Significant developments in early 1997 confirm Ecna's move from a trust-controlled organization towards a commercial company. Various pressures – including the loss of key administrative staff, internal pressure from DNA and a mounting financial crisis (a continuation of the previous year) – reached a climax. By June 1997 Ecna was virtually bankrupt and the Ecna trust met for the last time. DNA was separated from Ecna, reflecting an ideological split between the two organizations. Ecna changed to a registered company, the agency being renamed East Cape News (ECN). 'We felt we were not Ecna any more', says Mike Loewe, group editor.

This shift is also reflected (a) in the distribution of lead stories and the decline of the alternative press: in 1992 there were seven Ecna lead stories all in the alternative newspaper, *Mail and Guardian* (ECN, interview, September 1997); (b) in its changing relationships with the mainstream press. In addition to linking up with the national distributor of domestic news, SAPA, the agency is concentrating on 'group deals', where a single agreement is signed with the overall newspaper group rather than with individual newspapers; (c) structurally, with the chairman of the new ECN board based in Johannesburg 'with a good link with media trends' (Mike Loewe, group editor, ECN). Despite its weaknesses, Ecna/ECN, has managed to develop a weekend service (the biggest supply from January to September 1997 going to *Weekend Argus* (62 stories), and *City Press* (45) and *Sunday Tribune* (36) – source, ECN).

The Ecna training programme was taken over by DNA, now a new trust, Development Media Agency Trust (DMA). DMA is currently run by three freelancers. 'We don't believe in a standardized news service', says Rod Amner, DMA news editor. Its emphasis is on community news and community training for the emerging community radio stations.

TABLE 9.1   *SAPA bureaux and reporters*

SAPA bureaux	Reporters
Cape Town (city)	2
Parliament Cape Town	7
Johannesburg	30
Durban	1
Bloemfontein (Appeal Court)	1
Pretoria	1 (usually 2)
Pietersburg	1
Windhoek, Namibia	1

TABLE 9.2   *Major international agencies vs national agency*

Agency	SAPA	Reuters	AP	AFP	Ecna
Bureaux	6	3	3	3	4
Full-time reporters and editorial staff	44	23	19	8	10

Notes

1. A South African newspapers' syndicate, South African Amalgamated Press Agency, formed in 1908, aimed to supply cabled news from London to South Africa, but lasted one year.

2. Intergoverment Council for Communication in Africa, ICC/Res. 3, Resolution on the Legal Status of the Pan African News Agency (PANA), Sun City, South Africa, 3 October 1994.

3. SAPA report, 4 October 1994.

4. IMC/Draft/Res. 5: Draft Resolution on PANA Transmission Facilities proposed by South Africa, Sun City, South Africa, 4/6 October 1994. African
institutions are expected to conduct stock-taking exercises to evaluate capacities
that could be utilized; African telecommunications and expertise will be used before
non-African entities are engaged; where PANA management seeks external expert
advice, that advice will be sought from citizens of member states of the OAU, funded
from the PANA budget rather than through donations. Through the use of the satellite television transmission system of three African countries – Egypt, Tunisia and
South Africa – PANA will access most of Africa. Distribution is via the web page,
Internet, or alternatively from modem-to-modem or point-to-point communications.

5. Intergovernmental Council for Communication in Africa (ICC)/Res. 2, Resolution on the Activities and Budget Programme of PANA for 1994/95, Sun City,
South Africa, 3 October 1994. The scheme was backed by the European Union and
UNESCO who provided finance for technical aspects of the scheme. The projected
budget for 1995 was set at US \$4.3 million. Shares were offered over a two-year
period (1994–1996) on a proportionate basis to agencies, member states, NGOs and
financial institutions: 25% to member states and 25% to OAU, with the remaining
50% to African organizations and the national private sector – Intergovernmental
Council for Communication in Africa (ICC), Res. 3, Resolution on the Legal Status
of the Pan African News Agency (PANA), Sun City, South Africa, 3 October 1994;
IMC/Draft/Res. 6 and 7.

6. SAPA report 4 October 1994; Free Press, MISA, Oct./Nov. 1994, p. 16. The
new structure consists of PANA Foundation, PANAPRESS Ltd and PANA Communications Ltd. Sources indicate PANAPRESS Ltd shareholders consist of 60%
from the private sector and 40% by the public sector. PANA Communications Ltd
has a shareholding of: 51% PANAPRESS Ltd; 40% for African telecommunications
companies; and 9% for African financial institutions – source: PANA, Dakar,
Senegal, 27 June 1994.

7. ICC/Rpt VI, Report of the 6th Ordinary Session of the Intergovernmental
Council for Communication in Africa, Sun City, South Africa, 10 October 1994.
Since April 1993 PANA's volume of production increased from 2,000 words per day
to 10,000 words per day. By October 1994 it reached a level of between 35,000 and
40,000 words per day – Report of the Activities of the Coordinator-General of the
Pan African News Agency, PANA, ICC Rpt VI, Sun City, South Africa, 3 October
1994. By 1996 it produced 52,000 words per day in English and French (Arabic and
Portuguese are to be added in 1997) – PANA, Dakar, Senegal, telephone interview.

8. PANA, Dakar, Senegal, telephone interview, 1996.

9. Ibid.

10. *Sunday Times*, the biggest weekly South African newspaper, placed a reporter
in the region only in late 1993.

11. Veritas was established at King William's Town in 1982; in 1986 Elnews and
Pen agencies were set up at East London and Port Elizabeth respectively, followed
by the Albany News Agency at Grahamstown the following year.

12. Billing was centralized and all salaries paid from the head office in Grahamstown, Eastern Cape. A news editor was employed, allowing the group editor to
pursue other tasks such as individual coaching of journalists, besides his managerial
role.

13. Source: Ecna annual report, 1993.

14. Source: Ecna annual reports, 1992–1995.

15. Print production in 1993 was an overall total of 1,725 hard news stories, 279
features and 107 sports stories.

16. They included *Mail and Guardian, New (Sunday) Nation, Umafrika, Imvo*.
Clients in the mainstream press include the *Argus, Cape Times, Pretoria News,
Sowetan, The Star, Sunday Tribune, City Press, Daily News, Natal Mercury, Natal*

Witness and *Post*. *The Star*, a daily, has a 60.18% share of the greater Johannesburg area and 11.18% share of the national market, while its sister paper, the *Sowetan*, has 18.85% (Johannesburg) and 49.18% (national) share (*The Star*, 13 June 1994). Other major Ecna subscribers are the *City Press*, a Sunday paper with a readership of 232,518 and *Die Burger*, a daily with a Research Foundation, SAARF. Up to 1996 Ecna supplied 30- to 40-second pieces and 5-minute packaged pieces of radio news gathered around the province. Major radio clients included the commercial Gauteng station, Radio 702, and its affiliate Broadcast Resources, and their competitors, Network Radio News, a SAPA affiliate, SABC, Namibia Broadcasting Corporation, BBC Focus on Africa.

17. Source: All Media and Products Survey 1993 (AMPS).

18. The story of the so-called 'Cradock Four', Mathew Goniwe, Fort Calata, Sparrow Mkonto and Sicelo Mhlauti, goes back to June 1985 when the four political activists were found murdered in the Bluewater Bay area of Port Elizabeth. The first inquest, conducted by a magistrate, concluded that the men had been killed by unknown persons. In May 1992 the progressive press revealed that a top-secret military signal carried the order that the Cradock Four be permanently 'removed' from society, implying the South African Defence Force had carried out the killings (*New Nation*, May 1992). Judgement given on 28 May 1994, seen as one of the most important in South African legal history, found the South African security force (police and military) guilty of killing Goniwe (*Sunday Times*, *City Press*, 29 May 1994). And Ecna was credited with the lead front-page story on the final verdict in *City Press* (a national Sunday newspaper read mostly by blacks).

19. The Truth Commission's Amnesty hearings by former security policemen revealed the identities of the killers of Mathew Goniwe – *Business Day*, *The Star*, and *Citizen*, 29 January 1997.

20. Kruger, quoted in Forbes (1989: 93).

21. Four journalists left in 1994, including the editor and group editor. An Elnews reporter moved to *Pretoria News* after being offered a 'lucrative' salary in May. SAPA also made offers to Ecna staff. By June 1994 the group editor had left for SABC. A change in editor means a whole adjustment of relationships along the news gathering side. Continual movement of Ecna staff within the industry, moving up into the major media, together with the fact that Ecna-trained staff tend to leave for more lucrative jobs at SABC, *The Star*, Radio Transkei, etc., is a weakness. In 1997 two experienced reporters were 'bought off' by a commercial radio station.

22. In 1972 there were 112 SAPA staffers of whom 90 were journalists (and 32 were telex operators). The number of full-time journalists dropped to 60 in 1992–1993, and to 44 in 1996 (interview with ex-SAPA editor, E. Linnington, 1996).

23. SAPA is a highly centralized, non-profit, co-operative organization, with 68% of its workforce in the main Johannesburg bureau. The majority of the workforce is white, and only 8% black. The vertical structure is cumbersome and hampers the development of the organization. The board includes the English groups of Argus (Independent Newspapers) and Times Media Ltd, and the Afrikaans Nasionale Pers and Perskor and independent titles. The traditional Afrikaans–English divide is further complicated by the recent changes in ownership of the national press. The board argues that the newspapers around the country should supply news to SAPA. But most member newspapers are not giving their news to SAPA as required under the Articles of Association – that within their franchise zone news of spontaneous origin within 120 km of a newspaper should be given to SAPA for distribution to other areas. SAPA undertakes not to return that news to any of the originator's direct competitors.

24. The Reuters–SAPA relationship came to an end after more than 50 years. The original arrangement included the exclusive distribution (Reuters news) contract to the South African market. In 1992, the contract was renegotiated for a further three years. Reuters wanted to market its wire *directly* in the country, rather than through

an exclusive arrangement with SAPA. Thus a new contract was drawn up removing the exclusive clause. Referring to its domestic service, the international agency says, 'Reuters reports South Africa for South Africa' (source: Reuters).

25. Source: Reuters.

26. Under apartheid this was not possible because of political restrictions and boycotts. Full-time stringers are located in Namibia, Botswana, Malawi and Mozambique. Part-time stringers are in Lesotho and Swaziland. Reuters' head office in Johannesburg has 14 journalists. Two other key centres are located at Cape Town (two reporters) and Durban (one reporter) (source: Reuters).

27. Reuters is the only international news provider in South Africa which provides a domestic, economic service which appeals to most banks and brokers.

28. Reuters interview, 1996.

29. According to the contract, payment is split between SABC Television (TNP) and SABC Radio (*The Star*, *Citizen*, 28 May 1997).

30. AP clients include Sky TV, CNN, BBC World Service.

31. For example, ANGOP staff recently spent about two months at SAPA head office studying the agency's procedures (source: SAPA).

32. ANGOP policy has been essentially political – the journalist is seen to have a direct role in raising the consciousness of the people and the syllabuses of the courses included 'political education' (Forbes, 1989: 74).

33. Interview, 1995.

34. *Mail and Guardian*, 26 May 1995; *The Star*, 15 November 1995.

35. *Mail and Guardian*, 4 April 1996.

36. *Mail and Guardian*, 7 June 1996.

37. Ibid.

38. COMTASK (Communication Task Group) Executive Summary report, November 1996, included in its recommendations on restructuring the South African Communications Service the creation of a government 'news service' to local communities in the country (Rec. 50).

39. Thabo Mbeki, South African deputy president speaking at the OAU Conference of African Ministers of Information meeting, Sun City, South Africa, 10 April 1994.

40. Forty-seven per cent of contributions were recovered in 1993. Progress in implementing the Recovery Plan was 'seriously impeded' in 1994 with only 13% of contributions received, forcing the agency to resort to bank overdrafts – IMC/Draft/Report VII, Sun City, South Africa, 4/6 October 1994.

41. ICC/Res. 2, Resolution on the Activities and Budget of PANA for 1994/95, Sun City, South Africa, 3 October 1994.

42. SAPA, 4 October 1994.

43. Reuters, reported in *The Star*, 13 September 1996.

44. Reuters, reported in *The Star*, 13 September 1996.

45. SAPA, 4 October 1994.

46. Unctad, in *The Star*, 18 April 1996.

47. *The Star*, 18 April 1996.

48. Ibid.

49. IPS has agreements with PANA, MISA (Media Institute of Southern Africa) and SABA (Southern African Broadcasting Association) – see de Costa (1995).

50. NRS supplies national and international news to almost 40 community radio stations (source: SAPA, NRS, 1996).

51. This contract – worth R6,000 per month – is renewable annually (source: Ecna Radio Coordinator, interview, 1996).

52. Ecna Radio Coordinator, interview, 1996.

53. Ecna only recently found a solution to the problem by making an agreement with SAPA and allowing Ecna to distribute news more speedily. Ecna reports to community organizations were very occasional. It did supply information in the form

of news clippings on the Eastern Cape (drawn from the media with the Border Rural Committee) to local community groups which ended in 1995.

54. DNA, January 1995.

55. DNA provides a news network for the South African community media (about 18 community newspapers) as well as acting as a vehicle for media training (editorial, training service, and needs assessment). It also distributes community news/features to its members and to the commercial press (for example, *City Press* and *Farmers' Weekly*).

56. Under the current agreement, funding levels for DNA come down (July 1996) as the staff complement increases (from two to three).

57. DNA, interview, 1996. Eastern Cape's first development news 12-page supplement provided by DNA is produced in the *Daily Dispatch* and *Eastern Province Herald*. It feels news reportage has a limited impact as an educative tool, because it seldom conveys information which can be used in a practical way by the reader.

References ·

Blumler, J.G. (1992) 'News media in flux: an analytical afterword', in *Journal of Communication*, 42 (3), Summer.

Boyd-Barrett, O. and Thussu, K. (1992) *Contra-flow in Global News: International and Regional News Exchange Mechanisms*, London: John Libbey.

de Costa, P. (1995) 'Inter Press Service towards the year 2000', *Media Development*, No. 4.

Ehlers, C. (1993) 'Newspapers of the future: a marriage of marketing and meaning', *Rhodes Review*, December: 54–5.

Forbes, D. (1989) 'Training of journalism for developing countries', unpublished paper.

Forbes, D. (1994) 'Black advancement: an investigation into the training of journalists in the mainstream and independent press of South Africa', unpublished paper.

Forbes, D. (1995) 'SAPA – national news agency of South Africa', unpublished paper.

Forbes, D. (1996) 'Alternative news – the East Cape news agencies', unpublished paper.

Forbes, D (1996) 'Recent changes in Southern African media', unpublished paper.

Gurevitch, M. and Blumler, I.G. (1977) *Linkages between the Mass Media and Politics: a model for analysis of political communication systems, in Mass Media and Society*, J. Curran, M. Gurevitch and J. Woolacott (eds), London: Edward Arnold and Open University.

Jackson, G.S. (1993) *Breaking Story: The South African Press*, San Francisco: Westview Press Inc.

Malam, Mustapha (1992) 'Study of the Pan-African News Agency', Ph.D. dissertation, City University, London.

Malam, Mustapha (1996) 'NWICO and the "alternative agencies". An analysis of the Pan African News Agency (PANA)', unpublished paper, University of Maiduguri, Nigeria.

Musa, M. (1990) 'News agencies, transnationalization and the new order', in *Media, Culture and Society*, 12: 325–42.

Pinnock, D. (1992) 'It's time to bury "Alternative"', *Rhodes Review*, December: 49–51.

Read, D. (1992) *The Power of News: The History of Reuters*, Oxford: Oxford University Press.

Steinmann, B. (1994) 'A news service by children in Switzerland', *Media Development*, No. 1.

Storey, G. (1951) *Reuters' Century 1851–1951*, London: Max Parrish.
Tomaselli, K. and Louw, P.E. (1991) *The Alternative Press in South Africa*, London: James Currey.

Documents

Ecna Annual Report, 1991/2
Ecna Annual Report, 1992/3
Ecna Annual Report, 1994/5
Ecna Working Committee Reports 1990–1994
Ecna Group Editor's Reports 1990–1994

Part III

DEFINING NEWS: CONTESTATION AND CONSTRUCTION

Introduction

Oliver Boyd-Barrett and Terhi Rantanen

In this part we have set out to explore in some further detail and with more specific reference to news agency content, how it is that the news agencies have contributed to the prevailing western-originated concept of 'news', and then to look at attempts to establish news agendas and forms of organizing the delivery of news that challenge the dominant model. The three chapters of this part each separately stake out different terrains in this broad, important and very under-researched topic.

Following the argument of Musa (1997) we should say immediately that what distinguishes 'alternative' from 'mainstream' is not necessarily anything to do with size or scope of a news agency. Some small national news agencies, even when established with ambitious 'alternative' objectives in mind, seem in practice to share precisely the same premises, concepts and practices of news gathering as the established, western, mainstream agencies. Equally, a large international agency such as Inter Press Service (which is discussed in chapter 12) has a very distinctive philosophy of news, and is dedicated principally to serving the interests of the developing world. Or again, depending on definitions of 'development' it is possible that the developmental potential of some of the services of the major western-based agencies have been understudied and undervalued in the literature – which has tended to focus on 'hard general news' and print news, to the exclusion of other categories, including finance news, feature services, and video news services (which are discussed in chapters 5 and 6). Finally, even what counts as 'alternative' may change over time. In the earlier years of the development of the Eurovision News Exchange, for example, there was insufficient awareness, generally, of how this could constitute a public service style model, one that could challenge the increasingly powerful commercial models. We had to experience the consequences of media deregulation, liberalization and commodification to really begin to see its significance.

In his contribution to this section, Michael Palmer in chapter 11 looks at how the agencies have contributed to the development of western news practices, and at how they monitor, evaluate and codify approved practices or the 'canons' of journalism, which are related, in turn, to client requirements and the commodification of news. He compares the way in which the agencies reacted to problems encountered during coverage of Russia across two periods of considerable unrest in Russian history, 1904–1906 and 1989–1991. Of especial interest from 1904–1906 is the chronicle of how the agencies balanced the conflicting demands and practices of their own correspondents, competitor–client 'sensationalist' newspaper foreign correspondents, the official Russian news agency (both in Russia itself and in overseas bureaux), embassy sources, and clients. Reuters and Havas are seen attempting to instruct the Russian news agency in western news values of speed, accuracy and presentation, and trying to maintain a reputation for credibility in a highly competitive environment within which they themselves are not necessarily above corruption (for example, Havas dealt in the sale of its clients' advertising space, which the Russian government was prepared to buy). This is an unusual and significant study which opens a window on the very processes of the construction of what we now recognize as primordial western news values and news style. The only comparable windows we find in the literature tend to be ethnographic accounts of contemporary practice, but it is very rare to find good historical examples, especially ones that can encompass both the political economy and the textual components.

In the more confident and established environment of the 1980s the problem of competition is compounded by information glut which further accentuates the importance of supplying news that has 'impact' in client media. The agencies now appoint experienced journalists to monitor and evaluate their own services and those of their competitors. In addition to providing statistical 'impact charts' which monitor client usage of copy, these quality controllers are typically concerned with speed, accuracy, presentation and content. They also look at how well the story weaves together different sub-plots or themes, links together both domestic and international angles, whether it succeeds in etching vivid memories through effective headlines and leads, and they are tolerant, in appropriate context, of 'interpretative leads' and 'throw-forward angles'. They pass comments on logistics of coverage, and try to adopt the perspective of end-users.

It is against the established strength, global influence, and taken-for-granted solidity of such well-resourced, professional but essentially formulaic ideas about what constitutes 'news' that attempts to innovate different news agendas must battle. IPS (Inter Press Service) is probably still the largest and most credible of all 'alternatives' in the world of news agencies. In chapter 12, Giffard recounts its early history, its co-operative non-profit structure, its links with South America and UN agencies. He argues that the agency still confirms its radical credentials convincingly: its news service is dominated (three-quarters) by news of the developing world, in terms of topics, countries, sources and actors. It supplies services and manages projects on behalf of third world media and UN agencies which are serving the third world. The statistics of its global representation and of the usage of its services are impressive, even though in size it is still dwarfed by the major players. None the less, it has faced grave difficulties in recent years. These include a decline in the availability of aid (and the diversion of aid to eastern Europe), either directly to IPS or to its clients for purchase of IPS services; the increasing 'irrelevance' of the third world concept, following on the collapse of the cold war, at least in the minds of some western strategists and aid givers; the loss of what had been substantial aid from The Netherlands lottery, following disagreements as to long-term strategy between The Netherlands and IPS executive; declining demand for IPS telecommunications services in the wake of deregulation and the Internet. These economic problems have increased pressure on individual bureaux which are now encouraged to operate as businesses, gaining local revenue in order to offset local costs. In the meantime IPS believes that on-line services may offer a future source of new income. At the present time, however, complete self-sustainability is not considered a likely possibility.

In all, therefore, the prospects of 'alternative' provision still continue to look fragile and it seems that even though there is always likely to be scope and demand for such provision, it will continue to have only a relatively marginal status in the world of information and news providers. This is not to deny that even small initiatives can be very influential – Gemini News Service, based in London, for example. But it is possibly towards some of the older public service models, where these have managed to survive, that we should look for more ambitious developments. We can count IPS among these and, as Stig Hjarvard argues in chapter 13, we should also take account of the geopolitical regional video news exchanges between public service broadcasters; pre-eminent among these is Eurovision, followed by Asiavision, Arabvision and Afrovision.

Hjarvard focuses his attention on news coverage of the Eurovision news exchange, which he claims is a specifically European public service model, now fruitfully exported to other world regions, and which has also provided a conduit for electronic distribution of commercial news agency footage to European public broadcasters. As a consequence of satellite, however, the commercial agencies no longer require this conduit, and this threatens the future of the exchange. Hjarvard examines a central challenge of this model to its members – that they establish a degree of homogenization of news criteria. Outside of Europe this is still far from being resolved, where members differ as to what constitutes a threat to state interests, religious and other concerns about decency and propriety, and what they mean by 'development' news. Although individual nations may change, they do not move at the same pace or in the same direction. Hjarvard notes how the demands of member broadcasters sometimes impose pressure on state sources to be more co-operative and open to international demands for information than they would otherwise be. Most regions of the world interact only with Eurovision,

11   What Makes News

Michael Palmer

This chapter looks at three ostensibly unrelated objects: how news agencies assess their own output and that of their competitors; agency assessments from and about Russia at the beginning and the end of the 20th century; and the nature of news as a product, in the light of critiques of capitalism and of observations formulated day by day, by news agency journalists striving to show colleagues how to improve on yesterday's performance. Like a Chagall painting, or Shakespeare's *King Lear,* a sub-plot highlights the main theme – how standards of news values, categories and presentation developed by late 19th-century newsmen (accuracy, impartiality, speed and 'colour') set the canons of 'factual reporting' that would spread worldwide, even, ultimately, to Russia.

Words count; definitions clarify; and history is relevant – even for news agencies whose report of a news item, filed in the computer memory two minutes ago, is recycled as 'historic information' in the data bank. Etymologically, 'news' is a contraction of 'new things'; 'agency' derives from a Spanish term signifying 'fine, noble' and 'order', and, indeed, in Romance languages 'the imposition of order, classifications, arrangements'. Exercising their professional judgement and sense of news values, news agencies monitor and report developments worldwide as or when they become public knowledge; their flair for news of significance for various markets helps fashion the international news agenda; this, while constantly in flux, has identifiable 'top stories' at a given moment. Agencies offer a prodigious amount and range of news material for a large number of markets – in 1996, Reuters' English-language general service for media clients worldwide comprised 150,000 words daily. Agencies are information vendors: their advice on customizing the material so that clients access pertinent information helps set the international news agenda for media and non-media subscribers alike.

Who monitors agency performance? The long list of those who do so includes agency clients, sources of stories, and end-users of agency output. Within the agencies themselves, there are many control and evaluation systems. This chapter centres on how Reuters' agency journalists assess the copy of their own and other agencies. Such assessments are conducted rapidly, with a view to the total output of a given day or of a news cycle, and to apprise colleagues of successes or failures so that 'tomorrow's' output better meets production, distribution and presentation standards. Here, we shall focus on day-to-day agency assessments, made from editorial head-quarters, of coverage of Russia at the beginning and end of the 20th century. Such judgements are measured, strive to be Olympian – praising some bureaux *pour mieux encourager les autres* – but are by definition short-term. A longer-term perspective, suggested by critiques of the commodity nature of news, provides another angle on the commerce of ubiquity.

News gathering, processing and distribution is both a profession (included under the umbrella heading of journalism) and an industry. Inter-national news agencies helped make news a commodity by furthering the development of norms that systemize the content, categories and presen-tation of news worldwide – 'news brokerage', to use Richard Schwarzlose's (1989–1990) term. In the mid-19th century, when the founding fathers of today's news business first set up shop (Reuter – ultimately – in London, 1851; Havas in Paris, 1832 or 1833;[1] Wolff in Berlin, 1849), Karl Marx analysed the 'fetishistic character of commodities'. Like political econo-mists, he used the story of 'the lonely islander', Robinson Crusoe, to illus-trate his arguments about the production and exchange of commodities – use-value and exchange-value. In his correspondence (with Engels, for instance), he frequently assailed the workings of the capitalist press. In 1867, he observed: 'the commodity form is the most general and least developed form of bourgeois production', before proceeding to examine 'the illusions of the monetary system' (Mattelart and Siegelaub, 1979: 80–3). Later ana-lysts, sometimes associated with the Frankfurt school of the 1920s–1930s, considered news as a commodity when studying the serialization of the pro-duction and distribution of the content of other cultural industries.

News agencies, serving (and some times set up by) governments, the press, banks and financiers, may be studied with this *critique* in mind.

Journalists die in striving to obtain and file a story: on 17 March 1995, Adil Bunyatov, aged 36, was killed when working for Reuters Television, in Baku, Azerbaijan. He may, or may not, have read Reuters Holdings plc reports that state, justifiably, 'news moves markets'. Reuters, like other agencies, studies the impact of its news reports and varied information product on both its media and non-media markets. The revenue potential of non-media markets is infinitely greater – Reuters derives more than 90% of its annual revenue from such markets. But the visibility and credibility of the media products give them an importance greater than their contribution to company revenue suggests. The artificiality of the distinction appears from the range of Reuters products featured in a section of the 1991 company report subtitled 'News that moves markets': this highlights cover-age of 'sixty-one hours of uncertainty' – the August 1991 'Soviet coup attempt'. Material featured included news graphics, stills from television footage, spreadsheets and technical analysis charts, and extracts from news services ('dollar rises two-and-a-half pfennigs on Gorbatchev news'). Uncertainty generates demand and 'success on the big stories enriches all main Reuters products. 1991 was full of opportunities for Reuters' 985 journalists in 75 countries. None was bigger than the Soviet coup attempt in August; [it] touched off a chain of events that left the world a different place'.[2]

The deployment of news agency resources depends, *inter alia,* on assessments by professional newsmen, on relations within and between agencies, on perceived market demand, and on geopolitical and financial realities of the time. Here we look at the comments of professional newsmen and/or diplomats assessing agency coverage of Russia in 1904–1906, and in 1989–1991. How did agencymen assess production during two periods when the regime in power experienced external reverses and internal unrest? The choice of period – at the opening and close of the century – and of source material requires explanation: comparisons are odious. While the leading international agencies – London-based Reuters, Paris-based Havas/AFP, and New York-based AP – were major western news organizations covering Russia during both periods, the nature of the news flow and of agency relationships differed markedly. The official Russian news agency (SPTA or 'Vestnik') founded in 1904 considered the existing cartel, ring or alliance of the leading European and American agencies to be a 'natural', self-evident, partner; but tensions in the coverage of Russia appeared as early as 1904 both among the different 'western agency allies' and between the alliance and 'Vestnik'.[3] Some of the differences concerning the news flow from Russia during the two periods under review are glaringly evident; others less so. The volume and speed of agency output filed from Russia were much greater in 1989 than in 1904; in 1989 AFP and Reuters quoted TASS (with which they had news-exchange agreements) when they used its material; in 1904–1905, however, both Havas and Reuters replied negatively when Vestnik, with whom they were contractually linked, asked that they systematically quote it by name as a source.[4]

None the less, we shall argue that study of western agency coverage of 'Russia in crisis' at opposite ends of the century proves instructive: western agencies are themselves forerunners of democracy and of market forces. Messenger, message, media and markets are interrelated. This appears strikingly in times of crisis – and when access to news agency company archives is possible.[5]

For most of the 20th century, western news agencies (like western diplomats) sought to report from a Tsarist and subsequently Soviet empire that covered a sixth of the earth's land-mass and whose official news sources were headquartered in St Petersburg and, subsequently (1918), Moscow. In Tsarist St Petersburg and Communist Moscow, news values, news priorities and news presentation, as well as concepts of censorship and propaganda, differed from those in the west (to put it mildly); nor were they same under each regime. In 1904–1906, Tsarist Russia, an imperial autocracy with ties with western Europe (that news-exchange agreements reflected), experienced military defeat by an Oriental and Pacific autocracy, Japan, and internal unrest: strikes, repression and a peace treaty brokered by the USA, were followed by more violence, a quasi-revolutionary situation, and the summoning of a representative assembly, or Douma. In 1989, the Berlin Wall – symbol of the east–west divide – came down, and the process of what western media termed 'the fall of the Soviet empire', proceeded apace, as did *glasnost* ('openness' or 'proclaiming things loudly'); after the 'Soviet coup attempt' of August 1991, the USSR expired in December 1991. For much of the century most western media portrayed Russia as a government and society that were fundamentally different: for example, in pre-1914 France, allied to Russia during *la belle époque*, the socialist daily *L'Humanité* – one of the few Parisian titles not to carry advertising for Russian government loans and industrial investment – championed opponents maltreated by the Tsarist authorities just as western media in the 1970s championed the cause of dissidents in the Soviet Union.

1904–1906

In 1904, the leading news agencies in Paris, London and Berlin – Havas, Reuters and Wolff – admitted the newly reorganized Russian official agency, Vestnik,[6] to the alliance or cartel that they headed and which comprised leading agencies in Europe and elsewhere (including the American AP).[7] In January 1906 Reuters thanked the director of Vestnik, a career diplomat, for an interview with the Russian minister, Count Witte; because of the co-operation between the two agencies, the interview 'had been printed by every London newspaper and some 300 or 400 provincial papers'. Witte's observations included these words:

> Speaking of the situation at home, Count Witte admitted that the condition of affairs in Russia was perturbed but that if all were true that had been written in the foreign press concerning Russian affairs for the last few years, she would long since have ceased to exist. . . . The psychological condition of the majority of European society being such that it demanded sensational news, the correspondents of foreign journals were supplying them with reports of that nature from Russia, without enquiring into their source, merely to satisfy the caprice of fashion.[8]

Several factors placed strains on the news exchange between the Russian and European agency 'allies': the cost and logistics of covering Russian and Japanese (naval and army) troop movements, diplomatic developments, and the unrest in Russia: the competition from other news organizations – such as the London-based Central News agency, or the host of newspaper correspondents who flocked to St Petersburg and other news centres; and Vestnik's wish to modify existing inter-allied agency agreements that routed agency traffic through Berlin, where Wolff played a central, filtering role, in favour of direct ties between St Petersburg and Paris. The official news agency reflected Russian foreign policy goals. These included ending the perceived dependence on the German agency for its foreign news, and strengthening ties with the French agency; thus, in a letter to Havas in 1904, Paul Miller, the director of Vestnik, used the self-same formula, *'pays amis et alliés'* – 'friendly and allied nations' – used by Tsar Nicholas II in a celebrated toast to the French president in 1897.

Agency diplomatic niceties aside, Reuters and Havas strove to educate Vestnik in western news values. Each agency had its own representative in St Petersburg; but both relied on their Russian ally for coverage of official news which, it claimed, it should get first. In December 1904, Reuters stated its 'desire to publish with equal impartiality governmental announcements and events which may be regarded as unfavourable, such for instance as riots, disturbances, demonstrations and the like'.[9] Miller stressed that Vestnik wanted to provide: 'a complete regular "chronique" of the Russian politic [sic] and social life, without concealing or suppressing anything. . . . Until now, Russian agencies did not enjoy a good reputation in Europe'.[10]

Sometimes, he admitted defeat. Pressed by Reuters about delays in the reporting of the arrest of 'twelve socialist revolutionaries', Vestnik stated:

> as an official agency we have no right to transmit some kinds of news without a direct authorisation of the government. Your wishes are quite legal and righteous. The transmission of certain categories of information without the consentment of the Russian government can put our agency in a rather awkward position.

The solution was, for the Reuters' man in St Petersburg, 'in such cases to watch the events himself'.[11] Reuters concurred:

> we fully appreciate your responsibilities and would not for a moment seek to embarrass you by demanding what in the circumstances might be unreasonable.[12]

> In each of the great capitals of Europe, we have our own correspondents side by side with the official Agency. . . . It is the office of the English correspondent to look at things through English spectacles and to judge them from an English standpoint.[13]

In 1905, Reuters and Havas repeatedly, and politely but pointedly told Vestnik how to compress dispatches, and write them for their respective British, French and imperial customers: Vestnik dispatches proved wanting on several counts – speed, accuracy, news values and presentation. Thus, Havas rewrote dispatches sent it (in French) by Vestnik – 'you must summarise; for our part, we often don't give a full report of important meetings in France'; in November 1905, Havas sent Vestnik its 170-word version of a 368-word Vestnik report on the Congress of *zemstvos* (local government assemblies); it cut from six to three paragraphs a Vestnik account of how 72 St Petersburg companies had declared their unanimous opposition to the introduction of an eight-hour day.[14] In April 1906, Reuters explained how it cut down long Vestnik telegrams 'consisting very largely of argumentative statements which appear to have a semi-official character and to be intended to influence public opinion in this country'; Reuters was willing to publish provided 'either your Agency or an official representative, or a communiqué, "official or semi-official was cited as source,"' and that Reuters was not charged transmission costs.[15]

In December 1905, in the midst of many press reports about repression and revolution in Russia, Havas received a Vestnik telegram so drafted that it appeared the chief of staff in St Petersburg – *'haut état-major armée Pétersbourg'* – had been arrested. This, Havas said, fell into its category of 'big news' (*'grosse dépêche'*): on reflection in Paris, Havas decided the story concerned the arrest of a revolutionary leader (*'l'état-major révolution-naire'*).[16] Vestnik 'perturbed' Havas.

The 'colourful prose' and 'sensation-mongering reports', published in western newspapers that invested heavily in coverage ('on-the-spot' corre-spondents, transmission costs) of the then top international news story worried Havas and Reuters – as they did Vestnik, but for different reasons. For Havas and Reuters, the tried and tested arrangement of news exchange with the official agency and a local correspondent (wearing 'English', or 'French' 'spectacles') proved wanting: while Russian censors vetted even Vestnik reports, western newspapers published countless stories relating dramatic news from Russia. Time and again, Vestnik condemned 'private and unconfirmed rumours eagerly sent by private agents'. On 22 January 1905 – 'Bloody Sunday' – troops killed over 1,000 of the 150,000 people who sought to present a petition to the Tsar at his Winter Palace in St Peters-burg; in the strikes and disturbances that followed, speculation was rife – would the minister of the interior resign? Would the Tsar receive a 'workmen's deputation'? When the Central News beat Reuters with news that the Tsar had received the workers (1 February: he 'pardoned' them), Vestnik explained itself thus: 'The Central News published not a fact but only a rumour which in this case by chance found its realisation. "Hundreds of telegrams" had been "sent abroad" speculating about the two events: we abstained from communicating to you these rumours until they found realisation. If, however, you are willing to receive from us private and totally unconfirmed rumours we are quite prepared to supply you with them just to please you'.[17]

The French agency, Havas, likewise had difficulty in ensuring that its correspondent, Giaccone, adhered to factual news reporting, as he navi-gated between the Scylla of official sources and censorship, and the Charybdis of scoops and dramatic news output of Parisian newspaper correspondents. As early as March 1904, Havas noted how the numerous French newspapermen – who had only recently arrived and 'know neither the language nor the customs' of Russia – persistently scooped Havas. When Giaccone sent in reports of 'bad news', in colourful prose, Havas-Paris protested:

> a medium like ours must not attempt to forecast developments; we must not be judgemental or editorialize; we must not darken the situation. . . . Stick to the facts.

One of your dispatches yesterday began 'The mess persists [le gâchis continue]'. If such be the case, mere factual reporting should suffice; it's not for us to say so. . . . We are often accused of being hostile to Russia because your reports are over-pessimistic. . . . Your dispatches, which seem to us to paint the situation in too dark a colour, have already caused us serious problems. Facts without comment, please.[18]

Reports about Russia published by Havas, like those of the leading (and 'sensation-mongering') daily, *Le Matin,* were monitored by the French authorities and the Russian embassy in Paris (the Vestnik Paris correspondent had both an office in Havas and regular contacts with his diplomatic colleagues in the embassy). Havas was both a news and an advertising agency. The Russian authorities influenced the flow of both news and advertising 'budgets' to the French press. Indeed the Russian diplomat who advised on the allocation of advertising subsidies considered the French press 'abominably venal' and Havas as the 'pivot' (fulcrum or 'gatekeeper') of the news flow.[19] News reporting was influenced by geopolitical and financial considerations: it has been reckoned that, between 1887 and 1914, one French family in six invested in Russian government bonds or in companies participating in the industrialization of Russia, France's unique (before 1907) ally.

In March 1904, a month after the outbreak of hostilities, Havas wrote to its ally, Reuters, to deplore how the agencies had lost the dominant position in the international news flow that they had hitherto enjoyed:

we appear to be lagging behind English and French newspapers and indeed The AP. . . . We seem to give much space to dispatches from official sources, which are available to all and sundry. . . . Never before have our newspapers shown such zeal, and spent so much, so as to get their own news [informations indépendantes].[20]

Paris and London daily newspapers concluded or expanded news-exchange agreements with one another (*Le Matin* and *The Times,* for instance) (see Palmer, 1983). Vestnik, meanwhile, promised its allies privileged access to Russian official news. It wrote of its 'own fully organized staff of 9 [crossed out] many war correspondents and of its access to Russian military and naval head-quarters'.[21] Reuters, for its part, claimed it provided 'what has practically been the only continuous service of war news from the front on the Japanese side'.[22] But each allied agency found fault with the service provided by its partners.

Official News, Agency 'Contortions', 'Minute Globules' and 'Newspeak', 1917–1985

To western eyes, the concept of an authorized, official Russian agency, filtering the news released for 'outside' consumption, existed in Soviet Russia, and the Union, as it had in the Tsarist empire. For their part, the authorities in Russia sought to receive maximum information from western agencies, irrespective of censorship constraints within Russia, whether the official agency was Vestnik or TASS.[23] During the revolutions of 1917, the contortions of the Reuters–Havas-led cartel to keep the agency alliance functioning with the Russian Petrograd Telegraph Agency, provoked ironical comment in the press:

> as long as Russia had a Tsarist government, the Petrograd agencymen telegraphed pro-Tsarist dispatches ['tsaristement']; as soon as the provisional government became the master, the agency became anti-Tsarist – all this for a commission. A government considers the use of a semi-official ['officieux'] agency as its spokesman to be as normal as giving orders to the police.

The Dutch daily, *Nieuwe Rotterdamsche Courant,* portrayed the Petrograd agency as striving to serve two masters – the provisional government and the 'council of workers' and military delegates'.[24]

Thereafter the ups and downs of relations between western and Russian agencies mirrored, for the most part, the changing geopolitical relations between the west and the Soviet Union. The Petrograd Agency was transformed into an agency called ROSTA, in 1918: TASS, the state agency, replaced it in 1925. Lenin himself attended to the reorganization of Vestnik in December 1917, whereas Reuters' man in St Petersburg – the same person, Beringer, in 1917 as in 1904 – was an anti-Bolshevik and helped Vestnik correspondents escape from Russia. (Boyd-Barrett and Palmer, 1981: 257–8; Read, 1992: 142–5).

Reviewing changes 'in news-gathering and its transmission' in a brochure to celebrate 'Reuters' Jubilee', in 1915, the agency wrote of compressing news into 'minute globules'.[25] Condensing the essence of a story, as well as presenting it so as to respect agency canons of accuracy, balance, speed and interest together generate a 'creative tension' in news agency writing. Censorship restraints notwithstanding, agency output – even concerning Russia – was higher in 1915 than in 1865; the average monthly wordage that Vestnik expected from Reuters in 1905 – 10,000 words – was less than a single Reuters bureau might produce a day in 1985. For decades thereafter, the paucity of hard news, emerging rapidly from the Kremlin via TASS, led the limited staff of the Moscow bureaux of western agencies to have their own 'Kremlinologists', scrutinizing and deciphering what the cold war generations of correspondents who read Orwell's *1984* (published in 1950) sometimes called 'newspeak'.[26] Elsewhere, advances in communications technologies accentuated fears about an information glut.[27] Western international news agencies – with Reuters, AP and AFP to the fore – harnessed technologies so as to increase the flow of data for their customers, and to make the forms and range of agency output as 'user-friendly' and 'customized' as possible.

In Reuters, during the 1980s, the chief news editor Ian Macdowall developed various tools intended to aid staff worldwide to produce copy according to the same norms. He refined existing editorial notes and guidance and produced a 262-page handbook, built on previous international style guides. He also developed the use of quality control units that monitored, day by day, the output (and client-usage) of both Reuters and competing news agencies and services. We shall now highlight the observations of these quality controllers – known as 'quacs', a self-deprecating reference to quack-doctors – who comment on copy concerning Russia. The period concerns the years 1989–1991 (with a stress on 1989), and covers a period of internal reform and of overtures to the west, followed by the implosion of the Soviet empire, unrest within the Union and the decline and fall of Soviet power (see Crawshaw, 1992–1993; Pryce-Jones, 1995). We are concerned here, as before, with western agency assessment, day by day, of agency output. Clearly, the source material available, the nature of the agencies and the world they covered, and the volume and speed of international news flow, are not the same in the 1990s as in the 1900s. But, acting in both periods as the quintessential gatekeeper, agencies applied norms to impose order – '*agencer*' – on the international news flow. These norms govern both content and presentation. Indeed, as early as the 1880s, both Reuters and Havas instructed allied agencies and correspondents worldwide about the classification of news by category and priority.[28]

Quality Control: Russia, 1989

In the 1980s, with the revenue garnered from the success of financial products and services underpinning its media resources, Reuters 'charged . . . the quality unit with developing global standards of presentation and format'. How did the unit assess coverage of Russia in agency output for media clients?[29]

As the sample month of the quacs' world media comment, we have chosen July 1989 – a month during which developments in, or concerning, the Soviet Union constituted 'the top world story' (25 July). On 1 August, 'Q' announced: 'we topped world impact charts from Moscow (and other Soviet datelines) on cover of politics, labour unrest in July: RTR, 39.1%; AP, 30%; AFP, 10.3%'. As ever, events both foreseen and unpredicted made the international news agenda in July. The former included the scheduled travels of Mikhail Gorbatchev (including Strasburg, Paris, Moscow) and of the US President, George Bush (including Gdansk, Paris); Gorbatchev visited Paris shortly before the summit of 'Group Seven' leaders, which coincided with celebrations of the bicentenary of the French Revolution. The list of unforeseen international events, whose agency coverage 'Q' monitored, included air-crashes, a coup in Khartoum, and the death of the British actor, Laurence Olivier. Some stories were 'one-off', others 'ongoing serials'; many were the subject of reports from several locations, including usual and unusual news centres. 'Q's' remarks centred on speed, accuracy and presentation; he highlighted successes and failures in copy that sought to weave the strands of a complex story together, or to relate a development to 'the bigger picture'. This picture reflected western news values and presentational techniques.

July began with 'Q' both praising and criticizing coverage of the death of the former foreign minister and president Andrei Gromyko: RTR-Moscow beat competitors by two minutes with the announcement of the death, but the agency 'took nearly three hours to get to the wire with the full-dress obituary' (3 July). The month closed with 'Q' repeatedly praising 'Bob Evans and his Moscow team [who] stay right on top of the world story, grinding down the opposition with a file of unmatched range and depth. . . . To cap a winning all-round performance, Dominique Dudouble filed a telling picture of a perplexed Gorbatchev listening to critical speeches in the Supreme Soviet' (25 July). 'Q's' comments reflected the western media portrayal of Gorbatchev as a skilful operator abroad, beset by problems at home; the televising of the (new) Soviet Parliament and of the burgeoning miners' strikes – 'the biggest industrial action . . . the Soviet Union had ever seen'[30] – led to criticism of the authorities; *'glasnost'* ('proclaiming things loudly' or 'openness') had its obverse side. 'Q' monitored comparable output of different news organizations, often centring on 'leads' and interpretative material. He also monitored impacts and credits.

On 5 July, 'Q' commented on agency coverage of Gorbatchev's Paris visit and of an accident – the day he arrived a Mig-23 Soviet fighter crashed in Belgium after flying an hour without a pilot:

The Soviet Mig's ghost flight across Europe deflected the spotlight a bit from Gorbatchev's Paris visit. Brussels had a seven-minute beat over runner-up AFP on the break. Later efforts as pieces dropped into place looked sharper than AP's efforts. The intro to our AMs 4t hld wrap-up[31] was strengthened by spelling out that the plane 'flew across W Europe through NATO air defences'. AP just said it 'flew over three NATO nations'. One reservation – we could have lifted the TASS confirmation that the pilot ejected over Poland a bit high. This came in 6th para – after 5th para quoted W German/Dutch officials as saying bailout was believed to have been over Poland or E Germany.

That 'ghost flight' tag and throw-forward angle made for a good PMs wrap-up. Gorbatchev file read well. PMer – 'Mitterrand challenging Gorb's vision of common Euro home' – had more punch than AP's. They rather blandly said Gorb, professing adherence to ideals that sparked French revolution, 'has declared his readiness to safeguard human rights'. Subscribers (especially broadcast clients) might have liked a freshening lead sometime between our AMer at 1314 GMT and 1stld at 1856. Speed isn't the only measure of quality. Another test is to ask how often we succeed in etching vivid images on our readers' memories, perhaps even to the point of nightmare. Pictures that linger after looking into the past day's file – those patches of blood from victims of Stalinist purges floating down the Neva river past the winter palace (Soviet graves). Marie-Antoinette fainting as revolutionaries paraded outside her prison carrying the head of her companion Princesse de Lamballe on a pike (France-walks). Or, on a cheerier note, those elderly Tsarist bondholders clutching the worthless paper to their chests as they appealed to Gorby to pay up (Gorbatchev-bonds). . . .

'Leads' convey – and are of – the essence:

> those first 20 or 30 words make or break the story. . . . Many media subscribers scanning wire service directories on a computer screen will decide whether or not to use a Reuters rather than an AP or AFP story on the basis solely of the head-line and the first paragraph. . . . Ideally a lead paragraph should . . . stand as a self-contained story, complete with source if the subject is contentious.[32]

But 'quacs' appreciate 'interpretative leads' and 'throw-forward angles': this might appear to conflict with the earlier insistence – *pace* Reuters and Havas in 1904–1905 – on 'straight factual reporting'. The creative tension that results appeared in the 'quac's' comment on Reuters' coverage of Gor-batchev's Paris visit: 'the line that he seemed distracted by daunting prob-lems at home gave the lead of AM-Gorbatchev a boost' (6 July). Similarly, 'Q's' favourable comments on Moscow's 17 July output signalled the newsman's technique of linking the international and domestic aspects of a story. Moscow produced a 'Soviet strikes / unrest doubleheader' as the coal miners' protest spread. 'Q' recommended wrapping the 'the two serials together' and including 'high-up background and interp.'. He criticized a story that delayed until the 10th paragraph mention 'that this is the worst labour unrest since Gorbatchev came to power four years ago'. 'Spot copy', he added, 'should take a stab at assessing how serious the troubles are and relating them to the big economic/political picture' (18 July). 'Q' com-mented appreciatively on the next day's Moscow output: '. . . a good job of pulling together strikes/unrest and putting developments in perspective – "worst industrial unrest since the early years on the communist state" '. He added an aside: 'if anyone ever bans the word "unrest" Reuters have to go out of business' (19 July).

'The Wind-up of the Soviet Union', 1991

'Q' began his world media comment of December 18 thus: 'we'll keep the red flag flying here – well, until New Year's Eve'. At a meeting on 17 Decem-ber, Gorbatchev and Yeltsin had finalized arrangements for the transition from the Soviet Union to the CIS. 'Q' reviewed comparable AP, Reuters and AFP AM leads on the subject:

> AP: 'Boris Yeltsin and Mikhail Gorbatchev agreed Tuesday to dissolve the Soviet Union and proclaim a new commonwealth on New Year's Day, media reported. Even the hammer and sickle flag will be lowered from the Kremlin.'
> RTR: 'President Mikhail Gorbatchev has accepted that the fast-disintegrating Soviet Union will cease to exist by the end of this year, Russian President Boris Yeltsin said on Tuesday.' AFP's equivalent roundup didn't move until much later

and the lead could have been tightened / sharpened: 'At a two-hour meeting with Russian Pres B Y, Pres M G agreed Tuesday to abolish the Soviet Union as a union at the end of the year, when the red hammer-and-sickle flag will be lowered for the last time on the Kremlin' (You don't want to start such a story by telling readers that a meeting lasted two hours, and the union as a union repetition was pointless).[33]

'Q' signed off with an allusion to William Wordsworth's *The Prelude*, celebrating the French Revolution of 1789: 'Not much bliss was it in that dawn to be alive from hairdresser Lena Lemzikova, who told AP – "It's all the same to me. The only thing I care about is whether my children have medicine." '

But, before signing off, he pointed out that AP and AFP had beaten Reuters with the first news of the outcome of the Gorbatchev–Yeltsin meeting: 'Speed isn't always directly related to play, but there does appear to be some connection (Euro credits on the dissolution story today came up RTR 0, AP 3, UPI 0, AFP 2)'.

The Norms of the News: Accuracy, Speed, 'Interp.' and Colour – In Russia as Elsewhere

'The sun sets on *The Aurora*': this imaginary headline captures the scene from Liteiny bridge in St Petersburg at 22.00 hours on 28 July 1996: 'as the former imperial capital celebrated the 300th anniversary of the founding of the Russian fleet, the cruiser from which Bolsheviks broadcast in 1917 was engulfed in the pall of firework smoke and disappeared in the twilight. . . .' The subsequent issue of the English-language *Saint-Petersburg Times* featured its own report of the festivities but otherwise carried (and credited) Reuters stories on all its world (including ex-USSR) news pages.

Since the early 1990s, and the ending of the contractual obligation to distribute services essentially through TASS, Reuters has expanded in Russia. It produces services both in English and (since 1995) in Cyrillic, for the media and business communities; the latter includes traders in currencies – currency speculation was punishable by death only 10 years previously. Reuters staff in Moscow alone exceeded 110 in late 1994 – of whom three-quarters were Russian; Reuters needs no Russian agency 'partner'.

In general – as John Murray observes – Russian-language newspapers in the post-Soviet period draw their inspiration 'from a Western tradition that was in its fundamentals alien to the spirit of the Leninist press'. This is particularly true of international news.

> The foreign news story . . . has nothing in common with its distant and many times removed Soviet relative. For a variety of reasons, chief among them economic, Russian newspapers now rely almost entirely on Western European and American news agencies to fill their columns of foreign news briefs. (Murray, 1994: 144–5)

'Factual reporting and sensationalism' – Murray also writes – were 'the two foundations of the pre-revolutionary Russian liberal press.' Here, we have seen how Reuters and Havas in the 1900s tried to educate Vestnik, the Russian state agency, in factual reporting for European (and American) newspapers that included titles given to 'sensation-mongering'. In the 1990s, the reporting and presentational norms practised by agencies and other international news organizations are the common currency of professional journalism. As is the measurement of performance by market satisfaction.

Notes

1. Charles Havas opened a newspaper translation bureau in Paris in 1832 or 1833; the agency proper, 'Agence Havas', opened in 1835. Agence France-Presse, founded in 1944, inherited the premises of the news division of Havas, which had been nationalized and turned into an official news agency, OFI, in 1940.
2. Reuters Holding plc, Annual Report, 1991.
3. 'Vestnik' ('Messenger') was the journalistic title used by successive forms of the official news agency (Saint-Petersburg Telegraph Agency, etc.) in their dealings with foreign agencies. see Rantanen (1990). The 1995 'catalogue' of ITAR-TASS, celebrating the 90th anniversary of 'Russia's central official news agency' claims descent from the 1904 agency.
4. Havas to Vestnik, 5 April 1905; Reuters (RTR)/to Vestnik, 28 March 1905. Fond. 1358, the Central History Archives (TsGIA), St Petersburg.
5. We wish to thank AFP and Reuters for authorizing access to company archives of, respectively, Havas-information (Archives Nationales, Paris), and Reuters (London); and Galina Ippolitiva and Terhi Rantanen for facilitating access to Petrogradskoe telegrafnoe agentstvo archives (concerning 'Vestnik'), St Petersburg.
6. Rantanen (1990) explores the complex history of Russian agencies from 1856, and of their relations with the cartel.
7. AP joined the cartel in 1875. Hugh Hanna, a member of the US commission on international exchange, wrote from Indianapolis on 23 October 1903 to the Russian Finance Minister, Edouard de Pleske, enclosing a letter of introduction for Howard N. Thompson, then in Paris, 'who is going to St. Petersbourg to represent. . . The Associated Press; . . . if you would like to have some control of the despatches that go through the A.P. to the U.S. perhaps you would like to have the relation' Fond. 1358, TsGIA.
8. Reuters to Vestnik, 8 January 1906, TsGIA.
9. Reuters to Vestnik, 13 December 1904, TsGIA.
10. Miller to Reuters, 21 March 1905, TsGIA.
11. Miller to Baron Herbert de Reuter, 26 March 1905, TsGIA.
12. Reuters to Vestnik, 13 April 1905, TsGIA.
13. Reuters to Vestnik, 28 March 1905, TsGIA.
14. Havas to Vestnik, 22 November 1905, TsGIA.
15. Reuters to Vestnik, 23 April 1906, TsGIA.
16. Havas to Vestnik, 24 December 1905, TsGIA.
17. Vestnik to Reuters, 21 February 1905, TsGIA.
18. Havas to Giaccone, 16 March, 22 November and 2 December 1905, 5 AR 133, National Archives (AN), Paris.
19. . . . *L'abominable vénalité de la presse. . .*, (A. Raffalovitch), Paris, Librairie du travail, 1931.
20. Havas to Reuters, 23 March 1904, 5 AR 67, AN.
21. Vestnik to Reuters, February 1905, TsGIA.

22. Reuters to Vestnik, 20 March 1905, TsGIA.

23. In 1914, the Saint-Petersburg Telegraph Agency was renamed the Petrograd Telegraph Agency.

24. *Nieuwe Rotterdamsche Courant,* 24 March 1917, translated from the Dutch into French by the Dutch agency, Delamar. TsGIA.

25. Both Reuters and Havas, in correspondence with Vestnik, spoke of 'a brief summary of twenty or thirty words giving just the pith of the matter in hand' (Reuters to Vestnik, 13 December 1904).

26. Censorship, economic constraints, and diplomatic factors – western agency representation in the USSR was linked to numbers of TASS bureau chiefs (who had diplomatic status) operating in western capitals – limited agency representation in Moscow: Reuters withdrew its full-time correspondent in 1950, and had a two-man bureau in 1959.

27. Many western correspondents contrasted the news cornucopia outside the Soviet bloc and the state control of news and information flow within.

28. See Palmer 1983: 136; Read, 1992: 100–1.

29. Source material: *World Media Comment* (*WMC*) pages, compiled by as many as four different 'quacs' ('Q').

30. Crawshaw, 1992–1993: 85.

31. The fourth comprehensive lead on the story put out during the London morning news cycle. *'In the general news-service there is one news cycle each day, beginning with the world schedule issued at 23.00 London time. More loosely journalists will talk in terms of three eight-hour news cycles each day – the overnight GMT period when Hong Kong is in control and the London day and evening control periods'* (Reuters, 1991).

32. ibid.

33. *WMC,* 18 December 1991.

References

Boyd-Barrett, O. and Palmer, M. (1981) *Le Trafic des nouvelles*, Paris: Alain Moreau.

Crawshaw, S. (1992–1993) *Goodbye to the USSR. The Collapse of Soviet Power*, London: Bloomsbury.

Mattelart, A. and Siegelaub, S. (1979) *Communication and Class Struggle*, New York/Bagnolet.

Murray, J. (1994) *The Russian Press from Brezhnev to Yeltsin. Beyond the Paper Curtain*, Aldershot: Edward Elgar.

Palmer, M. (1983) *Des petits journaux aux grandes agences'*; Paris: Aubier.

Pryce-Jones, D. (1995) *The War That Never Was. The Fall of the Soviet Empire 1985–1991*, London: Weidenfeld & Nicolson.

Raffalovitch, A. (1931) '. . . *L'abominable vénalité de la presse . . .*, Paris: Librairie du travail.

Rantanen, T. (1990) *Foreign News in Imperial Russia: The Relationship between International and Russian News Agencies 1856–1914*, Helsinki: Suomalainen Tiedeakatemia.

Read, D. (1992) *The Power of News. The History of Reuters*, Oxford: Oxford University Press.

Reuters (1991) *A Handbook for Reuter Journalists*, London.

Schwarzlose, R. (1989–1990) *The Nation's Newsbrokers*, 2 vols, Evanston, IL: Northwestern University Press.

12 Alternative News Agencies

C. Anthony Giffard

Globalization is no abstract concept for Inter Press Service, the world's largest purveyor of information about the developing nations. Global issues and global interdependence are the core of the agency's news agenda and have a profound effect in shaping its philosophy, structure and financing. *IPS 2000*, a document laying out the agency's strategy, focuses the IPS editorial product on globalization as a key mechanism of the changing world order (Inter Press Service, 1996a). It notes that there is a 'mushrooming of threats to humankind at the individual and social levels . . . and these threats know no geographical or cultural boundaries. They range from environmental pollution, through the collapse of welfare values to denial of basic human rights'. In this context IPS decided in the early 1990s to update its role of making heard the voices of the developing world. 'Today, the challenge is to transform the agency into a truly global communication system . . . dedicated to offering a differentiated market systematic, continuous and in-depth coverage of global issues'(Inter Press Service, 1996b).

The emphasis on globalization is the most recent phase in the agency's evolution, which began with its founding in 1964 as an 'information bridge' between Christian Democratic parties in Europe and Latin America (Giffard, 1984). The cold war and growth of the non-aligned movement broadened the agency's focus to problems and priorities of developing regions generally. The emphasis then became promotion of horizontal, South–South information flows to encourage social, political and economic development and regional integration. IPS became associated with the Non-aligned Group's calls for a New International Information Order and its corollary, the New World Information and Communication Order. With its new allies, IPS quickly expanded in Latin America, the Caribbean, Africa, Asia and the Middle East. Having successfully established South–South communications, IPS turned its attention to enhancing its network for a South–North flow of news. Bureaux in Europe and North America provided coverage of events in the North of interest to the South, and enabled distribution of news about the South to northern media. By the mid-1980s, IPS had offices in about 60 countries: 23 in Latin America and the Caribbean, 16 in Europe, five in the Middle East and four each in Asia and North America.

The end of the cold war and related upheavals in international relations provided a new challenge as many developing countries adopted democratic systems of governance and free market economies. In the view of IPS, globalization has replaced the East–West and North–South conflicts of the post-second world war era as the single most important fact of international life, characterized by its ever-accelerating pace of cross-border economic, social and political interactions and the unprecedented expansion of private capital, free markets, advanced production and communications technology into virtually every corner of the globe. Yet, IPS believes, the broader issues raised by globalization go relatively uncovered in mainstream media that increasingly are geared towards entertainment, with coverage that 'careers from crisis to crisis, disaster to disaster and, increasingly, scandal to scandal' (Inter Press Service, 1996c).

Proponents of globalization see it as bringing the world closer together, making national economies and polities more interdependent, maintaining stability and ensuring economic growth. Others are more sceptical. As IPS points out, some argue that the forces of globalization have so weakened the nation state that it can no longer adequately protect its citizens, especially those who are most vulnerable – the poor, children, women, and minorities – from the excesses of private capital. Some believe that democratic participation is being undermined by the growth of the private sector and the polarization of wealth it appears to accelerate. Still others contend that globalization's pursuit of high rates of economic growth threatens the limits of what is environmentally sustainable. And some say that the kind of cultural, economic, and social dislocation brought on by globalization reinforces ethnic and religious identities, which further undermine the nation state's ability to safeguard the rights of its citizens.

IPS has tried to keep abreast of these historic shifts. Over the last several years it has directed an increasing share of its editorial resources to coverage of international agencies such as the World Bank, the International Monetary Fund (IMF), and the World Trade Organization (WTO), which play catalytic roles in the globalization process (Lobe, 1997). Once focused almost exclusively on the third world, IPS has also been paying more attention to trends – such as privatization and the polarization of wealth within countries - that are increasingly common to countries of both the industrialized North and the developing South, precisely because of their relationship to economic and technological globalization. Underdevelopment in the South is not a local problem: it is equally in the interests of the North to solve problems that could pose a threat to them (Kaul and Savio, 1993). For these reasons, IPS has set out to provide its own major constituencies – NGOs, interested media, research institutes, and UN and development policy-makers – with the information and analysis needed to understand and cope with these new challenges.

Structure

The IPS International Association is a non-profit, non-governmental organization with headquarters in Rome and bureaux in 41 countries. Professional journalists and others in the field of communications, whether staff or friends of IPS, are entitled to join the association. In 1997, there were 174 members, about 100 of them IPS employees. A board of directors comprising 10 distinguished international personalities (nominated by the regions); five members elected by the regions, and two elected from headquarters staff in Rome, provides overall policy direction. Oscar Arias, former President of Costa Rica and 1987 Nobel Peace Prize winner, is president of the association. The board appoints an executive committee and the director-general, who oversee day-to-day operations. The director-general is Roberto Savio, founder of IPS. He is assisted by managing director Giovanni Spinelli and a small, Rome-based management team. Regional editorial and management centres operate in Africa, Asia, the Caribbean, Europe, Latin America and North America. Five IPS offices are organized as independent foundations in Austria, Belgium, Finland, Norway and Sweden. IPS's articles of association stipulate that its main object is to contribute to development by 'promoting free communication and a professional flow of information to reinforce technical and economic cooperation among developing countries' (Inter Press Service, 1997). It aims to 'inform the public about vital global issues and events from a Southern perspective, to give a voice to those who traditionally have been marginalized by mainstream media, to bolster the institutions of civil society, and to self-consciously promote values of pluralism, participation and democracy' (Inter Press Service, 1996c).

To meet this challenge, IPS offers a range of services that go beyond the traditional functions of a news agency. Its products can be divided into three broad categories. IPS News Service, an independent global news wire, facilitates information flow among developing countries and distributes news about those nations to clients in the industrialized nations. IPS Projects designs and manages programmes for training, information exchange and increasing public awareness of global issues. IPS Telecommunications offers technical expertise in opening up communication channels for regions and people usually overlooked by mainstream media.

IPS News Service

IPS News Service provides news features, analyses and commentaries on events and global processes affecting economic, social and political development, especially in the South. Major themes covered regularly by IPS include human rights and democracy; environment, natural resources and energy; population; health and education; food and agriculture; international finance and trade flows; politics and conflict resolution; culture, arts and entertainment; science and technology; regional integration and sustainable development. IPS provides little spot news; it supplements coverage by the full-service agencies. The intention is to offer in-depth views of the major issues, explaining the complex processes that lie behind day-to-day events.

In 1996, the news service had permanent bureaux and correspondents in 41 countries. They covered events in 108 different nations. The main news product is the IPS World Service, which is transmitted, usually by satellite, to media and other clients in English and Spanish. The World Service typically carries about 30 items a day, with each geographical region represented. Regions can contribute extra items if desired. The Spanish Service in Latin America, for example, carries a number of spot news reports for media that use IPS as their primary agency. A selection of items from the World Service is translated into other languages, including Bahasa Indonesia, Bengali, Dutch, Finnish, French, German, Hindi, Kiswahili, Mandarin, Nepali, Norwegian, Sinhala, Swedish, Tamil, Thai and Urdu. These services are available by satellite, printed bulletins, electronic databases, and online computer facilities such as the Internet and the World Wide Web.

In a project designed to provide in-depth coverage of international conferences, IPS published *Terra Viva*, an independent newspaper, at each of the major UN conferences from the Rio Earth Summit in 1992 to the World Food Summit in Rome in 1996. *Terra Viva* provided conference participants with a daily roundup of key issues on the agenda. Reports written for *Terra Viva* were also distributed on the IPS news services. A related publication, the *Terra Viva Daily Journal*, is produced at the United Nations in New York and focuses on development issues. It is distributed to policy-makers in the United Nations, development agencies and foundations in North America and Europe.

IPS media subscribers in 1996 included 615 newspapers and magazines, 79 news agencies and databases and 65 broadcast media. Another 549 NGOs and institutions were subscribers – a number which does not include about 20,000 NGOs who can access the IPS service through computer nodes of the Association for Progressive Communication (APC), Peacenet, the Global Information Network (GIN), One World Online and other networks.

IPS's biggest client base is in Latin America, where it serves media in Argentina, Brazil, Bolivia, Chile, Colombia, Costa Rica, Ecuador, El Salvador, Honduras, Mexico, Nicaragua, Panama, Peru, Uruguay and Venezuela. In Asia, IPS is used by subscribers in Bangladesh, China, Hong Kong, India, Indonesia, Malaysia, the Philippines, Nepal, Thailand and Pakistan. United Press of India distributes a daily selection of IPS reports to 1,000 media clients. In Southern Africa, IPS reaches almost all news outlets through the South African Press Association. A package of IPS reports, ready for use in radio newscasts, is transmitted twice a day to national broadcasting corporations in 10 Southern African nations. In

Europe, media that buy the service are found in Austria, Belgium, Britain, Finland, France, Germany, Hungary, Italy, The Netherlands, Norway, Portugal, Spain, Sweden, Switzerland and Turkey. The GIN distributes IPS material to more than 300 alternative ethnic and minority media in the United States and Canada, and reaches hundreds more clients though the Lexis/Nexis online database every month. GIN also supplies IPS copy to schools, which use IPS reports in language-training programmes.

It is not easy to track media pickup of IPS materials with precision. Because of the high cost of clippings services, and the fact that there are no such services in many of the nations in which IPS operates, reliable figures are hard to come by. In several countries, news agency stories are not normally credited with their byline. Nor would clippings reveal the audience of radio news services that use IPS, or the number of NGOs that access it via computer databases. IPS monitors a sample group of media subscribers regularly to check on pickup of its services. In 1996, this produced 36,700 clippings.

Studies undertaken for other purposes provide additional data. One analysis, commissioned by the UN Food and Agricultural Organization (FAO) and conducted at the School of Communications at the University of Washington, examined print media clippings that covered FAO activities in calendar year 1991 (Giffard, 1992). Almost 9,000 clippings were gathered by clipping services in Europe and North America, and by FAO offices in other regions. These clips appeared in 13 different languages (primarily German, Spanish and English) and were published in newspapers and journals in more than 100 countries. Reports about FAO activities generally dealt with such global issues as food production and malnutrition, warnings of imminent food shortages, deforestation, the environment, population growth and sustainable development – the kinds of topics typically covered by IPS.

Of the 2,932 clips that carried a news agency credit, 13.2% were from IPS, making it the third most often cited agency for this specific kind of news, behind Deutsche Presse-Agentur (19.1%) and the Associated Press (18.8%), but ahead of such traditional news agencies as Reuters, Agence France-Presse and Spain's EFE. The IPS reports were found in 138 separate publications in 39 countries – a greater number of countries than any other agency. More than 70% of the IPS clips were published in Latin American papers, especially in Venezuela, Mexico, Bolivia and Ecuador. Of all FAO clips that appeared in Latin America with an agency credit 72% came from IPS. But IPS also had substantial numbers of clips in Asia (primarily India, the Philippines and Thailand) and in Europe, where papers in The Netherlands and Norway, and, to a lesser extent, Finland, Belgium and Germany were frequent users. IPS, which has a contract to cover FAO activities, was unique among the agencies in its balance of clients in the developed and developing nations.

Annual analyses of IPS copy undertaken at the University of Washington since 1991 show that it does indeed focus primarily on the developing world (Giffard, 1991–1997). Typically, they find that two-thirds of the reports carry datelines of cities in developing countries. Samples of AP and Reuter reports carried on their international news wire in the United States include, on average, less than 50% of third world datelines. IPS reports filed from European and North American capitals tend to deal with their policies that affect the developing regions, or with the activities of international organizations headquartered there.

When one counts the number of times individual nations are mentioned, about 70% of the IPS references are to countries in Africa, Asia, the Caribbean and Latin America. The actors and sources in IPS reports likewise are twice as likely to be from the South as the North. Analysis of the topics covered shows that the most frequent category on the IPS services relates to economic issues – trade, business, industry – either within nations or in relation to regional groupings such as the North American Free Trade alliance or the Latin American customs and excise union, Mercosur. Other frequent topics are domestic politics, and particularly democratic processes and institutions; social issues, including women, families, education, housing, health and nutrition; and development, with reports on investment, debt, financial aid and structural adjustment. Compared to the AP and Reuters wires, IPS has proportionately more references to development, culture and social issues, and fewer to crime, disasters, military activity and political violence.

IPS Projects

Training journalists is one of the IPS project department's most important activities. Projects typically train IPS contributors and other journalists to provide information on development and international co-operation. A recent project involved managing a daily news service in Zimbabwe to train journalists and disseminate news from member stations of the Southern African Broadcasting Association (SABA). Another was training 32 journalists in Africa, Latin America and the Caribbean on reporting population issues. The European Union supported a project to develop a network of journalists and media organizations in central and eastern Europe as a means of reinforcing democratic practices in the region.

Clients have included government agencies such as the Canadian International Development Agency (CIDA), the Danish, Dutch, Finnish, Italian and Norwegian ministries of foreign affairs, the German Ministry for Economic Development and Cooperation, and the Swedish International Development Agency (SIDA). United Nations agencies have been major supporters of IPS projects, particularly the Food and Agriculture Organization (FAO), the Children's Fund (UNICEF), the Development Fund for Women (UNIFEM), the UN Development Programme (UNDP), the Educational, Scientific and Cultural Organization (UNESCO) and the

Environment Programme (UNEP). United Nations contracts usually call for IPS to report on projects undertaken by the agency. They usually specify that selection and treatment of the topics are left to IPS, which distributes the items over its network.

Several foundations also have funded projects, among them Germany's Carl-Duisberg-Gesellschaft and the Friedrich-Ebert-Stiftung, the Dutch Federatie Nederlandse Vakbeweging and The Netherlands Organization for International Development Co-operation (NOVIB), and the US-based Charles Stewart Mott Foundation, John D. and Catherine T. MacArthur Foundation, Ford Foundation and W. Alton Jones Foundation. These contracts usually involve funding for reporting on specific topics in development, the environment, women and democracy, among others. Recent examples include a UNDP-funded programme to create awareness for sustainable development in Asia through training of journalists in 11 countries. UNDP also funded a project to strengthen information flows on Haitian issues to promote democracy there. The Diocese of Graz in Austria supported a project to create a flow of information on rural development in East Africa.

Several projects furnish the North with contextualized information from the South. The Environmental Reporting Service covers environmental organizations, and is supported by the US-based W. Alton Jones Foundation. The Ford Foundation supported a fellowship for an African correspondent to report on African issues from Washington DC, a key news centre on issues of concern to the region.

Other publications include the *G-77 Journal*, a fortnightly information bulletin for the developing countries. Inter Press Service Features is a fortnightly package of features, special reports and columns that is mailed to media clients in the Asia-Pacific region. The package, distributed in English, is translated into Bahasa Indonesia, Bangla, Hindi, Nepali, Tamil, Thai and Urdu for local distribution. The agency produces weekly or monthly bulletins for issue-specific organizations on development, drugs, human rights, religion, environment, investment, energy, population, arts and entertainment, technology and Latin American integration. An example is *Tierramerica*, a bimonthly supplement for newspapers, published by the UNEP using IPS news services and intended to encourage protection and sustainable use of resources in Latin America and the Caribbean. The IPS Columnist Service provides analysis and commentary by statesmen, officials, opinion-makers, cultural leaders and experts.

IPS also assists projects aimed at development co-operation. Among them is the Technical Information Promotion System (TIPS), a South–South network that collects and disseminates technology and trade information to thousands of users in Africa, Asia and Latin America (Giffard, 1994). TIPS is funded by the Italian, Austrian and Netherlands governments, the EC Commission and UNDP.

In 1994, IPS began a three-year project to create gender awareness among its own journalists, with the aim of improving understanding of the roles of women and men in the development process. The project is supported by the UN Development Fund for Women (UNIFEM), the Danish Ministry of Foreign Affairs (DANIDA), and the Swedish International Development Authority (SIDA).

Impact of Globalization

The same process of globalization that shaped the mission and editorial policies of IPS in recent years precipitated a crisis in its operations. Funding for IPS comes from three main sources: sale of its news service to media and other users; grants and projects paid for by outside organizations; and carrier services. All three revenue streams have dwindled. By comparison with traditional international agencies such as the Associated Press or Reuters, IPS is a shoestring operation. At its most affluent, in 1992, the agency's annual budget totalled $15 million. By 1997, this had shrunk to $5.8 million, resulting in severe reductions in expenditure in every region.

The financial crisis can be attributed in large measure to the end of the cold war, which resulted in a sharp decline in official development assistance (ODA) from donor nations to the developing regions. With the end of East–West rivalry, the notion of the third world had become largely irrelevant; it was no longer of strategic importance. Most donor countries cut back the percentage of GNP devoted to development aid, which is now at its lowest level in two decades. Part of what remained was diverted to eastern Europe, or to new activities like peacekeeping operations. For IPS, this meant fewer grants for third world communications projects, which also supported the agency's regular operations.

Such constraints are common among alternative news agencies trying to compete in the global marketplace (Boyd-Barrett and Thussu, 1992: 109–10). Some factors, however, are unique to IPS. Starting in 1992, IPS had received part of the proceeds of a public lottery in The Netherlands, which yielded almost $3 million a year to expand the European network. However, policy disagreements between the Dutch foundation that ran the lottery and IPS management in Rome (among other things, over the foundation's proposal that IPS buy the bankrupt United Press International), resulted in a phasing out of the relationship, loss of the lottery revenue and a sharp cutback in IPS's expensive European staff and operations. At the same time several major projects were completed, or failed to get continued funding. Some promised grants did not materialize. Revenue from telecommunications declined as deregulation and advances in technology decreased reliance by third parties on IPS technical services. Another global trend – deregulation and privatization of media – undercut IPS's traditional links with national news agencies.

IPS management responded to the financial crisis by adopting a 'structural adjustment plan' that involved closing down loss-making affiliates in several countries, decentralizing management functions from Rome to regional offices and aggressive cost-cutting, particularly in Europe and North America. One successful strategy involved switching some bureaux to 'franchising' contracts, in terms of which IPS correspondents also handle sales of the service. Under this arrangement, offices are expected to cover increasing portions of their expenses through local income. First implemented in Latin America in 1995 (thereby avoiding the threatened closure of half the bureaux in the region), the system is being introduced where feasible in other regions.

The cutbacks also had an effect on the news service. The number of countries with permanent bureaux dropped from 44 in 1995 to 41 in 1996; the number of permanent staff from 192 to 140; and the number of stringers from 351 to 233. The survival plan called for concentrating money and staff on the editorial product, and particularly the production of a news service focusing on key global issues, while preserving quality by limiting output to 30 news features a day. Despite the cuts, IPS appears to have retained most of its major subscribers and has added a significant number of new clients.

IPS Online

IPS offset losses in revenue from telecommunications by itself embracing the new technologies. Satellite distribution has replaced fixed lines, radio teleprinters and telex machines. IPS now uses the Internet to reach such groups as NGOs. The resulting savings have contributed to the very survival of the agency. IPS regards the new technologies as not only slashing telecommunication costs, but as a means to advance its mission to promote understanding among the world's peoples and to ensure that the voices of all groups of actors are heard. An IPS Online Policy document, adopted in 1996 after much internal discussion, posits that IPS has a role to play in promoting a democratic and participatory, rather than top-down, communications system. The paper calls for creation of a 'development mall' that would provide a new source of revenue, distribute IPS products, implement communication projects, promote development dialogue and cement relations between the agency and its partners and donors. As of 1997, the IPS Web site consisted of two servers, one in Rome, the other in Norway. The Rome site (www.ips.com) contains institutional information and samples of IPS products, and is free. The Rome server links to the Norwegian site, which contains the entire IPS news service in several languages for the past three years, organized by region and topic and searchable by keyword. Access to the full text of articles requires a subscription. IPS has successfully marketed the database to schools, universities and other institutions in Scandinavia.

Even if IPS succeeds in raising substantial revenue from online services, it is not likely to become self-sustaining. The numerous media clients served by the international agencies in the North have large circulations or audiences and can afford to pay substantial amounts. But the kind of background news that IPS provides, while useful and important, is not particularly attractive to market-driven commercial media. Two-thirds of IPS subscribers are in developing regions that have fewer and less affluent media. Operating the IPS news services costs more than half the annual budget, but less than one-third of revenue is from subscribers. The balance must come from funding for projects, or from donors who consider it important that alternative views should be heard.

In the case of United Nations agencies that contract with IPS to report on their activities the motivation clearly is to publicize and mobilize support for their work. Much of their effort goes into development projects in remote areas that take place over an extended period and have no news peg to attract coverage by mainstream media. These agencies typically get the world's attention only when they are involved in disasters – famines, floods, epidemics or refugee crises. Covering their unspectacular but vital everyday activities dovetails neatly with IPS's editorial mission – although it opens the agency to charges that it cannot be fully objective when coverage is commissioned.

Other supporters have more generic motives. European governments and foundations, particularly in Scandinavia, Germany, The Netherlands and Austria, have demonstrated a sympathetic interest in third world concerns – as evidenced by the Brandt Commission report, with its central thesis of the mutual interdependence of developed and developing nations. Typical motives for supporting IPS emerge clearly from a 1997 report prepared for the Norwegian Ministry of Foreign Affairs (Norwegian Royal Ministry of Foreign Affairs, 1997). Norway is the third largest contributor to IPS's core programmes, after The Netherlands Organization for International Development Cooperation. Norway has supported IPS operations, particularly in Africa and Asia, since 1987, and the report evaluates the desirability of continued funding. It recognizes that IPS is unlikely ever to become economically self-sufficient, and will need continued subvention. It points out that one of the main objectives of Norwegian foreign policy is contributing towards peace, human rights and democracy, and that media have a central role in promoting these ideals. It notes that Norway's policy is congruent with IPS's credo that

> as national boundaries are obscured, news services must convey the impact of international systems on local peoples, so they are empowered to understand their own world and the effect of the outside world upon them. It is only by ensuring an informed global civil society that peoples everywhere will share equitably in the development process.

The report recommends continued funding from nations in the North that find the 'value systems and thematic choices and priorities of IPS important as well in a political North–South and South–South relation as in a broader context where democracy and the plurality of opinions in the world becomes a value in itself'.

References

Boyd-Barrett, Oliver and Thussu, Daya Kishan (1992) *Contra Flow in Global News*, London: John Libbey.

Giffard, C. Anthony (1984) 'Inter Press Service: news from the third world', *Journal of Communication*, Autumn: 41–59.

Giffard, C. Anthony (1991-1997) *The World of Inter Press Service*, Rome: IPS.

Giffard, C. Anthony (1992) *International Press Coverage of the Food and Agriculture Organization*, Rome: FAO.

Giffard, C. Anthony (1994) 'The Technical Information Pilot System', *Journal of Development Communication*, June: 34–44.

Inter Press Service (1996a) *IPS 2000*, Rome: IPS.

Inter Press Service (1996b) *Notes for an IPS 2000 Plan*, Rome: IPS.

Inter Press Service (1996c) *Draft Document for Global Project*, Rome: IPS.

Inter Press Service (1997) *Articles of Association*, Rome: IPS.

Kaul, Inge and Savio, Roberto (1993) *A Political Framework for North–South Relations*, New York: UN Development Programme.

Lobe, Jim (1997) Interview with Jim Lobe, IPS Washington bureau chief, 4 October.

Norwegian Royal Ministry of Foreign Affairs (1997) *Review of Norwegian Assistance to IPS* (draft report).

13 TV News Exchange

Stig Hjarvard

The Eurovision News Exchange is a distribution network for television news pictures and a part of the general Eurovision programme exchange system that is organized by the European Broadcasting Union, EBU, the European organization of national, public service broadcasters. The Eurovision News Exchange distributes news items between all national public service broadcasters in western and (since January 1993) in eastern Europe. The Eurovision News Exchange was initiated in the late 1950s and has been a prominent actor in the field of international TV news distribution ever since. There are other actors in the wholesale TV news business in Europe, and, in particular, private agencies such as WTN and Reuters TV have expanded their activities during the 1990s. However, the Eurovision News Exchange continues to be a very important TV news distribution system in Europe.

The Eurovision model of co-operation has spread to many parts of the world. During the 1980s it was adopted by a majority of the other regional broadcasting unions. Only North and South America seem to be immune to this kind of co-operative model. The regional broadcasting unions and their respective exchange networks are:[1]

Regional organization network	*TV news exchange*
Arab States Broadcasting Union (ASBU)	Arabvision
Asian-Pacific Broadcasting Union (ABU)	Asiavision
Caribbean Broadcasting Union (CBU)	Caribvision
European Broadcasting Union (EBU)	Eurovision
Union of National Radio and Television organizations of Africa (URTNA)	Afrovision

In this chapter I will first give an outline of the historical development of these exchange networks, based on the Eurovision model, from the early initiatives in the 1970s to the satellite-based systems of the 1990s. The reciprocal influence from specific interests of broadcasters and the general political debate on inequalities in global information flows are emphasized. The chapter then moves on to analyse the content of the news flow and discuss some of the major problems connected to the question of different conceptions of news value.

Before I move on to the historical analysis, I shall briefly specify the main characteristics of the Eurovision model:

- The Eurovision news exchange is a co-operative venture between *national, public* broadcasters, either independent public service institutions (European stations such as ARD/Germany and DR/Denmark) or government-controlled institutions (primarily the North African stations such as LJB/Libya and some east European stations). Thus the TV news service of the national participants is typically of a non-commercial nature and subject to public obligations (typically demanding an unbiased news service of high quality). In some few cases the news service is subject to direct governmental censorship.
- The television news pictures are exchanged on a non-profit basis. The TV news item is *not* considered a commodity but a *public good*. Thus the participants only pay for the use of technical and administrative facilities, not for the news items.
- The Eurovision system also operates as a distributor between agencies and their subscribers among the national participants. These items are paid for on a traditional subscription basis. Thus the Eurovision system is financially speaking a dual system: partly a non-profit exchange system, partly a distributor of agency items. Until the spread of satellite technology in the 1980s the Eurovision system was the only network through which agencies could reach their subscribers by electronic means. Thus the subscribers could in many respects – via the Eurovision system – control the the agencies' operations *vis-à-vis* their subscribers in western Europe. The subscribers have now lost most of this influence because satellite technology allows the agencies to reach their customers directly.
- The costs of operating the system (technical and administrative costs) are shared between the participant according to a *collective cost-sharing system* in which larger TV stations *subsidize* the use of smaller stations.
- The participation of the national newsrooms is based on a *voluntary principle*. There is no contract that specifies how many news items the individual station must offer or receive; this is up to the individual newsroom in question to decide for itself. However, there is a general 'moral' obligation to offer pictures that are considered to be of interest to other countries.
- The national newsrooms maintain *editorial independence* in the sense that they are free to offer and receive items and can use the news pictures in any way they want. However, the final news packages distributed among the members of the system are put together by a *supranational* news coordinator and part of the news in these packages is selected by the news coordinator alone. The national newsrooms do not maintain full control of the system at the supranational level in the detailed selection of news, but they can influence the composition of the news packages by giving a request to the coordination center in Geneva by electronic mail or during the daily radio conferences between all participants.

- There is a higher degree of user influence on the performance of the system compared to a traditional agency–buyer relationship. Representatives of the national newsrooms meet every half year to evaluate and discuss problems and possible improvements of the system.

These characteristics of the Eurovision system may sound rather idealistic, and indeed there is a certain democratic ethics inherent in the principles and practice of the system. None the less there is also a more pragmatic reason why these principles have been adopted in the first place. At an early stage in the development of the Eurovision system it was recognized that if the aim was to create a large pool of interesting news from many countries it was necessary to create conditions that allowed countries to participate regardless of size and financial capabilities and to offer and receive on the basis of journalistic reasons only. The voluntary principle and subsidizing arrangements helped to create these conditions.[2]

The Eurovision model has spread to many regions of the world but it varies in the extent to which the principles have been implemented. This reflects both an adjustment of the model to specific socio-geographical circumstances and a historical disadvantage for the regional newcomers. The Eurovision system was established at a time when commercial TV news agencies did not yet play a prominent role. The new regional news exchanges have been trying to establish themselves at a later time when agencies have not only been active for several decades but are also experiencing a considerable growth in activity thanks to the same satellite technology that enabled the regional exchanges to proliferate. The competition today is much harder than in the 1950s and 1960s, when the European broadcasters had a *de facto* monopoly on electronic news distribution in western Europe. A collective non-profit system is much more difficult to establish when a commercial service is available to the potential participants with often more favourable conditions. In order to acquire the benefits of a collective system (for example control of distribution system) it is often necessary to give up immediate and individual benefits.

The Eurovision model of co-operation obviously differs from the agency model of commercial enterprise. However, the purpose of this chapter is *not* to argue that a non-commercial model necessarily or in all cases is superior to an agency model. Both models have advantages and disadvantages, and a mixed or dual system with both models represented is perhaps the best solution. The experience of regional news exchanges using the Eurovision model of co-operation also demonstrates the weaknesses of this model and implicitly signifies some of the advantages of the agency model. But the global spread of the European public model provides a useful case to discuss – on the basis of practical experience – the possibilities of such a non-comercial organization of news distribution. Furthermore, the case provides an interesting corrective to the general assumption that the global TV news flow is entirely dominated by commercial agencies.

The Development of the Regional Exchanges

Attempts to build up regional exchange systems date back to the beginning of the 1970s when more formalized co-operation between the broadcasting unions began to take place. The first World Conference of Broadcasting Unions was held in Rome in 1972 on the initiative of the EBU and has been held subsequently every three years. The conference both deals with inter-union questions on possible areas of co-operation (technical, programmes, etc.) and serves as a global forum for the coordination of broadcasters' interest in other international organizations and interest groups such as ITU, Intelsat, UNESCO, etc. The question of usage of satellite technology for broadcast purposes has been a predominant concern at these conferences.

The establishment of the International Broadcast News Workshop has been of particular importance for the development of TV news exchanges. The first workshop was held in Cologne, Germany, in 1973 and has continued to take place every four to five years. The workshop is partly a forum for professional discussion between foreign TV news editors and correspondents, partly a kind of informal sub-committee between the world broadcasting conferences. In addition to the broadcasting unions a single private organization, the German Friedrich-Ebert-Stiftung, FES, a social and cultural institution of Social Democratic orientation, has played an important role for the International Broadcast News Workshop. The FES has promoted new ideas and taken many initiatives in the workshop and has provided financial support for many activities; to some extent it has also served as a secretariat for the workshop.

The discussions in UNESCO and other international bodies about the global inequalities in information flows have been important for the development of regional exchange mechanisms for TV news. In the first place these discussions about a New World Information and Communication Order, NWICO, provided a political framework for understanding the necessity of alternative distribution networks and later – in the 1980s – UNESCO and similar bodies became more practically involved in these initiatives providing organizational and financial support. However, it is characteristic of the history of regional TV news exchanges, that when the NWICO debate was in its early stages in the 1970s some of the broadcasting unions had already begun to take the first practical steps to change existing inequalities in international news flow.

Although other international entities have supported the development of TV news-exchange mechanisms the broadcasting unions have been the main actors and it is within their professional co-operative framework that the exchange mechanisms have been developed. Thus the choice of the Eurovision model of the European Broadcasting Union was a very natural one, being in accordance with existing organizational and professional preferences in the broadcasting and TV news sector. Furthermore, the basic characteristics of the Eurovision model were also considered to be supportive of the development of a more independent flow of news pictures. The principle of freedom to offer and freedom to accept was considered important. Thus the recommendations from the second International Broadcast News Workshop in Cairo in 1977 stated:

> The Workshop believes that TV news exchanges between broadcasters on the basis of the principle of freedom to offer, or not to offer, to accept or not to accept have great potential for redressing the existing information imbalance, and notes with satisfaction the progress made in organizing TV news exchanges in the Arab countries and in Asia and the improvement in exchanges in Ibero-America since the Cologne-workshop.[3]

The support for this principle reflects several interests. First, the experience of the European model clearly demonstrated that the principle was important for editorial reasons because it allowed journalistic criteria to play a prominent role, in contrast to a system based on compulsory offers and receptions. Second, it was an important principle that protected the editorial autonomy of the individual national broadcaster. For the large group of broadcasters who either directly or indirectly were subject to governmental control it would have been impossible to give up any kind of editorial authority to a transnational entity. Finally, the voluntary principle was favoured because it was considered a non-commercial principle, and as such a counterpart to the operating principles of private TV news agencies. Hence, ABU argued at the fourth International Broadcast News Workshop in Malaga in 1986:

> TV news agencies are there to sell visual news material. Broadcasters are there to broadcast visual news material. If supply meets demand, it is only a question of money to keep the mechanism working. The establishment of direct broadcaster to broadcaster relations in terms of news exchange was, therefore, a challenge to this traditional concept of supplier–consumer relations.[4]

The principles of the European model fitted well with the needs and visions of third world broadcasters at that time. However, and I shall return to this later, these principles were not without problems when applied to a non-European context.

A crucial factor for the development of regional exchange mechanisms has been the advent and spread of satellite technology. Contrary to the situation in Europe and the USA the transmission facilities for broadcasting purposes in the 1970s were poorly developed in many third world countries and regions (and in some places this evidently continues to be the case). The huge distances both within the national borders and between the countries in the different regions made it extremely expensive to built a regional transmission system via terrestrial facilities. Satellite technology offered an opportunity to overcome this geographical barrier. Thus it was the experience with a large-scale satellite TV experiment in 1983, the so-called

'Global Satellite System Project', that gave an important impetus to the further development of regional exchange networks.

The Global Satellite System Project was a result of the co-operation between broadcasting unions, UNESCO and Intelsat. In continuation of UNESCO's establishment of the IPDC programme, UNESCO arranged a symposium in October 1981 about 'regional and international mechanisms for the dissemination and exchange of information'. At this meeting the representatives of broadcasting unions proposed that concrete plans for a worldwide satellite TV network should be developed. Such a network should be permanently available for exchange of TV news and programmes of general interest such as transmission of major sports and cultural events. UNESCO supported this proposal but the broadcasting unions made it a condition that they had the sole responsibility for the project so the involvement of UNESCO was limited to financial support for weaker third world participants and an intermediary role in the early stages of the project.

As a first step towards such a worldwide TV network the broadcasting unions decided to conduct an experiment of TV news exchanges both inside different regions and between the regions. This experiment was carried out in March 1983 with participation from the Asian, Arabic and African unions: ABU, ASBU and URTNA. In total 27 TV organizations participated in the experiment and more than 500 news items were exchanged.[5]

Although the experiment was forced to stop earlier than initially planned because of financial limitations it was very important for the subsequent development of news exchanges. It demonstrated in practice that third world countries could take advantage of satellite technology for both intra- and inter-regional exchange. ABU, for example, stated in its newsletter after the beginning of the experiment:

> March 1, 1983 will go down in the records of broadcasting history as the day on which 22 broadcasting organizations in Asia and Africa made their first attempt to establish a South–South dialogue in television by satellite. . . . [The] ultimate aim is to establish a global satellite network for the exchange of television news and programmes as a practical means to reduce the imbalance in the flow of information.[6]

Although the exchange was only an experiment, the idea of a global system had now acquired so much impetus that a discussion of the organizational and editorial structure of such a global system seemed necessary. The fourth World Conference of Broadcasting Unions, which was held in Algeria during the experiment, recommended the establishment of a central structure to coordinate the further development of a global system and to manage the system when implemented. The conference recommended

> the creation of a minimum central inter-union coordination structure responsible for planning, developing and coordinating any regional and interregional action judged necessary for the implementation of the Global Satellite Project, at union

and inter-union level and *vis-à-vis* any international organization concerned (UNESCO – ITU – Intelsat – Intersputnik etc.).[7]

It turned out, however, that it wasn't possible to create such a central coordination group at that time. Some of the unions did not have the required resources or authority to undertake a more binding inter-union co-operation. Furthermore, the most urgent problem was not the development of an exchange *between* the unions, but a more basic one: the development of organizational and technical structures to support the development of *intra*-regional exchange. In recognition of this a meeting between the directors general of broadcasting unions in July 1983 underlined that there was a need for 'a first stage in the course of which each union concerned will endeavor to set up and/or develop regional television news exchange systems'.[8]

This brought the planning at the global, inter-regional level to a temporary standstill. Meanwhile there was considerable progress at the intra-regional level; during the next few years both ABU and ASBU introduced a daily exchange of news via satellite, in 1984 and 1986 respectively. The African region, however, was still without any TV news exchange. In the light of this development the EBU at the fifth World Conference of Broadcasting Unions in Prague in February 1986 called for a renewed initiative to coordinate the exchange between the different regional exchanges. EBU suggested that the 'building bricks' of a global system were ready: 'the elements of a coordination of news exchanges on a planetary scale are now in place, except for the African continent'.[9]

As a consequence a working group later to be known as the Inter-Union Satellite Operations Group, ISOG, was created. ISOG became a very important forum to represent the interests of broadcasting unions *vis-à-vis* Intelsat and other entities concerning technical, financial and operational aspects of broadcasting satellite technology.

In the late 1980s a global news exchange system between broadcasters no longer seemed a remote vision but a possibility within a limited span of years. Thus it seemed necessary to clarify the organizational and editorial management of such a global system. The recommendations from the 1983 conference in Algeria (quoted in part above) pointed towards a centralized system: the implied model was the regional exchange system, now elevated to the global level with a central coordination committee to organize the daily TV news exchanges. The sixth World Conference of Broadcasting Unions in 1989 in Washington reconsidered these principles. Centralized coordination was now considered undesirable for both editorial, political and organizational reasons:

> However, the central flaw in the Algiers proposal was identified as the proposition that the exchange should be centrally coordinated. As one speaker put it, 'If it is to be centrally coordinated, it will fail. If we are talking about every union downlegging each other's exchange, we are on the right track.'

A global news exchange should be governed by two principles:

- each union must develop its own regional exchange expressly to serve the interests of its own members;
- each union should have equal access to the news exchanges of the sister unions, in which each remained free to use or not to use the available news material.[10]

As a consequence the vision was no longer to replace the regional exchanges with a global exchange system. Instead, the global system should become a *network* between independent systems that on a continuous basis provide and receive news items to and from each other. The voluntary principle also became the basis of inter-regional exchanges. The individual region was to have neither editorial influence upon nor financial responsibility for the offers to and receptions from other regions.

Current State of Development of the Individual Networks

The level of development varies considerably in the different regions. The following overview summarizes the development of the individual regional networks.[11]

Afrovision   URTNA was formed in 1962 and today it has members in 48 countries. Exchange of radio programmes began quite early, and from 1974 an exchange of TV programmes began. In 1977 a permanent centre for programme exchange was set up in Nairobi. The exchange of TV programmes was primarily carried out by exchange of videotapes and to a small extent via the terrestrial network. Until 1991 exchange of TV *news* was not a systematic activity but was carried out on a bilateral basis through exchange of videotapes. A systematic exchange of TV news began on 2 January 1991 between nine members. In 1997 the number of partipants was eight.[12] During 1992 1,244 news items were exchanged; approximately 100 of these came from Eurovision. There is not, as is the case of Eurovision, a collective cost-sharing system; each station pays the same amount to cover international costs and all of the national costs for the use of the ground station, etc.

Arabvision   ASBU was formed in 1969 and today it has members in 21 countries. In the early 1970s they began to exchange TV news on terrestrial network and by tape. In the period from mid-1973 to 1975 the news exchange intensified, but after 1975 the activity declined rapidly. In 1973 a five-day experiment using satellite exchange (Intelsat) was carried out in which 39 news items were distributed. With the launch of Arabsat 1 and Arabsat 2 in 1985 a new opportunity for systematic and continuous exchange of TV news appeared. A six-month experimental news exchange between 14 Arab countries was carried out between 1 October and 31 March and this led to a permanent exchange of TV news. In March 1987 the ASBU News Exchange Center was opened in Algier. By June 1993, 13 members were affiliated with the news exchange but on average only six members participated in the daily exchange.[13] Arabvision also receives the daily news packages from Eurovision and redistributes these to their members. Arabvision has a collective cost-sharing system that among other things takes into consideration the gross national product of the country, that is, the relative economic wealth in the different countries. In 1991 the volume of the exchange was about 2,500 news items.

Asiavision   ABU was formed in 1964 and today it has members in 30 countries. A limited exchange of TV news began in 1977 between NHK/Japan and TVRI/Indonesia. This exchange of news on videotapes gradually extended to five countries. In January 1984 a permanent TV news exchange via satellite was set up. During 1996 nearly 6,000 news items were exchanged in Asiavision. In principle all offers are distributed, but occasionally a few items are omitted by the coordination centre in Kuala Lumpur if they are considered propagandistic or simply of poor quality.[14] Ten ABU members participate in the news exchange on a regular basis but occasionally some other TV stations participate.[15] It is possible to receive Asiavision on a subscription basis; for example the American network and CNN subscribe to Asiavision. There is no collective cost-sharing system; each member pays the same amount to cover the mutual, international costs, namely central coordination in Kuala Lumpur, international satellite costs, etc.

Caribvision   CBU was formed in 1970 and today it has members in 17 countries and territories. Satellite exchange began in January 1986 between three members, three times a week. In 1997 the regular group of participants had grown to six members with exchanges five days a week.[16] A few other TV stations in the area occasionally contribute to the exchange. In 1991 a total of 1,148 news items was exchanged; in 1992 the number was 1,087. Caribvision has no regular exchange with other unions. CNN, WTN and Reuters TV occasionally take some news items but agency items are not transmitted in the Caribvision exchange. According to CBU-coordinator Sharon Marshall, the coordination centre does not serve an editorial function; most of the offers are exchanged but practical circumstances can cause cancellations. No content analysis of the Caribvision exchange has been made, but according to Sharon Marshall the news content is varied: 'the stories exchanged run the gamut from politics, disasters, economic issues, occasional culture and art items, and sport'.[17]

News Values and Cross-cultural Exchanges

In order to establish exchange systems in third world regions the broadcasters have been forced to tackle many difficulties and problems of which many continue to hold back the development. Some crucial problems concern lack of adequate equipment, poor technical and journalistic education, difficult relations with national Post Telegrammes and Telephone Services (PTTs) and Intelsat, etc. The problems are not only related to the specific media environment in the countries but also to more general societal conditions. Thus it was no coincidence that Afrovision was the last network to be established; it can best be described as a result of the general political and economic problems in Africa.

In the following I will go into more detail over one very important and recurrent problem: the editorial problem related to the exchange of news between countries and regions with different political systems and different conceptions of news value. The basis of the exchange system is the contributions from the individual national TV stations. Consequently the system relies on a certain homogeneity of news criteria between the countries. If a certain degree of consensus is not present because of different conceptions of news value, the participants will not consider the offers of the others relevant or usable.

The institutional foundation of journalism, including broadcast journalism, determines the basic framework for the work of the individual journalist and news medium including the application of news criteria. In western countries (western Europe and the USA) journalism in both print and electronic media is guaranteed a relatively high degree of independence from state institutions, and from legislative, judicial and executive powers. Ideally journalism is to serve as the fourth power of the state, that, independently of both state and market forces, ensures the exercise of public debate and provides a critical function by scrutinizing the sayings and doings of social actors in state and market. In short, journalism serves the exercise of citizenship. The aim here is not to discuss whether or not journalism and the media also serve this ideal function in practice in western societies, nor to discuss the different obstacles that impede journalism and the media from serving such a function in western societies. The aim is only to point out that journalism has considerable independence from state power and this is a central part of the journalistic profession's understanding of its own work, and, subsequently, is of importance for the conception of news value and news criteria.

The institutional basis of journalism in many third world countries differs considerably from the western ideal and this has been a serious obstacle to the development of both intra- and inter-regional exchange. In many countries in Africa, Asia and the Arab world the press is not independent of state power, but on the contrary is either directly or indirectly controlled by the government. This is especially true for broadcast news, whereas the printed press often maintains a higher degree of independence. In the following I shall briefly specify the consequences of this for the development of TV news exchanges, taking the Arab region as an example.

In almost all Arab countries the press is subject to severe government control. The press has different organizational structures, namely private, public or semi-public. Abubakr (1980) points out that the Arab press was typically not established so much from commercial objectives but in association with national liberation movements and as such has strong national, social and religious objectives. National news agencies are government organizations whose purpose is to support the projection of state policies to the domestic population and the outside world. Consequently the Arab news agencies have a much more official character, and the form and content of news differ from western agency material. A UNESCO report characterizes this in the following way:

> This link between government and agency is most often manifest in the somewhat stilted presentation of news by comparison with the 'lighter' presentation in, for example, American and European agencies. The tendency is for a disproportionate amount of space to be devoted to what can be called 'protocolarian' news (that is, the doings, sayings and travels of political elite figures).(Harris, 1981: 6)

The electronic news media play a considerable role in the Arab world. Turkistani (1988) has examined the news criteria and news conception of Arab TV news journalists. His conclusion is that Arab TV news journalists adopt a highly official attitude towards domestic news, whereas a more 'western' attitude is often taken towards foreign news. This is among other things a result of the different sources available for domestic and foreign news; foreign news often comes from western news agencies or Eurovision and because of this has a more 'western' character and deals with more critical issues. However, the difference in source is not the only explanation for this variation. Turkistani (1988) reports that foreign news is subject to a higher degree of independent rewriting and re-editing by Arab journalists, while domestic news typically is broadcast in a 'raw' form, as simply a presentation or reproduction of official statements and actions.

The national objectives of television in the Arab countries were strongly taken into consideration when the regional exchange system was developed. In a charter by ASBU from 1973 about the purpose of news exchange it is specified:

> The system shall devote its greatest attention to the content of the news material exchanged through it, and in all cases, shall ensure:
>
> 1. That this material shall reflect the interest of the Arab man, deepen his belief in the unity of objective and destiny of the Arab nation, develop common trends in the Arab homeland by disseminating information thereon, its message and potentialities, while stressing and supporting the causes of its struggle.
> 2. That this material shall abide by the provisions of the Arab Broadcasting Charter, namely to conform to the truth, to be accurate in the selection of sources, to be just and unbiased, to avoid sensational or exciting details which are not necessary for the realistic rendering of news items.
> 3. That this material shall not be confined to hot news but cover all fields of social, cultural, economic and other activities.
> 4. That this material exchanged with other regions of the world, either incoming

or outgoing, shall reflect the necessity of acquainting peoples with one
another and of deepening the spirit of human brotherhood.[18]

The requirements in paragraph (2) (to conform to the truth, be accurate,
unbiased, etc.) are very similar to the guidelines for the news service of west
European public service broadcasters and indeed corresponds with a
general western news conception. The stress on non-sensational news is,
however, in this context, an implicit criticism of western news agencies'
alleged preference for so-called 'negative' news, that is, accidents, scandals,
etc. The demands in paragraphs (1) and (3) differ from traditional western
news criteria and news conception. Paragraph (1) underlines the role of the
news service in fostering national unity and in creating popular support for
national development. The idea of national unity is extended to the regional
level to create unity in the Arab world for the Arab man, and this reflects
the fact that ASBU and Arabvision are built up within the framework of
the Arab League. The purpose of paragraph (3) is to contrast Arabvision
with the commercial TV agencies and Eurovision by underlining the need
for what is often called 'development news', namely news about general
societal questions, economic, cultural, educational affairs. The universal
declaration of intent in paragraph (4) is so vague that it really doesn't say
anything substantial; it can however be interpreted as a demand for more
'positive' news and as such it is a criticism of western news values.
   Turkistani (1988) has carried out a quantitative content analysis of TV
news items in Arabvision during the experimental period from November
1985 to March 1986. The result of his analysis is presented in Figure 13.1.
Results of the content analysis largely confirm the editorial principles that
are expressed in the ASBU charter. News about official and governmental
matters predominates ('protocol', 'politics', etc.), and news about accidents
and 'light' topics is almost non-existent. However, the intention to have a
large supply of 'development' news has not been fulfilled. The strong
emphasis on official news is shown by the fact that nearly half of the news
is categorized as 'protocol' news, defined by Turkistani in the following way:
'News involving the mere reception, greeting, honoring, visiting, and seeing
off of officials or delegations from inside or outside the country with no
details beyond public relations. This does not include receptions which are
accompanied by negotiations or other political activities' (1988: 168).
Turkistani concludes that

> it is obvious that projection of the state is the principal function of news, even
> though it comes in various types. Projection of the state (whether inside or outside
> the country) constitutes over three-fourths of the contributed items. (1988: 184)

   The fact that news serves the purposes of the state makes it less acceptable to other countries' news services unless they for some reason want to
support another state ideologically. In the ASBU region this has been a particular problem for intra-regional exchange in periods of political conflict

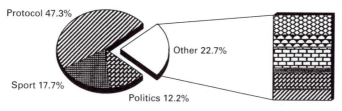

FIGURE 13.1 *Arabvision News Exchange, 1 November 1985 to 31 March 1986*

(*Source*: Turkistani, 1988: 183. Number of exchanged items: 1128)

between the Arab countries. Controversy about the Arab policy towards Israel caused a drop in news exchange in 1975 after a good start in 1973. In the case of inter-regional exchange with western countries the problem is that the very notion of protocol news is incompatible with the conception of the role of the press. Thus the different institutional foundation of the broadcast news media is a barrier to exchange of news pictures between the Arab world and Europe and the USA. Seen with the eyes of western broadcast journalists, Arabvision is encumbered with a serious problem of legitimacy,[19] and the result has been a limited usage of news items from Arabvision.

These political and institutional problems have also – with certain differences – afflicted the ABU and URTNA exchange systems. Quantitative content analyses can give some indications of the kind of news that is exchanged in Asiavision and Afrovision. An analysis of Asiavision covering the period 1 June 1992 to 31 May 1993 shows that politics makes up around 30% of all news; there is also a moderate representation of news about conflict issues (violence: 2.36%; disaster/tragedy: 6.79%), broader social topics (arts/culture: 8.75%; economics: 9.10%) and human interest (4.9%). The category 'general interest', which represents 26.4% of all news items, is unfortunately so vaguely defined that it to some extent invalidates the whole analysis.[20] However, a considerable proportion of non-political news may also be interpreted as a sign of very mixed news values and perhaps an emphasis on 'development' news. A comparison with the Arabvision analysis, which for methodological reasons can only be speculative, shows that Asiavision in some areas looks more like western news and also has more news about broader ('development') social issues.

A quantitative content analysis of Afrovision for the year 1992 (Figure 13.2) shows that political items make up a considerable part of the news. There is also a significant segment of news that deals with broader 'development' issues (economy: 10.3%; culture: 9.08%; environment: 2.73%; social/others: 7.56%). In contrast to the analysis of Arabvision these content analyses only indirectly suggest something about governmental influence on the content of Asiavision and Afrovision. But this problem can be further illustrated by looking at the evaluations from people closely related to the exchange practice. Lansipuro, who assisted

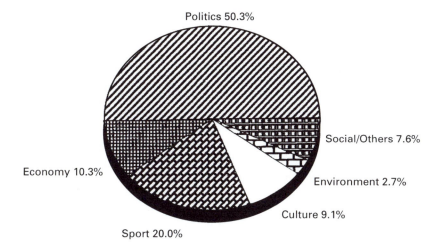

FIGURE 13.2   *Afrovision News Exchange, 2 January to 31 December 1992*
(*Source*: URTNA statistics. Number of exchanged items: 1244. Approx. 100 of these are
Eurovision items)

Asiavision during the construction phase in the 1980s as an EBU expert,
and who generally has expressed support for the Asiavision project and
achievements, evaluated political news in Asiavision in this way:

> The majority of political items from any country are about the activities of the
> government, with a heavy dose of official visits and ceremonies. Coverage of
> opposition activities is rare, and in the case of some members completely absent.
> (Lansipuro, 1987: 25)

Luc Leysen, a journalist from the German ARD and FES consultant for
Afrovision in the 1990s, gave a corresponding statement in 1992 about the
news content in Afrovision: 'Inhaltlich ist noch nicht alles perfekt. Der alte
Reflex der Hofberichterstattung sitzt tief.'[21] This criticism was repeated by
the director of Afrovision, Harald Georg, in an evaluation report in 1996:

> Since its launching, the network has been subjected to 'abusive use' by making
> offers covering speeches of heads of states or the daily activities of his spouse or
> public ceremonies on the inauguration of one or other landmark of national
> progress. The real events on the continents which are of interest to the public at
> large and those outside the national borders such as disputes between the govern-
> ment and opposition parties, natural disasters, successful programmes of multi-
> national co-operation, major cultural and other events are rarely offered for the
> exchange.[22]

These political problems have hampered the development of the news
exchanges in the sense that they have made the news less attractive and consequently have impeded the participation of other TV stations. In this respect
the regional exchanges suffer a handicap compared to the agencies. The

agencies will often be able to film a controversial event in a country in the region and distribute the news pictures to other parts of the world. But the national TV station in the country where the event takes place will often not be allowed to distribute similar pictures because it is a national institution.

The regional exchange networks are aware of these problems but the possibility for change in the regions obviously differs. The ABU News Study Group, which oversees the Asiavision exchange has, for instance, continually encouraged more offers of 'hard news' and criticized when governments have tried to restrict the offer of news items dealing with domestic conflict. A recent content analysis of Asiavision covering March 1997 (Figure 13.3) signifies that conditions may be gradually changing. In 1997 there is much more emphasis on political and hard news compared to the 1980s and early 1990s. Indeed the general distribution of items in Asiavision in 1997 resembles the general priorities of Eurovision. A similar development can be traced in the content of Caribvision. Francine Alexander, assistant manager at CBU, reports 'two significant improvements' in 1997:

> We are able at times to actually have same day stories on the exchange, which was almost impossible in years gone by.
> Stories being sent are much more 'hard news' in style and regional in slant, rather than very local and parochial reports.[23]

Although political and hard news may also be subject to government control, the very stress on these news topics indicates that western news values are gradually gaining prevalence.

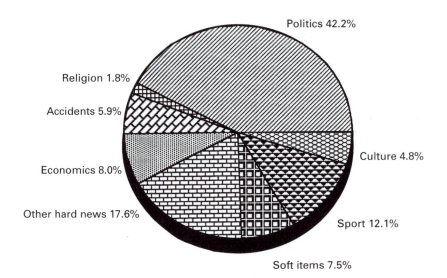

FIGURE 13.3 *Asiavision News Exchange, 1–31 March 1997*
(*Source*: ABU. Number of exchanged items: 438)

In this connection it is interesting to note that the development of inter-national exchanges can influence the political relation between national broadcaster and state. In the Asiavision exchange there have been incidents where a repeated request from other TV stations about a news item has led the government to allow the national TV station to distribute controversial news pictures via Asiavision, even in cases where the national TV station was still not allowed to show them for the national audience.[24] In these inci-dents the national TV station has acted as an intermediary between state interest and international opinion (as expressed by other national foreign news editors through Asiavision). The existence of an international network such as Asiavision can in this way contribute to a new point of professional orientation for broadcast journalists.

Reinhard Keune from the German Friedrich-Ebert-Stiftung (Keune, 1991) states that ASBU and URTNA have a particular problem of depen-dency on governmental policies. The national newsrooms in the ASBU and URTNA regions are not only subject to national governmental control but the regional co-operations are themselves subject to control from regional inter-state co-operations (OAU, Arab League). It is now being discussed whether URTNA and ASBU should try and detach themselves from inter-governmental authorities and become solely professional organizations like ABU and EBU.

Keune (1991) considers these signs of independence as a contributory cause of the establishment of Afrovision in January 1991. Apart from more specific explanations of what made the Afrovision exchange possible, he also put forward a more political and ideological cause:

> At the same time there was already appearing on the horizon in the mid-1990s a far-reaching change of African political paradigms which encouraged quite a number of broadcasting people to orientate themselves newly and more profes-sionally. (Keune, 1991: 21)

These changes of general political paradigms are of course related to the changes in the Soviet Union and eastern Europe. With the collapse of the communist bloc, east–west opposition suddenly declined and the develop-ment paradigm of intensive state planning lost its attraction. In Africa these changes were followed by the abandonment of apartheid in South Africa and this signalled a new future for the whole of Southern Africa. This region would no longer be locked into a permanent conflict between South Africa and its neighbouring countries. As a consequence of these general developments a new situation arose in many African nations in which tra-ditional models of development and the institutional organization of society were no longer adequate. In this new situation journalists have experienced a higher degree of independence *vis-à-vis* national authorities, allowing a more professional attitude to the production of news to develop. Although this tendency has been most visible in the area of printed news, it has to a more modest extent also been noticeable in broadcast news.

Attempts to exchange other types of news have been carried out especially by Asiavision and Afrovision but it has not been without problems. So-called 'development' news differs from traditional news in three ways: in content, form and politics. As to content, it deals with broader social topics (economy, culture, education, etc.) and as to form, it will often have the character of background information told in a non-sensational style. Politically it will often have a bias, either being critical of existing policies, or alternatively, serving as a projection of government interest. The political bias is certainly not a necessary consequence of the focus on development issues; it is of course quite possible to discuss development topics in a neutral or analytical manner. The experience of the independent 'alternative' news agency Inter Press Service (IPS) also demonstrates that it is possible to develop a critical but still professional attitude to these issues. General governmental control of broadcasting in many third world countries does, however, often entail that the treatment of development news will be subject to the policies of the ruling elite and hence development news becomes a demonstration of 'progress' rather than serious information or discussion.

Apart from the political aspect, development news constitutes another problem for the regional exchanges. The idea of development news implies a redefinition of the traditional concept of news and this – together with the absence of a more strict positive definition (actually it is mainly defined negatively, in opposition to western news values) – makes it difficult to achieve consensus about criteria of relevance. Seen from the point of view of the individual country that offers an item of development news it perhaps looks important but this evaluation is seldom shared by other countries' newsrooms. Lansipuro (1987) reports on the exchange of development news in Asiavision:

> Every organization is ready to offer but others are not keen on receiving and using these items. The dilemma was explained well by a participant in the recent workshop of AVN news coordinators: 'if I show a new irrigation project in a neighbor country, they'll ask me next morning why. As if there aren't enough such things in our own country'. (Lansipuro, 1987: 26)

These problems of reaching consensus on news value become even more pronounced in inter-regional exchanges because the cultural differences become more pronounced. The experience of, for instance, Inter Press Service indicates that it is necessary not only to redefine the content of news but also to change the format of this kind of information. The heart of the problem is that you cannot bring non-news (as regards content compared to western standards) in a traditional news format. This kind of information is much better suited for other kinds of journalistic formats, genres and programmes (commentary, analysis, current affairs magazines, etc.).

The Eurovision model is very suitable for exchange of material that emphasizes the news dimension of a social occurrence, that is the *immediacy* aspect of news. However, the model is less suited for material that doesn't accentuate this temporal aspect of news. Thus, there is a built-in contradiction in redefining the news concept *and* using the Eurovision exchange model. The distribution of development information or other types of journalistic non-news material will perhaps – at least in the broadcast field – have better chances of being disseminated through other kinds of exchange mechanisms.

Towards a Global TV News Exchange System?

The regional networks have gone through an impressive phase of development since the Global Satellite System project in 1983. All geographical regions are now – apart from the American continents – covered by network exchanges between national public broadcasters. A foundation has been made for an alternative – or perhaps more correctly a *supplement* – to the news service of commercial TV news agencies. However, intra-regional exchange is still far from being fully developed in most of the regions. In some of the regions only a quarter or a fifth of the union's members participate in the exchange on a regular basis. And the journalistic content has to be improved considerably if a more extensive exchange is to be developed.

An exchange *between* regional networks has only in a few cases been developed to a more regular and comprehensive practice. As discussed earlier, the idea of a centrally coordinated global exchange system has been abandoned. Instead an uncoordinated global network structure has been adopted. Each union remains an independent entity and exchanges with other unions on a voluntary basis.

In Figure 13.4 the degree of interaction between the regions is illustrated.[25] The model distinguishes between four degrees of interaction: (a) systematic exchange practices and a high exchange volume (black arrow); (b) regular exchange practices and a moderate exchange volume (white arrow); (c) ad hoc exchange and low exchange volume (dotted arrow); and (d) no interaction at all (no arrow). From the figure it appears that Eurovision is engaged in exchange with almost all other regions but the degree of interaction varies. The other regions interact mainly with Eurovision – it is only Afrovision and Arabvision that have a mutual exchange with each other. Because of this unequal relationship the inter-regional exchange with Eurovision is relatively of far greater importance for the other regional networks than it is for Eurovision.

Because of the low level of interaction between other regional networks, Eurovision comes to function as a connecting link, a kind of relay station, between the other networks. Several regions take all of the daily Eurovision packages and through this they have access to news items that Eurovision has included from other regions. This is, however, not an ideal solution for the other networks because Eurovision items from other regions are selected with special reference to the needs of European newsrooms and

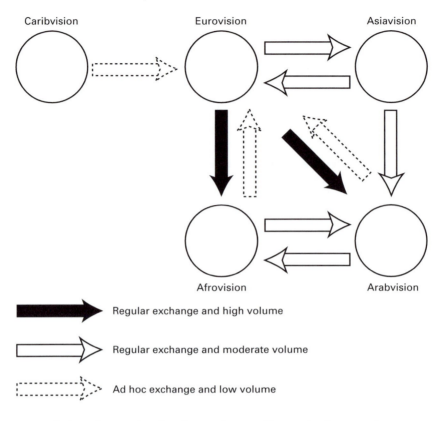

Caribvision   Eurovision   Asiavision

Afrovision   Arabvision

Regular exchange and high volume

Regular exchange and moderate volume

Ad hoc exchange and low volume

FIGURE 13.4 *Inter-regional exchange: degree of interaction between the regions*

they only represent a fraction of the TV news items that are potentially available from the other regions.

Eurovision's role as a connecting point for the inter-regional exchanges makes its news coverage of non-western countries very important. Eurovision does not take many items from other regional exchanges apart from Asiavision. However, Eurovision still has a considerable coverage of non-western affairs. A content analysis of all Eurovision news during one month in 1990 showed the following geographical distribution: Europe 56.3%; North America 10.5%; other highly industrialized and/or western countries (Japan, Israel, Australia, etc.) 7.4%; international organizations 0.8%; third world countries 25.0%. There was an even distribution of the 25% among the four different regions: Africa, Asia, Arab countries/Middle East and Latin America.[26]

At this general level Eurovision news about third world regions is at least not marginally represented. However, the coverage of third world countries could nevertheless be very much influenced by a European or at least western viewpoint. In order to examine this the same 1990 sample was analysed in order to see if news about third world countries was predominantly selected because it related directly to European or western affairs. Most news in Eurovision, including news about third world countries, does only deal with events in one country at a time. This indicates that news about third world countries is not closely related to western interests, at least not at the individual story level. The same conclusion can be drawn from analysis of Eurovision news items dealing with more than one country. In Table 13.1 there is a cross-table distribution of all Eurovision news items dealing with more than one country. News items dealing with one European country interacting with another European country is not surprisingly the most frequent occurrence in Eurovision. However, of 129 items dealing with a third world country and another country, this other country was in almost one-third of the cases another third world country. Of 213 news items dealing with a European country and another country, this other country was in 17.8% of cases a third world country. News dealing with interaction between Europe and North America was actually less frequent (16.0%).

This analysis only considers interaction between countries in news at a very concrete level (countries depicted and/or referred to in the news item). The analysis does not rule out a western bias in the selection of third world news items at a more general level. Such a bias could for instance be a general interest in specific regions because they are vital for western economy. Neither does the analysis rule out a stereotypical coverage of third world affairs in the individual news item. However, the analysis does suggest that Eurovision coverage of third world affairs is not always limited to news that has a European angle. Some Eurovision news actually deals with third world affairs alone, including third world countries interacting with each other. Thus Eurovision does provide some material through which different third world regions can learn about each other.

The level of interaction between regional exchange networks and TV news agencies differs considerably. The Eurovision system has a high degree of exchange with the agencies. Arabvision receives material from WTN but Asiavision and Afrovision have no or only limited exchange with

TABLE 13.1 *Eurovision news exchange: interaction between geographical regions (distribution in per cent according to source locations)*

	Europe %	North America %	Other western %	Global int. org. %	Third world %	Total %	News items numbers
Europe	58.2	16.0	6.1	1.9	17.8	100	213
North America	38.6	2.3	21.6	0.0	38.6	100	89
Other western	28.3	41.3	2.2	4.3	23.9	100	46
Global int. org.	28.6	0.0	14.3	21.4	35.7	100	14
Third world	29.9	26.8	8.7	3.9	30.7	100	127

Note: News items involving more than one country in the period 16 February to 1 April 1990. N = 329. The table is read horizontally.

Source: Hjarvard, 1995a: 235

agencies. The agencies have seen the rise of regional networks as a potential threat to their market shares. Keune (1991) reports that the former Visnews (now Reuters TV) tried to avoid the formation of Asiavision as a broad-caster-to-broadcaster co-operation by suggesting that the exchange became organized by Visnews. This failed and Asiavision has been in competition with the Asian services of Reuters TV, WTN and others since its inaugura-tion. Today, however, Asiavision would like to develop regular exchanges of news with the agencies because it could supplement and improve its regional coverage.[27] At present there is no stable pattern of co-operation between regional networks and TV news agencies.

The international TV news market is undergoing considerable change and expansion as a result of technological innovation, deregulation of com-munication technologies and societal changes. A series of new actors is entering the market. First, new agencies have been formed: European News Service, ENS, and Associated Press Television. Second, a number of satel-lite channels, specialized in news or with a high proportion of news such as American CNN, British BBC World Service TV News and Sky News, Spanish-language ECO News, Japanese GNN and others, have expanded their activities to a regional and global level. These channels do not only compete with the news bulletins of national broadcasters but are also used as sources for news pictures by broadcasters, thus becoming, in effect, news wholesaler. How the relation between the three kind of actors – agencies, regional networks and transnational news channels – will develop in the future is uncertain. Perhaps a more stable system will develop that allows all types of actors to coexist on a complementary basis with a high degree of exchange between them, but it is perhaps more likely that competition will increase and limit the exchange between the different actors and con-sequently lead to the elimination of, for instance some of the regional exchange networks.

The present highly dynamic situation with many new actors in the field bears witness to the relatively weak position of regional exchange networks *vis-à-vis* the agencies – at least when one makes a comparison with the early years of Eurovision. The new regional exchange networks must consolidate themselves in a situation where TV news agencies and dedicated news chan-nels feed news packages directly to their clients via satellite 24 hours a day. Competition is not only increasing at the wholesale level. In many of the regions the national broadcasters face new competition from local and regional commercial channels and this will gradually transform the kind of services and news that the exchange networks must provide for their national participants. National broadcasters are not only looking for more and better news from their own region but are increasingly looking for news content that will compete with that of the commercial newcomers. The exchange networks are forced to adapt to this new situation but it may be difficult because changes at national level happen at a different pace in indi-vidual countries. Thus the needs of NHK in Japan and CCTV in China may certainly not be the same, but they are both part of the same exchange network and Asiavision must be able to cater for them both if they are to continue their participation in free exchanges.

The present structure of interaction between the regional networks (Figure 13.4) could be interpreted as a traditional dependency structure, that is, that TV news flow is locked in a unequal relation of domination in which news goes from north to south and not south to north or south to south. However, this would be a far too simplistic way of understanding the development of inter-regional interaction. At a very general level the exchange structures can of course be said to reflect unequal development, but seen from a more historical and concrete point of view the exchange relations are not signs of domination. Neither Eurovision nor any other of the regional networks has anything to benefit from a limited south–north or south–south flow of news pictures. It is quite the other way around. Eurovision has actively helped the formation of other regional networks, not with the intention of dominating them, but in order to create organizational structures that in the long term could establish regional pools of news from which everybody, including Eurovision, could benefit.

The present structure of exchanges is the temporary result of an on-going process that so far has resulted in the formation of regional exchanges and limited inter-regional exchanges. For economic, political and technical reasons (some of them discussed above) the level of interaction has not developed further so far, but it is possible that this will change in the future.

Today there is no single global system for wholesale distribution of television news if by that one understands a stable, unified and coherent system covering the whole world. What we see instead is a structure consisting of parallel systems (regional exchanges, agencies, transnational news channels) working side by side with different levels of coverage and interaction between them in different parts of the world. The regional exchange networks which have been the focus of this paper are only beginning to connect into a global unbound network structure. Television news is increasingly being distributed around the globe but organizational and editorial control is still very much located at the regional and national level.

Notes

The chapter is based on the analysis of internal documents from the different broadcasting unions, from the World Conferences of Broadcasting Unions, from the International Broadcast News workshops and a 1993 survey of regional television news exchanges undertaken by the author. This survey was updated in spring 1997.

1. There have been – and still exist – other exchange networks between public or state broadcasters, for instance between Islamic countries. They are typically of less importance and are not modelled on Eurovision. For an overview of exchange mechanisms see Boyd-Barrett and Thussu (1992).

2. For a detailed account of the history of the Eurovision News Exchange see Melnik (1981), Eugster (1983) and Hjarvard (1992, 1993, 1995a, 1995b). For an overview of activities in the 1980s and 1990s see Hjarvard (1995a, 1998) and Cohen et al. (1996).

3. Second International Broadcast News Workshop, Cairo, 2–6 June 1977, EBU document SPG 291, app. 7, p. 2.

4. 'Broadcaster to broadcaster relations. Experience by Asiavision', presented by ABU, in Keune and Bauer (1987: 6).

5. EBU document SPG 2297, 28 June 1983.

6. 'News exchange trial by satellite', Asian-Pacific Broadcasting Union Newsletter, March–April 1983.

7. Recommendations, Fourth World Conference of Broadcasting Unions, reproduced in EBU document EBU/52–02.

8. EBU document SPG 2323, Luxemburg, 18 July 1983.

9. Working document presented by the EBU, fifth World Conference of Broadcasting Unions, Prague, 17–23 February 1986, EBU document EBU/52-02, p. 3.

10. Report of the Sixth World Conference of Broadcasting Unions, Washington, 12–16 March 1989, p. 35.

11. The overview is based on the results of a written survey conducted in mid-1993 by the author. The overview was updated in spring 1997.

12. In 1997 the contributors were: ENTV/Algeria, ERTU/Egypt, GBC/Ghana, NTA/Nigeria, RTI/Ivory Coast, RTS/Senegal, ERTT/Tunisia and TPA/Angola. A few other TV stations receive the Afrovision exchange without contributing themselves.

13. In June 1993 the following countries participated in Arabvision news exchange: Jordan, United Arab Emirates, Bahrain, Algeria, Djibouti, Saudi Arabia, Iraq, Oman, Qatar, Kuwait, Libya, Morocco and North Yemen.

14. According to Dennis Anthony, senior officer, news, at Asiavision coordination centre in Kuala Lumpur: 'Generally no editorial control is exercised by the coordinating centre but weak or propaganda items are screened out'. Reply of 27 May 1993 on written questionaire.

15. In 1997 the following TV stations contributed with news items to the exchange: RTM/Malaysia, NHK/Japan, CCTV/China, DDI/India, TVRI/Indonesia, SLRC/Sri Lanka, IRIB/Iran, BTV/Bangladesh, TCS/Singapore and RTB/Brunei.

16. In 1993 the regular participants were CBC/Barbados, TTT/Trinidad, JBC/Jamaica, ATM/Curaçao, ATV/Surinam and ICRT/Cuba. In 1997 regular participants were Trinidad and Tobago Television, CBC/Barbados, CVM/Jamaica, JBC/Jamaica and CBU itself.

17. Reply of 8 June 1993 on written questionaire.

18. ASBU document: 'Charter of the Arab TV News Exchange System', article 7, adopted at the second meeting of the founding group of Arab TV news exchange centres, Baghdad, 3–5 September 1973.

19. In 1982 a meeting took place between the news coordinators of Eurovision and representatives of North African TV stations. One of the conclusions was: 'The viewing [of Eurovision News Exchange and North African news bulletins] also made it clear that the philosophy behind the editing of news bulletins is quite different in the Arab world and in Europe', EBU document SPG 1974, September 1982. The meeting took place because of North African dissatisfaction with the way they were treated by the editorial system of Eurovision News Exchange. An EBU employee at management level in Geneva, who was interviewed by me in 1990 and who wanted to be anonymous, characterized Arabvision as 'a disaster'; according to him Arabvision never distributes news about political controversy in the Arab region and he considered Arabvision to look like Intervision (the former east European counterpart to Eurovision) did 20 years ago.

20. Source: statistics provided by ABU.

21. 'Stories von Afrikanern, über Afrikaner, für Afrikaner', *Süddeutsche Zeitung*, 23 October 1992.

22. Harald Georg, 'The development of a pan-African TV news exchange network', presented at the 'Brainstorming workshop: the future perspectives of the Afro-Vision network', 23–24 September 1996, Kalahari Sands Hotel, Windhoek.

23. Letter of 22 April 1997, from Francine Alexander, assistant manager of programme operations, CBU.
24. The incidents are mentioned in 'Asiavision as an example of regional TV news exchange in the South', presented by the Asia-Pacific Broadcasting Union, Fourth International Broadcast News Workshop, Malaga, 12–16 April 1986, in Keune and Bauer (1987).
25. Data for the volume and direction of regional exchanges are reported in Hjarvard (1995a).
26. The Eurovision analysis covers the period 16 February to 1 April 1990. Reported in Hjarvard (1995a).
27. See ABU document, 'Asiavision Review Team. Recommendations', October-November 1996.

References

References to internal documents from the broadcasting unions are mentioned in the notes.
Abubakr, Y. (1980) 'Towards an intra-cultural news exchange in the Arab states', in UNESCO: *News Values and Principles of Cross Cultural Communication*, Reports and Papers on Mass Communication no. 85, Paris: UNESCO.
Abubakr, Y. et al. (eds) (1983) *Development of Communication in the Arab States: Needs and Priorities*, Reports and Papers on Mass Communication no. 95, Paris: UNESCO.
Boyd-Barrett, O. and Thussu, D.K. (1992) *Contra-Flow in Global News*, London: John Libbey.
Cohen, A.A., Levy, M.R., Roeh, I. and Gurevitch, M. (1996) *Global Newsrooms, Local Audiences*, London: John Libbey.
Eugster, E. (1983) *Television Programming across National Boundaries: The EBU and OIRT Experience*, Dedham, MA, USA: Artech House.
Harris, P. Malczek, H. and Ozkol, E. (1980) *Flow of News in the Gulf*, New Communication Order Series no. 3, Paris: UNESCO.
Harris, P. (1981) 'Reporting Southern Africa', Western News Agencies Reporting from Southern Africa. United Nations Educational.
Hjarvard, S. (1992) ' "Live". On time and space in television news', *Nordicom Review*, 2, Göteborg: Nordicom.
Hjarvard, S. (1993) 'Pan-European television news. towards a European political public sphere?', in P. Drummond, R. Paterson and J. Willis (eds) *National Identity and Europe. The Television Revolution*, London: British Film Institute.
Hjarvard, S. (1995a) *Internationale TV-nyheder. En historisk analyse af det europæiske system for udveksling af internationale TV-nyheder* [International Television News. A historical analysis of the European network for exchange of international television news], Copenhagen: Akademisk Forlag.
Hjarvard, S. (1995b) 'Eurovision news in a competitive marketplace', *Diffusion*, autumn 1995, Geneva: EBU.
Hjarvard, S. (1998) 'Deregulation Policies and European Media Cooperation', in Sekvens *Yearbook of Film and Media Studies*, Copenhagen: University of Copenhagen.
Ishadi, S.K. (1986) 'From Asia Vision to Global TV News Exchange', *Media Asia*, 13.
Keune, R. (1991) 'After the Gulf War and the fall of the Berlin Wall: television news and news exchanges in the 1990s', in Keune and Bauer (1991).
Keune, R. and Bauer, H.D. (eds) (1987) *International News Exchange. Reports and Recommendations of the Fourth International Broadcast News Workshop*, Köln: Friedrich-Ebert-Stiftung.
Keune, R. and Bauer, H.D. (eds) (1991) *TV News and News Exchange in the 1990s.*

Reports and Recommendations of the Fifth International Broadcast News Workshop, Köln: Friedrich-Ebert-Stiftung.

Länsipuro, Y. (1987) 'Asiavision News Exchange', in *InterMedia*, 15 (1).

Melnik, S.R. (1981) *Eurovision News and the International Flow of Information: History, Problems and Perspectives* 1960–1980, Bochum: Studienverlag Dr N. Brockmeyer.

Turkistani, A.S. (1988) News Exchange via Arabsat and News Values of Arab Television News People, Dept. of Telecommunications, Indiana University.

Index

Page numbers in italics refer to tables and figures